WITH A
ROYAL
ENGINEERS
FIELD
COMPANY
IN FRANCE & ITALY

The author on "Snuffles," France, 1916

WITH A
ROYAL
ENGINEERS
FIELD
COMPANY
IN FRANCE & ITALY
APRIL 1915 TO THE ARMISTICE

V. F. EBERLE

Pen & Sword
MILITARY

First published in Great Britain in 1973 by Pitman Publishing

Republished in this format in 2020 by
PEN & SWORD MILITARY
An imprint of
Pen & Sword Books Ltd
Yorkshire - Philadelphia

ISBN 978 1 52675 132 4

Printed and bound in England by CPI Group (UK) Ltd, Croydon, CR0 4YY

Pen & Sword Books Limited incorporates the imprints of Atlas, Archaeology, Aviation,
Discovery, Family History, Fiction, History, Maritime, Military, Military Classics,
Politics, Select, Transport, True Crime, Air World, Frontline Publishing, Leo Cooper,
Remember When, Seaforth Publishing, The Praetorian Press, Wharncliffe Local History,
Wharncliffe Transport, Wharncliffe True Crime and White Owl.

For a complete list of Pen & Sword titles please contact:
PEN & SWORD BOOKS LIMITED
47 Church Street, Barnsley, South Yorkshire, S70 2AS, England
E-mail: enquiries@pen-and-sword.co.uk • Website: www.pen-and-sword.co.uk
Or
PEN AND SWORD BOOKS
1950 Lawrence Rd, Havertown, PA 19083, USA
E-mail: Uspen-and-sword@casematepublishers.com • Website: www.penandswordbooks.com

Preface

In August 1914 I embarked unexpectedly on the uncharted and uncertain venture of taking part in a twentieth-century war.

This is a factual account of my own experiences following enlistment on the outbreak of the war in an R.E. Field Company of the 48th South Midland (Territorial) Division. It covers the whole war period of the Division from mobilization, including four years' service overseas in Belgium, France and Italy.

Despite the personal nature of my story, it is hoped that it will convey a more general understanding and portrayal of the role and tasks undertaken by the R.E. Field Companies, and of the conditions in which they worked, both in the trench warfare and major battles.

The narrative is extracted to a large extent from my letters, diaries and other records *as written at the time*, and I have retained the original wording, however unpolished. It will be evident, also, that the views and reactions expressed in the earlier days of the war underwent very considerable changes as the number and intensity of the weapons employed increased.

For the blatant egotism of the narrative I can only recall in my defence Carlyle's words, "Every mortal is a microcosm; but to himself a macrocosm. Universal Nature would barely hold what he could say about himself."

Finally, I should like to thank my friend Charles Carrington, who encouraged me to quote from his book *Soldier from the War Returning*.

V. F. EBERLE

STRAITS OF DOVER

ANTWERP

OSTEND •BRUGES

GHENT
R.Schelde

DUNKIRK
CALAIS
PASSCHENDAELE
ST. JULIEN
R. Yser
YPRES
ST. OMER
MESSINES
PLOEGSTEERT
ARMENTIÈRES
R.Lys

BRUSSELS

BELGIUM

BOULOGNE

MONTREUIL

BÉTHUNE•
LILLE
•LA BASSÉE
LOOS•
•LENS
ST. POL
VIMY•
•DOUAI
•MONS

VALENCIENNES
R.Sambre

DOULLENS
ARRAS
GOMMECOURT
CAMBRAI•
MAUBEUGE
LE CATEAU

ABBEVILLE
FONQUEVILLERS
BAPAUME
SAILLY•
OVILLERS•
POZIÈRES
R.Somme
ALBERT•
FRISE
•PÉRONNE
AMIENS•
ST. QUENTIN
R. Oise

FRANCE

NOYON
•LAON

•BEAUVAIS
R. Aisne
SOISSONS
RHEIMS•

CHANTILLY
CHÂTEAU
THIERRY
R.Marne
ÉPERNAY•
CHÂLONS•

R. Seine

PARIS

Scale of miles
0   10   20   30   40   50

VITRY le
FRANÇOIS

━ ━ ━ British Line ━━━━ French Line ★★★★★★ Belgian Line

THE WESTERN FRONT

The British and French General Headquarters are
indicated by flags

Before the Somme Battle, 1916

Contents

Contents

1   Early Days

August 1914–March 1915

On the evening of 30th March 1915, with a near-full moon to follow, the SS *Matheran* steered slowly down Southampton Water. She was an old Calcutta-run ship of 16,000 tons, able to do a steady eleven knots. On board were four officers and seventy other ranks, with seventy horses and the transport vehicles of the 2nd Field Company South Midland R.E. The remainder of the Company were following in a faster ship, the SS *Munich*. A short distance ahead another transport, and on either side a long dark shadow, with a single shaded light visible at the stern, denoted an escorting destroyer.

For a long time I stood alone by the *Matheran's* rail, watching the receding English coast-line. Inevitably perhaps, in common with those of my fellow voyagers, and countless numbers who preceded and followed us, I had conflicting thoughts of the future and the past racing through my mind. Should I see England again? How would I react to active-service conditions?

I was setting forth on the biggest and perhaps the last venture of my life. Unexpectedly I had been taken from a happy, but relatively humdrum, life in my family's oil manufacturing and merchanting business, and exchanged it for that of a combatant on active war service.

I recall clearly how, as I watched the waves sweeping past the side of the ship, my thoughts traced out the changed course which my life had taken over the last eight months. The declaration of war on the previous 4th August; our hurried return from the beginning of a holiday in Wales; my interview on the following day with Colonel E. S. Sinnott, Commanding the South Midland Royal Engineers; my asking to be enlisted as a Sapper in the No. 2 Field Company. My eldest brother, George, was then Captain in the Company, and in my school days I had spent three years as a cadet and volunteer in the School Corps, which was attached to the S.M.R.E. After the interview I had

1

hurried down to seek permission from my uncle, who was chairman of our family business, intruding on his luncheon in a well-known Bristol restaurant. Duly enrolled—under the rating of "Clerk"—and "kitted out" the next day, I had spent that night—once more in uniform—sleeping somewhat uncomfortably in the balcony of the Colston Hall. A few days later my first billet was in a small terraced house in Swindon, the concentration point for the South Midland Division on mobilization. Here "Ma," the widow of a railwayman, cooked for three of us the lump of raw meat, hacked off by the Company cooks at the daily distribution of rations.

The first two months of the war were to prove the most carefree that I was to experience for the next five years. In the lowest rank of my Corps, with no responsibility for dependants or business, an open-air life, a fair knowledge of army drill and R.E. training gained as a cadet N.C.O., and with a small group of Clifton friends in a similar position, life was indeed carefree and enjoyable. Responsibility had come gently by the transition, early in October, from sapper to second-lieutenant.

In my thoughts of what the future might hold for us, as the English coast faded from sight, there was one which certainly did not occur to me. It was—that out of the twelve officers who went overseas with the two original Field Companies in the S.M.R.E., I should prove to be the only one left in them at the conclusion of hostilities, nearly four years later.

After mobilizing in the Swindon area, the Division was ordered to move to the Chelmsford area in Essex for training, and work on the outer defences of London. I was one of an advance party of ten who set off by train at 5.45 a.m., without any breakfast, for Leighton Buzzard. I recorded in my diary a trivial incident, but one typical of the spirit which in those days showed itself in every section of the British people. While we were waiting on the platform at Oxford, the appearance of one of our party, a member of a well-known Bristol family, and a natural pessimist, but possessed of much dry humour, was so woe-begone that an elderly lady was prompted to hurry out and return with two large bags of apples and bananas. This was our first experience of a welcome which we received on our march by stages, covering some 60 miles, from Leighton to Chelmsford. In every village the inhabitants waved on the marching troops, running alongside with offerings of fruit, flowers and drinks. The route lay via Tring, Waltham Cross and Chipping Ongar. The days were hot, the roads (mostly pre-tarmac) were dusty, so much so that the lusty singing of 'Tipperary' and other popular songs of the day readily resulted in dry throats. Similar acts of kindness were repeated when we were billeted for the night in village schools or private houses.

A wave of patriotism and enthusiasm was sweeping over the country, and found public expression in a way which was not repeated in 1939.

On arriving at Chelmsford the whole Company was located in a large empty house called "Springfield," on the outskirts of the town. Here for the next five weeks my bedroom was the straw-bedded loft over a stable, shared with half a dozen other sappers.

Under their original obligations, men who were embodied in the Territorial Army were liable for home service only. It was recognized at once, however, that the Territorial Units, who were already trained soldiers, and embodied in Divisions similar to those of the Regular Army, should be made available for overseas service forthwith; but also that a number of the men were unsuitable for active service overseas. In consequence the whole Company was put on parade, and each man called up before a senior officer, out of earshot of his comrades, to declare if he would volunteer for overseas service. Those who did not do so were sent back to the Bristol Depot, and their places filled at once by new volunteers.

Thus a number of individual units, e.g. a battalion, or, in our case, No. 1 Company of the S.M.R.E. were sent out to France, for attachment to the British Expeditionary Force, during the last three months of 1914. Also the formation of a second-line South Midland Division was started. This included in Bristol the raising of a Field Company, who were sent out to France to make a third company in our Division in June 1915.

As a result of the need for more officers in the S.M.R.E., I was offered a recommendation for a commission by Colonel Sinnott. I was exceptionally fortunate in obtaining a posting to No. 2 Company, in which I was already serving, and which my brother was by then appointed to command. Three of the four other officers were friends with whom I had been associated over many years, and most of the N.C.O.s and sappers had become known to me.

The winter months passed quickly in training and working on the outer defence line of London in Essex. The latter gave us useful experience in handling infantry working-parties, in preparing trenches and wire entanglements, strong emphasis being laid on working at night. Around Christmas we trained in the handling of our pontoon and trestle bridging equipment at Brightlingsea, under conditions of bitterly cold winds.

In March 1915 came the final preparations for the Company going overseas with the South Midland Division, henceforth referred to as the 48th Division, with a white diamond as its symbol on its transport vehicles. This included the careful checking of all equipment and tools, comprising over 6,700 separate items, excluding rations and

3

harness, and listed under some 400 headings in the classification of Ordnance Stores. Thus the total road weights of each of the three bridging wagons exceeded 5,500 pounds, and were pulled by six-horse teams. Each of the four Sections' double tool-carts was over 4,000 pounds, and had four-horse teams.

On the evening of 29th March 1915 the Company set out on the first stage of its journey—an 11-mile march from Braintree for entrainment at Chelmsford. By 9 a.m. the following morning, the two trains carrying the Company had arrived at Southampton Docks, and embarkation on the two transport ships was carried out.

Our destination, which had not been disclosed to us until we were embarked, proved to be Le Havre. We turned into our bunks early, my brother and I sharing a cabin. About 1 a.m. I awoke and felt an urge to take a "look around" from the deck in the bright moonlight. I tried to let myself down quietly from the upper bunk, without waking my brother. As I swung myself down by the top rail it broke off, and I and the rail landed heavily, with a loud clattering, on the floor. My brother seemed uncertain at first whether our ship had struck a mine or was merely involved in a collision, but took it very calmly. In the morning, as we passed into Le Havre harbour, we saw in the "Roads" outside a big cargo ship half-submerged. It was our first evidence of the toll taken by war. She had been recently torpedoed, but had managed to crawl back, only to sink in shallow water.

In slinging our vehicles on to the quay the G.S. wagon and trestle-bridge wagon were damaged. Within half an hour they were replaced from the vast ordnance stores housed in nearby sheds. The horses stood the sea journey well, but disembarking them down a very steep gangway made heavy demands on the muscles of their handlers.

For our first night in France, officers, other ranks and horses "dossed down" on the floor—mostly concrete—of one large transport shed at the Docks.

One further incident may be recalled as expressive of the spirit which animated at least the younger men who had enlisted. On distributing the blankets, carried in each section's forage-limber, one sapper reported that he had not received one. The Section Officer, G. S. Perry, was thoroughly perplexed, as he had personally checked and re-checked the number. On investigation, Perry ascertained that it was not a case of one blanket deficient, but of one man surplus. The explanation: just prior to our leaving England a young sapper, named Hill, was found to be under age for overseas service, and orders were given for a substitute to take his place. In his keenness not to be separated from his friends he had fallen in, as usual, with his section, when the Company paraded for entrainment. His presence had not been detected by superior authority. To his bitter disappointment he was sent back to England, and when he came out later on was killed in action.

Up at 4.30 a.m. next morning the Company entrained in one long train, consisting mainly of about 60 trucks. The Company had a total establishment strength of 6 officers and 209 other ranks. It was divided into a Headquarters and Mounted Section, and four Sapper Sections. The latter, each under a subaltern, comprised 37 sappers, with 6 attached drivers from the Mounted Section, for its transport of equipment and baggage. Out of the total of 76 horses required, 17 were riding, the remainder heavy or light draught for the Company's 19 vehicles.

After twenty-two hours in the train, with a couple of half-hour halts for watering the horses, the Company detrained at Cassel. From there they marched by two stages to Ploegsteert—universally referred to as "Plugstreet." This was a village about $1\frac{1}{2}$ miles inside the border of Belgium, and about 8 miles due South of Ypres.

It fell to my lot to go forward, a day in advance of the Company, with two cyclists, to arrange billeting accommodation. On finding Brigade Headquarters—this was the 11th Brigade of the 4th Division, whom we were to relieve—I was taken in charge by a very pleasant officer, and given an excellent lunch. Under my guide's direction, accommodation in farm barns, about a mile West of the village was found without difficulty, except for getting all our horses under cover. The result was that a number of them had to go in parts of the barns occupied by the men. Our wagons were no longer to be parked in precise lines, but tucked away in odd corners and disguised from air observation.

My first impressions, after a general view of the front-line trenches, are recorded as follows: "At last we are right there! I have had my first glimpse of war as it is out here, and watched our shells bursting on the German trenches; and, in return, their shells pitching within a few hundred yards of us. The Germans made a perfect hit on a fine château about $\frac{3}{4}$ mile away. When the black smoke had cleared, we could see that it had taken off one corner completely. Old shell-holes scattered around and shattered houses and church in the village mark the shelling. What strikes one at first is that everywhere there is a splendid absence of fussing. The Brigadier calmly reading his *Telegraph*, and then going off to a concert party, provided by men in the Division, in a town not far away. Women in the village hanging out their washing while guns are pounding away over their heads. It seems strange that a number of the civilian inhabitants have been allowed to stay there."

The following day, 7th April, the Company arrived, and took over their billets in three farms. The 48th Division were thus one of the earliest Territorial Divisions to take over a sector of the long, entrenched battle front, as a complete self-contained formation.

2   Front-line Impressions ("Plugstreet")

April 1915

It may be recalled that extreme cold and heavy rains, in January and February 1915, had made active operations on a large scale impracticable. The opposing armies faced one another along a line which stretched from the Belgian Coast near Dunkirk to the Swiss border. The British forces were holding trenches North of the Somme River, where the line ran East of Ypres, Armentières, Arras and Albert. The conditions under which the British men lived in the front-line trenches in that period is thus described in one of Sir Philip Gibbs' dispatches: "After the earlier winter campaigns, that long period of dark wet days was the most tragic ordeal of our time. In Plugstreet and other lines of trenches they stood in water, with walls of oozy mud about them, until their legs rotted and became black with a false frost-bite, until many of them were carried away with bronchitis and pneumonia, and until all of them, however many comforters they tied about their necks or however many body-belts they used, were shivering sodden, scarecrows plastered with mud; and they crawled with lice."

By the time our Division reached Plugstreet the spring weather had greatly improved the conditions, but water and mud were a constantly recurring enemy. The sector which our Brigade was to take over lay on the North-East side of Plugstreet village. Four battalions of the Warwickshire Regiment—the 5th, 6th, 7th and 8th—made up the Brigade. They all had good officers; the men were stouthearted, and later proved themselves, both in raids and big operational attacks, to be good fighters.

Compared with the standard reached as the static war continued, the defensive barrier provided by the trench system was weak and incomplete. A long Divisional frontage comprised a number of separated fire-trenches, with a thin belt of barbed-wire entanglement along the whole front. Behind these were support-trenches which had to be

7

linked up with the front line by communication-trenches. Dugouts in many cases were merely small box-like burrowings into the wall of a trench, with a sheet of corrugated iron and two or three rows of filled sandbags on top. They were alleged to be shrapnel-proof, but gave no real protection against even a small 3-inch high-explosive shell. Behind this trench system a second line composed partly of what were called "strong-points" or "defended localities" was being prepared. Also further back, and outside normal shelling range, Belgian civilian workers were employed on a "Reserve" line.

The left, or more Northern, sector of our Brigade front was on low ground, with a small river—the Douve—flowing through it. Owing to the wet subsoil it was not feasible, in some parts, to dig deeper than about 3 feet, and the parapet had to be built up, with sandbags, a further 3 feet above ground level, and made bullet-proof. It was also necessary at some points to build-in sandbags, or provide some form of revetment for the trench walls.

A bad feature was that the trenches were at the bottom of a forward slope, leading down from a prominent hill, known as Hill 63. The approach was thus under full observation by the Germans, and no communication trench existed. Hence reinforcement, or evacuation of the wounded to the rear, could only be carried out after nightfall. Similarly all rations and stores had to be carried for nearly a mile over rough ground pitted with shell-holes usually full of water.

Conditions in other parts of the Divisional front were quite different. On higher ground trenches could be dug to a greater depth, and they could be reached by day through relatively short communication trenches.

From this point the narrative will consist largely of extracts from my diary and letters, as originally written, except that minor additions or explanations such as place-names, omitted at the time for security reasons, have been added. They were usually scribbled by flickering candle-light, on a roughly made table or a packing case, or by day in the open field or in a trench, under conditions of noises and interruptions from messmates or enemy sources or both.

"*12th April 1915.*   It is Monday midday and we are having a rest day after four nights of fairly strenuous work—three on the second-line trenches, and one in the front. I am lying at full length in a field watching a bombardment. A battery on each side of us is in action, and the Germans are replying every now and then, and I can watch the busting of the shells about 800 yards away. Last night was a very quiet night so they are apparently making up for it, and using up their normal daily ration.

"Thursday night was fairly quiet. It was the first time the Sappers had come into the rifle-fire zone, but we were high up (on Hill 63), and about 800 yards away from the German trenches, so that we only got an occasional zip-zip from wild shooting near us.

"Friday night was quite lively. The Germans spotted one of our working parties near the front line and started shelling them. It was a dark night and our own gun flashes show up very brightly. Four flashes followed quickly by bang-bang, and then a softer 'plump' as the shells burst down below. A battery behind us had opened up and given them 'zip'. As they did not stop, one of our 5-inch howitzers lent a hand. The game, however, seems to be played this way—if 'A' starts shelling 'B's trenches, 'B' phones back to his gunners to say that his rest is being interrupted. His gunners promptly retaliate on 'A's trenches—*not* the battery. That upsets 'A' and he tells his gunners, politely or otherwise, to shut up! There is also a kind of mutual-obligation element in the front line. It often happens that A does not fire from his trench on an enemy working party, e.g. putting up wire entanglement in front of his trench, although he knows just where they are—the reason being that if he does so, he knows that B will return the compliment on his own men, who are doing exactly the same job in front of his trench. Sometimes it is a sort of race as to who will get their working party finished first, so that they can have a blaze at the others. [It should be noted that these early impressions rapidly became out-dated.]

"At first it is not easy to keep one's attention, and that of the Sappers, on the job in hand, when the guns are at work just behind us. There is a crash, with a second report just after it, and the shell goes screeching over our heads. The sound is a kind of cross between a screech and the tearing of a huge piece of calico. In the darkness you can see, apart from the flash, the line of the shell's flight like the trail of a red shooting star. Then you hold your breath till you see it burst on the German side. It was our first experience of shells passing over our heads, and I was thankful that there was no retaliation on the batteries behind us, till we are more acclimatized. Rifle-fire at short range is comparatively child's-play, though last night I found myself continually ducking as they pinged overhead. We ought to get out of that habit soon, as it serves no purpose, except to make the neck muscles ache. Already we are learning to distinguish between the sharper, whip-like crack of a rifle bullet when it is close to you, as compared with the whizzing or whistling sound when it is further away. Similarly we are learning to differentiate between the bursts of German shells, as to what kind they are, and how far away. There is all the difference in the world between the 'plonk' of the Germans' 'Little Willie' and the deep note of a heavy 'Jack Johnson' shell, which produces a sizeable crater. 'Little Willie' is a nasty little fellow who seems to take a delight in popping over in unexpected places, and to arrive in a tearing hurry, but does not do much damage.

"A building on my right has just been set alight by a shell, and is smoking hard.

"Saturday night was quiet again with us, though I think there must have been an attack a few miles to the North of us, as there was a big 'hullabaloo" with plenty of machine-gun firing.

"Sunday was the strangest sabbath day I have spent so far. We did not get up till about 11 a.m., as we had been on trench work till 4 a.m. By one o'clock we were in a shattered red-brick château [this was the Villa Roozenberg on Hill 63, owned by a member of the Hennessey family]. Three sides of the tower about 80 feet high, and about half the outside walls remained standing. I had been ordered to blow down all that remained, as bricks were in considerable demand for horse standings and other purposes. It was 'some demolition'! A great black smoke at the base, then the loud report, and a side wall toppled first, while the tower, after a momentary hesitation, gave a kind of waltz turn and came down with a crashing grunt. Two more small charges and a landmark for miles around was gone."

My brother has told me that later on the same day he had gone to report at Divisional Headquarters. On entering the room he overheard an irate regular Gunner Colonel demanding to know why some blankety Sappers had destroyed the tower, which his guns used as an aiming aid. The brother discreetly left the reply to the C.R.E. It did not take us long to learn that a trench war high-lights the truth of the old saying "One man's meat is another man's poison."

"I was told to use, for the explosive, the guncotton slabs from my Section's tool-cart, in which we carry some 700 slabs. The latter are rectangular, 6 inches long by 3 inches wide, and it is essential that each slab should be in actual contact with the next slab. In order to economize, as all explosives and shells were in short supply, each slab was to be sawn in half, down its length. This was something we had not previously envisaged when training. My Section carpenters were markedly dubious as to the likely result of the shock or heat generated by sawing through them, a view which I must confess to sharing at first. However, by standing at their elbow with as nonchalant an air as I could muster, confidence gradually grew, and the operation on the large number required was satisfactorily completed, and we had learned another lesson.

"It was a glorious sunny afternoon and while waiting for the sappers we lay and basked on the hillside, watching some daring aeroplane work. Four of our aeroplanes, marking for our gunners, were circling around, and dodging over the German and our lines, with the German anti-aircraft guns plugging away at them. Such a pretty sight, with the biplanes glistening in the sun, and the little fleecy puffs of white smoke from the busting shrapnel showing up all round them.

"After a hurried meal at the billet, Mark Whitwill, who is in charge of No. 4 Section, and I set out to meet a subaltern of the 9th Field Company. He was to conduct us round part of the front trenches which we are taking over from them. We had to wait till it was sufficiently dark, as they could only be reached over open ground. There was very little firing activity. The German trenches opposite to us were about 200 yards away, but one felt wonderfully safe when in the trench, and it is only by very bad luck, or lack of reasonable caution, that one gets hit by rifle-fire."

"At intervals in the trench a look-out at night stands on the firestep watching the front. The rest of the men, for the most part, sit around on the firestep or in little shelters cut into the sides of the trench, except at the evening and dawn 'stand-to' periods. Part of the time they may be required to go out on a patrol in no-man's-land, or to strengthen the wire in front, or make good any damage to the trench. At night if there is no shooting they walk about freely behind the trench. We could hear very clearly the German transport rumbling along a road just behind their lines.

"One of the troubles that beset us when walking over open ground at night is to avoid falling into shell-, or as they are more usually termed, crump-holes. They are everywhere, and usually full of water. On the way back two nights ago I came across one of our other sections' tool-cart stuck in a slimy shell-hole. It took about 15 men twenty minutes to haul it out. Some of the crump-holes are 10 feet across the top, and 4 or more feet deep."

3   "Plugstreet" Trenches

April 1915

"*16th April 1915.* I have just woken up from a most peaceful sleep in a dugout in the front line, with the Germans occasionally sniping and our men in the trench replying. It is a great asset to be able to sleep under unusual conditions, and I have only had one night in which I went to bed—so called—before 3 a.m. for the past week.

"In official language we have been 'carrying on,' having taken over full responsibility for our sector of the Divisional front.

"Our only change has been to move our Company Officers' billet to more comfortable quarters in a house. [This was in a row of small terraced houses in a main road in Plugstreet village.] The owner is still in nominal occupation, but does not appear by day, and we have the full use of the kitchen and sitting room, and we all doss down in a room upstairs. There is not a pane of glass left intact in the windows, which are stuffed with sacking upstairs. The door and outside shutters on the ground floor have a number of peep-holes, where shrapnel has paid a visit. The Authorities will only allow the actual owners to continue living in the village. The remaining inhabitants seem extraordinarily unconcerned, and when shelling starts merely retire to a cellar till it ceases.

"The past week's work has been almost entirely night work on the second line for the Sappers, combined with nightly tours of the front trenches for us. One night my brother and I went overland with the C.O. and Major of one of our battalions. The Major distinguished himself by twice falling into shell-holes. The first time he went crash into a big one up to his chest in water, and very nearly had to swim out. I came down to this trench last night, or to be more exact in the early hours of this morning, with the intention of spending the day here and making a daylight survey of it. It is part of the line for which my section is to be responsible from the R.E. point of view. Unfortunately it

12

is one which can be reached only under cover of darkness, and my journey to it did not go quite according to my plans.

"I was alone and called in at the farm headquarters of the Battalion of the 4th Division in the line to report and ask for a guide. Here I found the C.O. and Major of one of our Battalions in reserve also expecting to pick up a guide. The Adjutant, a Regular officer, however regretted that he could not provide one, as his battalion were all on the point of being relieved. He then brightly remarked: 'This officer', indicating me, 'has been up there, he can guide you. There's a track from the farm gate, follow that till you reach a narrow trench across it. There's wire also in front of it, so you can't walk into the Boche lines.' I had previously been taken up by another route on a dark night. Last night was darker still, with no moon and a black sky, so that one could only see a yard or two in front. When we reached the trench across the track, I found that the C.O. was expecting to go in the opposite direction to that of my previous visit, and a part where the trenches also were not joined up. When we reached the end of the first trench we asked for the whereabouts of the next one. The only answer we could get was 'It's somewhere over there,' with an airy wave of the hand; 'We don't really know, as we've only just come in.' The rest of our journey was quite exciting. I was somewhat dubious as to the reception awaiting three unheralded figures who might appear either in front or behind the trench, or merely fall into one of its drains, especially as this was the occupants' first night in the front line. The occasional flares which the Boches sent up—and we went down on our stomachs—enabled us to keep our general direction, and to spot the trenches we were looking for, over about half a mile of open country. The return journey was considerably easier, and my two companions were deposited back safely at the Battalion headquarters. By about 2 a.m. I had ended up in this trench. I found a little cubby-hole shelter which was vacant, and was soon fast asleep on an air-pillow and straw, oblivious of occasional shooting by over-zealous sentries at phantom figures in no-man's-land. My dugout (so-called) is about 5 foot by 4 and 3 foot high inside. The roof is a sheet of corrugated iron with two rows of sandbags on top; the front is made up of sandbags also except for a narrow entrance, through which it is possible to squeeze on hands and knees. It is really quite snug."

Later in the day I added the following: "I have been writing this while sitting outside the dugout, and basking in the sunshine. So long as you are not being shelled, day-life in the trenches may be boring, but in glorious weather such as this it is far from being insufferable. This morning the Germans expended a few rounds of their daily shell ration on the front lines near us. Later they dropped a few further down the line, after our gunners had stirred them up. Then they lengthened the range, apparently trying to find a battery nearly in line behind us. Provided they do not drop them short, we are quite satisfied with hearing them 'swishing' over our heads.

"I have been fairly well occupied in taking copious notes and drawing rough diagrams for trench work, which it is hoped to carry out as soon as possible. [This referred to priority number one, the joining up the separate trenches, to give a continuous front line trench; number two; a new long communication trench to the rear.]

"The three Infantry officers and I have been feeding together, squatting round a sandbag table outside my dugout. For breakfast— sausages and bacon; for lunch—a stew from tinned rations. Our appearance from the smartness point of view would be quite laughable. Caked with mud from the eyebrows downwards; hardly any of the puttees and boots visible under the mud plaster, and I have not washed since early yesterday morning. At night we wear an old and muddy trench mac and cap-comforter, the latter a much loved and indispensable item. A long stout stick for spotting crump-holes is at present our most valuable weapon, but we usually carry a loaded revolver in the front line, more from the comforting feeling it produces."

Those of us who slept on the straw in the front-line dug-outs quickly learned that the louse is an unpleasant parasitic creature, and no respecter of persons. Hence the unedifying spectacle could be seen of subalterns sitting outside the billet in the sunshine, carefully searching the seams of their undergarments. In default of a hot iron, a positive satisfaction was achieved by firmly squashing the intruders between two thumb-nails.

"*21st April 1915. Wednesday*.   Last Saturday, just as I was setting out to meet my brother at Divisional Headquarters about 7 p.m., a tremendous cannonade broke out in the direction of Messines, to the North of us."

It turned out to be an attack on the Germans for the possession of Hill 60. This formed part of a ridge about 5 miles North of our sector. Six mines were exploded under parts of the hill. Fierce fighting lasted for the next four days. It was followed in the last week of April and in May by attacks on a large scale in the area between us and Ypres, including the German attack using gas, known as the Second Battle of Ypres. One anomaly that was borne on us was that, though we were close to the scene of the fighting, we were in complete ignorance of what was happening. Apart from rumours which reached us from the rear, through the drivers of the wagons bringing up rations, we had to wait till the newspapers from England reached us.

"I have seen my first German soldier at close quarters. He was a prisoner captured by one of our night patrols, who came across two Germans in no-man's-land. They lost the other, and had one of their own men shot at about two yards' range. I had called in at the Battalion front line headquarters about mid-night. It was a strange scene in the kitchen of the old farm. The German standing bare-headed, close-cropped, sullen-looking, with two mud-bespattered Warwicks, with fixed bayonets, behind him. An officer sitting in front of a packing case table interrogating him in German. The big room with a cavernous fireplace, was lit only by two flickering and smelly candles. On the whitewashed walls some previous artist among the British occupants had drawn, almost life-size in charcoal, delightful sketches of the Dana Gibson Girl type, and copies of *La Vie Parisienne* drawings. The prisoner apparently expected to be bayoneted forth-with, but made a request that he might smoke a cigarette, which was not granted.''

The drawings referred to were by Bruce Bairnsfather, who had been at the Farm when the 4th Division were in the line. Shortly afterwards his realistic drawings of "Old Bill," taken from his experience of the trenches and the area round Plugstreet, were first published in England, and became widely known.

"Mark Whitwill and I have come into the trenches for a thirty-hour spell. It is 8 a.m. and he is sleeping soundly in a small shelter. After three or four hours of being wedged together like tinned sardines we decided to repose more peaceably by taking turns to occupy it.

"We have brought up a good supply of provisions with us this time. Last night supper was served in the Infantry Major's dugout at 3 a.m. It consisted of sardines, followed by jam and chocolate. For breakfast we have tongue plus marmalade, tea, etc. Our enjoyment thereof is not impaired by the presence of the adjectival Huns sitting in their trenches, which are about 300 yards away.''

"It has just turned cold and wet. I am hoping for a dark night to-night, as we have a big job to do with a big working party. It is an attempt to dig and join up the front-line trenches under our jurisdic-tion in one night, so that it will become a continuous line. Between us Mark and I have five trenches. Last night we had a number of parties from the reserve battalion carrying up stores, including gabions, pickets and tools, to a point concealed behind the trench, and also filling sandbags. Many improvements have been made already, and we find the Infantry very willing to work hard on this front-line type of work, which will make it safer and more comfortable for them. We are responsible for taping out the line and supervising the work, as well as the organization for tools and materials. Our sappers help with the supervision and doing some of the more technical revetting work, and bonding in the sandbags forming the top part of the parapet.''

15

"*22nd April 1915.* We had a splendid night's work last night. I was quite expecting some trouble from the Boches, owing to our having parties, much bigger than usual, working above ground so close to them. We connected up all our trenches, so that we have communication along the whole of our sector. It involved digging over 250 yards of deep trench, with only six hours of darkness available, as the nights are getting shorter, and we have to allow an hour for the working parties to get out of sight over the hill, before the light gives them away.

"There is still a lot of work to be done on the new trenches, but I did not regret the time spent on previous nights, in the taping-out and preparations in general. With 450 men to control, in two reliefs, between Mark and myself, fully exposed to the German trench, we might easily have run into trouble and confusion. As it turned out there was hardly a shot fired in our direction, and it was the quietest night I have experienced. I think it must have been a relieving night for the opposite German battalion.

"On one of the previous nights we were lucky also in bringing down a German sniper who had been worrying us. We knew roughly the direction from which the shots were coming, but could not locate him. Then one of our infantry covering party spotted him up a tree about 150 yards away, when a flare went up, and promptly brought him down. The German let out a double yell which we all heard.

"Whenever we have a working party, e.g. on wiring in front of the fire-trench, a small covering party, from the infantry holding the trench, always lies out on either flank, ready for immediate action, in case of an enemy raid. The working party also have to keep their loaded rifles close to their hand.

"Similarly when a patrol is sent out at night, or if anyone goes out in front, two very necessary precautions have to be taken. The senior officer on duty must be told, and he in turn has to see that all the sentries on the front affected are warned. Secondly the point of exit and of return must be predetermined. Otherwise accidents resulting from trigger-happy sentries are liable to occur.

"The firing of 'Véry lights' or 'star shells' from the front trenches to light up no-man's-land is adopted by both sides. They can be an accursed annoyance or a help, according to the position you happen to be in. Fortunately they leave a trail of sparks as they ascend in an arc, before bursting into a brilliant light at the apex, and then float slowly down to the ground. This gives time to prostrate oneself and hug mother earth. Although the light is very bright, a party of men lying flat on the ground, and thereby casting no shadows, can remain undetected, provided that they stay motionless. If flares drop fairly close they are apt to induce a feeling of nakedness, and that the whole

German army are looking at you. I was not very happy on a recent occasion when I was out in front with a few sappers. I had gone flat on my tummy when a flare went up from the German trench. As I screwed round my head to watch its descent, I realized it was not far from the ground, and apparently dropping plumb on top of me. Actually it missed me by about 4 feet, and the long wet grass put it out as it fell.

"Life out here is expressed with a splendid wealth of humour from all ranks, although punctuated with adjectival additions. When a shell or bullet passes fairly close, the stock remark is—'Ah! that one was allright, it hadn't got my number on it.' The expressions 'luck in' or 'luck out' are favourites. An example of the former occurred a few nights back. I was leading a party of my Section sappers across country, and had reached a gap between our front-line trenches, where we wanted to erect some canvas screening. Strict silence had been enjoined just previously. A heavy roll of thick 6-foot-wide Willesden canvas was being carried on the shoulders of two of the sappers. I heard a loud swear, followed by mutual recriminations from the two carriers just behind me, each demanding of the other 'what he was playing at.' This brought a sharp, but I hope low-voiced, reprimand from me, as I did not want our presence there made evident to the German trench opposite. The explanation was found, however, when the canvas was unrolled. There was a round hole in it, and about two-thirds through the middle of the roll a German bullet imbedded in it. Two feet to left or right would have been exactly head height of one of the carriers. That was a case of 'luck in'."

24th April 1915. Notes in my diary record that my Section had changed over from night work to day work—that is in the back area. Also that our C.R.E., Colonel E. S. Sinnott, had been transferred for work on the Vth Corps Staff, and had been succeeded by Lieut.-Colonel H. J. M. Marshall as C.R.E. He was a regular officer with considerable service in India. I took an opportunity with G. S. Perry to visit Armentières, where the 4th Division "Follies" gave an evening performance. "It was such a change; as we sat in a little concert hall, watching a pierrot troupe quite equal in talent to a Musical Hall Show at home, it seemed hard to realize, that the moment we put foot outside the door, we should hear the sound of rifle-fire. In fact, a short distance outside the town, we had to dismount from our bicycles to cross fire-brigade hoses. A khaki brigade were pouring water on a large farmhouse adjoining the the road, set on fire by a shell a couple of hours earlier. The casualties were two horses and a mule.

"After seeing the Follies, who included an attractively dressed—alleged—girl, something we had not seen for weeks, we 'found' a dinner at the Station Hotel. There we met what was to us another strange species—to wit—a tablecloth. True, we had to use the same knife and fork through the dinner, but a tablecloth! We were quite civilized!

"I recently passed a half-ruined row of houses in a village. One of them was the equivalent of one of our pubs at home. It bore the sign 'Estaminet au Cheval Noir.' The roof and upper floor had, for the most part, been demolished by a shell, but the two rooms on either side of the front door were each stabling a team of Gunner horses. I think the original setter-up of the sign could hardly have imagined that the equine species would take his sign so literally, and make themselves comfortable in the bar parlour.

"There are two very small villages [Le Gheer and St Yves] close to a big wood, and within a few hundred yards of our present front line. They had been taken and re-taken several times in the fighting earlier on. I passed through one for the first time on a bright moonlight night, which threw into heavy relief the gaunt remains of walls and roofs. I can hardly imagine a more deserted scene, and the sudden 'Halt! Who goes there!' from a sentry hidden in the shadows seemed only to accentuate it. When a cat suddenly appeared in the roadway in front, it seemed like a visitant from another world."

"*28th April 1915.* My Section has changed over for a period of day work. It has the added pleasure that we are sufficiently far back for me to ride round on my blue roan mare 'Girls' to the various points where they are working. These include putting some farm buildings into a state of defence. We are not hampered in what we can do, but we try to worry the inhabitants as little as possible. It is slightly embarrassing at times. For example, today, having strolled into an upper room, with the intention of knocking a hole in one of the walls, I found an old dame fast asleep in bed.

"Those inhabitants who have remained are wonderfully plucky and phlegmatic. I found in another case that, in the daytime, two small shells had passed through the wall, against which the farmer's bed was placed. He had begged some sandbags from the R.E., which he filled and dumped into the holes, and continues to sleep there nightly.

"Today three young girls were collecting sticks in front of their cottage as we passed, and suddenly one called to the others and pointed. It was to a farm about 450 yards away, with its roof blazing from end to end—a lucky hit by a German long-distance shell. After a few moments they quietly resumed their stick-collecting, although they knew that it might be their own homes the next time that would suffer. When our guns nearby barked a fit and proper reply, how dearly one wished that they would pitch on German homesteads rather than those of our allies.

"On the other hand, all these tales of shell- and rifle-fire, unless you are in an attack or particularly 'warm' corner, sound very much worse than they are actually. Once out of the immediate front line one is only a flea on the landscape, and the betting against a shell knocking you out is more than a thousand to one.

"To give a general view of the varied nature of our Company's work, here are some of the jobs we have been doing this week: First and foremost superintending trench-making and communications, building dugouts and repairing portions of trenches blown in. Making wood pickets and X-frames for barbed-wire protective belts. Blowing up damaged buildings in the back area—this included some further successful experiments with my Section. Putting other buildings in a state of defence. Supervising about 70 Belgian civilian labourers on back trenches and roads. Then we have been acting as water-supply and sanitation advisers, constructors of destructors, making huts and slatted trench-boards. As intensive horticulturists, Perry's and my Section induced a 10-foot high hedge, 30 yards long, to spring up in the space of two hours, where before there was none. Other tasks include clearing field of fire, and bridging small dykes and streams. Our 'Stores' and carpentry shop acts as a local 'Harrods,' from which the Gunners and Infantry can draw materials. Making sketch maps of the trench systems and design drawing also fall to our lot.

"*1st May 1915.* Mark Whitwill has been wounded. Our two Sections were working together at night on one of the back support trenches. I had been bringing up a relief party for digging, and found that he had been hit by a stray bullet through his arm. He was able to walk to an ambulance, but has been evacuated. I shall miss him more than I can say, as he is one of my oldest friends, and a first-rate officer. The place where we were working was in a fold of the ground, where rifle shots, probably aimed at the front line but too high, came down to earth in a tired condition. We had several men hit and in one case a bullet—very tired—hit one of the sappers in a soft spot below the spine while bending down. There it stuck with its back portion protruding, until it was pulled out.

"The Germans have been much more active in shelling Plugstreet village, including the area round our officers' billet. Two afternoons ago I had intended to spend the afternoon in the field behind it, but in a zealous mood had walked over to my Section's billet to check up on some details for the night's work. On my return I found our next-door neighbour busily engaged in sweeping up muck and debris from the pavement in front. At the back of our billet, within half a dozen yards of our garden, there was a 5-foot deep crater, where a big 5·9 shell had landed. We recovered the buried nose-cap. Three pitched in the road

19

40 yards further down, and half a dozen in the field opposite. The Infantry also reported over 70 shells on our part of the front line. Net result—casualties nil, and all damage to the trenches repaired the same night.''

By this time we had joined up all the front-line trenches in the Company's Brigade sector, and greatly improved the communication approaches from the rear, with the exception of daylight approach on our extreme left portion. It was decided to start on remedying the latter. It entailed digging a long trench of approximately 3,000 yards, leading from Hill 63 down to the River Douve trenches. In addition it was essential to dig draining-trenches leading away from it at frequent intervals. We were allocated large working parties from the Battalions in reserve, but owing to front-line reliefs these were not available on some nights. We had to keep one of our four Sapper Sections to run the workshop and certain back-area day work. By the 15th May the Company's War Diary records that communication from Hill 63 to the front line was now practicable in daylight. Considerable further work, such as completing the layout of trench-boards for the whole length was necessary, but direct reinforcement of the front line and evacuation of men wounded was then possible.''

"*4th May 1915*. Our Infantry working parties have been as many as 1,200 per night. The O.C. and 2nd in command of our Company give us our instructions, and keep a watchful eye as far as it is possible, but the actual supervising, and preparational work, falls on the three subalterns. We all have to make careful preparatory arrangements to avoid wasting the labour available. The exact lines of the trench to be dug have to be marked out beforehand with white tapes, with appropriate traverses or dog-leg layout. It entails the provision of the right number of picks and shovels, sandbags, wood pickets, gum-boots and other items required, at the right time at a predetermined rendez-vous for the various parties, and the careful briefing of sapper guides.

"By day in the back area parties of men must not exceed 15 in number, without a substantial gap between parties. At night this does not apply. The main source of our 'cussing' is near a road, suitable for transport, which leads to one point through which all parties from the different units have to pass. Here they have to be sorted out, tools pressed into unwilling hands, others loaded with stakes or other materials, and then led away by sapper guides across country. On the way they may run into a cross-current of a ration or water party from the trenches, and in the dark follow the wrong party. If they get out of touch with the man in front they may disappear into the nearest bit of trench, or shell-holes, if sufficiently dry. Not being over-anxious for hard physical work, they are quite content to 'lie doggo,' and in the darkness may well evade discovery for some time. Last night I experienced the delights of half my party going astray, through not keeping close up to the man in front of them. 60 men, including a sapper tail-dog, wandering off on their own, and then having to be guided back across country full of shell-hole traps. To make it more realistic it rained hard, and the ground had become more like a mixture of ice and quagmire. Each man, in addition to his rifle and equipment, carried a waterproof sheet and a bundle of stakes or alternative tool or load, and our uncharted course was a fair imitation of a steeplechase course—so we had some fun, and there was no bar on the use of the infantryman's expressive vocabulary."

We received an unexpected visitor—the Bishop of Pretoria. As Dean of my brother's College at Oxford, he was an old friend. "An old rowing blue and coach, he is a man of outstanding physique and personality. He lunched with us, and a short service was arranged for the men available outside my Section's farm billet. We gathered round him close to 'Archie,' our anti-aircraft gun mounted on a lorry. Two men a dozen yards away continually sweeping the sky with their glasses—a lovely sunny day, and the guns booming in the distance—a striking change from the atmosphere of our church services at home. The Bishop—Mike Furse as we knew him in earlier years—gave us a splendid talk straight from the heart, and straight to the point of why we are fighting. Halfway through the service a nearby battery started banging, and before we finished German shells were plumping down not far away from us, punctuating the 'Rock of Ages,' sung without an organ accompaniment."

On his return to England the Bishop wrote a long and forceful letter to *The Times*, on the conditions at the Front; in particular the lack of support from home in the supply of shells. This had a considerable impact in rousing public opinion.

In a leading article *The Times* described it as "a singularly impressive letter confirming all that we have been saying on the urgent and imperative need of national service in the very broadest sense of the words."

The following brief extract from the Bishop's letter is, perhaps, particularly significant as indicating the view which we as Christian Members of the overseas British Forces held in those days, and also explanatory of comments in my early written records. He wrote: "Recent events have clearly shown, even to the most phlegmatic, that we are in a perfectly real sense up against the Devil incarnate. What else is it when we are fighting against an enemy who will stop at nothing, however mean and cruel and disgusting—an enemy who will use gas, *sink Lusitanias*, put arsenic in running streams, and sow disease."

21

Throughout the Bible the inevitability of wars, and resistance against evil aggression owing to human frailty is indicated. It is unfortunately true that the spur of hate for their enemy makes the vast majority of men more useful as soldiers, and hate is inculcated in their training. We hated the German soldiers, not as individuals, but as upholders, willing or unwilling, of the actions of their country's leaders. Ours was not merely the spirit which animated the Knights of the Crusades, although the British Army retained the unwritten elements of chivalry to a foe. We were fighting for the safety and future freedom of our country; for maintaining its way of life. I do not think many of us subscribed to the claim that it was a "war to end wars." It is only natural that the younger generations of today should look upon the two twentieth-century world wars as merely episodes of history. It is, however, surely right that they should be able to realize the cost in human life and suffering that their predecessors paid in securing the freedom they have today. It is right also that, with the passing of time, the spirit of hate, among those who experienced and suffered from those wars, should be wiped away. To "forgive—but not to forget" comes easier, perhaps, for those who were actively combatant.

The "Padres" attached to the Divisional Units had only a limited scope allowed them in their activities with men actually in the front line. Sundays were no different from other days in respect of work or shelling. An occasional Communion Service was available in the back billeting area. These services were usually held in a barn, everyone standing, the Chaplain with spurs sticking out below his surplice, and a packing-case for an altar.

4 Carrying on ("Plugstreet")

May 1915

"*8th May 1915.* We are carrying on along normal lines for this type of trench warfare. Shelling and being shelled, sniping and being sniped, urging on sweating infantry working parties, repairing sandbagged trench parapets, dispensing materials from stores and workshop. For the rest—we sleep well, eat well, drink well and cuss well! The Germans opposite us are now more 'chatty.' On our battalion relief nights the incoming troops are greeted with 'Hullo the Blanks.' An officer vouched for the following being shouted across no-man's-land: 'Hullo the Glosters! What are they saying about you in Bristol? When is this war going to stop? I have a wife and four children in Flax Bourton.' Night patrols are also more active. The Germans had been seen working in front of their line. One of our patrols investigated the following night, and pinched the tools which they had left on the job.

"Our Sappers have settled down splendidly, and take a real pride in seeing that the various jobs are done properly, when working alone or supervising others. There are plenty of tricks for which they have to watch out. A favourite one, when the job is to fill a quota of sand-bags, is to stuff one or more empty sandbags into one they are filling.

"The Sappers have also become quite ingenious in improving their barn billets, and making themselves comfortable. No. 2 Section have built themselves a summer-house, with deck-chairs, and other useful embellishments, and the gateway proclaims in neat letters 'The Kursall.' My Section, having been temporarily driven out of their barn loft by the effect of the warm weather on a pigsty underneath them, not inaptly countered with a black board artistically painted with white lettering 'Paradise Lost.'

"Yesterday was my rest day, and as usual it worked out that I was on various jobs for eleven out of the thirteen hours before retiring to sleep. We always view rest days with grave suspicion, but on this

occasion it was largely my own fault. Taking advantage of the progress made on our long communication trench, I was able to reach,
and roam by daylight, over a large farm building. Not without reason
it is officially labelled on our maps 'Stinking Farm.' Inside the
dwelling part there were obvious signs of a hurried flight, and its
occupation and defence in the earlier fighting here. Dresses strewn
about on the floor, pots and pans pulled down, or blown down by
shells which had hit the building, empty cartridge cases and equipment, with broken brick and tiles scattered over everything. In one
loft into which we climbed we found large stacks of tobacco on the
floor, and strings of leaves still hanging up to dry. It was a perfect
hiding place or nest for a sniper, and on our arrival we had been told
numerous stories of snipers operating behind our lines. If a mouse had
squeaked I certainly should have jumped! Inside and outside, rifles,
ammunition, equipment, farm implements lying where they had been
discarded, and now rusty and rotting. Close by, three cows and a mule
lying stiffly on the grass, in a very advanced state of decomposition.
The wastage just in this one farmhouse brings home the toll taken by
war on the civilian population."

There is an old saying, "Live and Learn." A more appropriate
rendering for those at the Front was "If you live you learn." Thus a
radical change came over our early light-hearted views of being under
shell-fire. Hitherto we had experienced only sporadic shelling. We
now learned what a moderately concentrated bombardment involved.
Even then we had no conception of the intensity of bombardments
such as we were to see in the battles of the Somme and Passchendaele.
The entry in my diary for 9th May is headed "Black Sunday." This
referred only to our own small sector of the front. We knew little of
the critical nature of the fighting on that day in the second battle of
Ypres, or of the opening attack on Festubert to the South of us. News
of the sinking of the *Lusitania* also had not yet reached us.

I wrote on the 11th May: "About 4.30 a.m. on Sunday (the 9th) we
were woken up by very heavy firing. It was not unexpected, as our
night working-parties had been cancelled, but when it developed into
clearly heard incessant rifle- and machine-gun fire, it seemed rather
absurd to stay in our sleeping-bags with a battle apparently raging
only a few miles away, and we got up. We had received no orders, and
as there seemed to be no firing on our front we retired to rest again;
and the firing to the North of us slackened down though still fairly
heavy. Presumably the Germans opposite us were not going to take
all this without retaliation, and just about noon the ball opened, with
Plugstreet village as their indiscriminate target.

"Fortunately for us our billet was in a row of houses end-on to the
line of fire, so that any shells, at the relatively short range, would hit

24

other houses first, as actually happened. Our little cellar with its brick arching had been reinforced with steel joists. The bombardment continued till after 3 p.m., but in a lull we slipped away to the men's billets, which were outside the target area.

"The next afternoon the shelling was repeated. Over 100 shells fell within a radius of about 500 yards of our billet, and the roof of the kitchen, which was built out at the back of the house was badly knocked about. I never want to see a fairly heavy bombardment again when there are civilians still in the neighbourhood. It was the sickening sight of these shells raising clouds of dust as they crashed into houses or roadway, the continual whistling of the next one almost before the last one had burst, the smoke and flames of a whole row of cottages near us, and another area of some 50 yards square was still blazing. Later, motor ambulances making a periodic dash up the road, and a stream of inhabitants, women weeping, including a party of nuns being escorted on foot into at least temporary exile. Part of the front of the nuns' home opposite our billet had been blown out. In one period of the shelling our cellar, with barely sufficient space for our batmen and ourselves, was invaded by a weeping civilian family. It included a girl slightly wounded in the face, and moaning 'Mon père! Mon père!' Later we found that they had come from the end house of our row, where a shell had penetrated the end wall, and wrecked the room in which the old man lay dead. Two little kiddies had been killed within fifty yards of our billet."

Unfortunately the casualties included one of my best Corporals killed and two sappers wounded from my Section.

"*12th May 1915.* We have migrated to a country residence which we designate 'The Cottage.' Our Plugstreet billet had become too hot for us, and the village is now deserted. Our new residence, about ¾ mile further back from the front, is a pretty little farmhouse, composed of a thatched cottage with a barn adjoining it, in which we live. One end of the latter has been cleared out to form our mess-room. The middle part is partitioned off, and contains the tobacco-drying straw mats. Our batmen sleep here, and we store our belongings. At the far end we climb up to a small loft where the six of us can just find room to sleep. The ladder is a bit shaky, and also the floor, so we may on some night give the old mule who lives below an unpleasant surprise. We intend building a sleeping hut, and the sappers and drivers will also turn out into huts or some form of tented cover. In our late billet we had rather a warm time. There was a continual strain to catch the heralding whistle of a shell, and if the wind got up, or a passing wagon squeaked, it disturbed our pleasure in a meal or rest. The area round this farm has so far been quite clear of shell-fire, and it is quite cheering to feel that one can carry on without having to make a bolt for the cellar. The old farmer is very willing to help, and probably thankful for the small billeting payments he will receive.

"*16th May 1915*.   Today I change to a prospective eight days' day work. That should mean a so-called hot bath tonight. Quite a welcome change, after seeing the dawn come up for nearly three weeks before retiring to sleep. Our work here has been exceptionally interesting and varied, and on the whole we come off easier than the Infantry, who are being worked very hard in their out-of-the-line periods. While on the job it is tiring, especially during the last fortnight, when the nights have been very dark. That means more of a strain as I am moving about all the time from one place to another, but I can leave far more of the supervision now to my Section N.C.O.s and sappers. For instance, two nights ago I had 530 Infantry, in two reliefs, as working parties to supervise, with about 25 sappers. The principles we learned in our training have given us all a sound foundation, but a few weeks' practical experience out here are worth months of training at home.

"*18th May 1915*.   The weather has changed to a gale and rain. Last night I was nearly blown out of my sleeping-bag. One side of our barn loft is open, and I sleep on that side for the sake of the fresh air. We have laid tobacco-drying straw mats on the sloping floor under our valises, and these are made with two long strips of wood to bind the straw. The result is that it feels as if one was sleeping across a railway line. I have also found a use for the two body-belts I brought out. Instead of a 'dado round the dining room,' they make an excellent pillow-slip round a sandbag stuffed with straw, and you have the finest pillow imaginable.

"Here follows an account ot today's happenings for a Sapper subaltern, on a quiet day, on this part of the British line. Aroused by a tug on my big toe, in time to eat a hearty breakfast I am found trudging off at 8 a.m. to my Section, who do the required stiffening exercise on my arrival. With them tacked on behind me, we wander on till we find a hundred infantry, sitting by the roadside, and looking distinctly tired after a four-day duty in the front line. The officer in charge is well known to me from our joint training days in England. Together we split the men into various parties, tack a sapper or two on to each party, and pack them off down our new long communication trench. After a short interval the officer and I follow them. First we call on a party of about 20 starting to dig an enclosed defence work, on the back line, which we had taped out the previous day; next a small party trying to persuade water in the trench to flow down a drain. Next a party putting up wire entanglement, which calls for

26

some correction. On the way I spot a 'blind' 5·9 shell, weighing about 90 pounds, lying in the open nearby. He would not do any damage where he lies, and it does not seem worth wasting explosive in blowing him up. The officer and I discuss the best positions for a couple of machine-guns on the flanks of a 'strong-point,' which is to be constructed. We find a party laying trench-boards, carried up the previous night, and further on another one wading, with gum-boots on, and (occasionally) depositing some of the mud from the bottom of the trench over the top. A few well-chosen words of exhortation are called for here. Close by, some of the sappers are revetting a bad patch in the trench wall, and cutting and boarding steps out of it. We collect a few men to bury, or at least deposit a modicum of earth over, the carcases of the cows outside the farm house, whose presence is wafted to us over the air. [This was Stinking Farm.] I call one of the sappers to act as my escort, and he and I continue towards the front line. Now we are splashing again through mud and water, as trench-boards have not yet been put in position, although we have been turning them out by the hundreds at our workshop. After passing 'Gabion Farm' and 'Snipers' Home,' our stroll lands us in the front line and we are able to stand upright more freely.

"We pass under a low arch erected as a screen, with a narrow trench leading off it, and labelled 'This Way to Dover,' presumably because it would deposit us in the little River Douve. Two more arches are labelled 'Post Office Bridge' and 'Marble Arch.' These are overhead bridge traverses, as the trench is exposed to enfilade rifle-fire from the German trenches. On our left we notice 'Rose Dale' and various other similarly named cottages—I should say dugouts. At the entrance to one of these is the notice 'Please wipe your feet.' This, however, does not strike an answering chord, as we do not wish to waste half an hour in removing mud. We next hurry past a notice, 'Catch'em Corner. Beware!,' a point which is unhealthy, as being a favourite aiming-mark for a German sniper; but ease up to have a chat with the Infantry officer in charge near 'Snipers' Rest.' It is very different now that the front-line trenches have been joined up. Where, in our early days here, in passing from one to another at night, we had to flatten ourselves on our tummies, if a flare went up, now we move freely by day. A board proclaiming the 'King's Head Hotel—Good Dinners, etc.' is inviting, as it is nearly lunch time, but we pass it resolutely, to pay our respects to the Company Commander at the 'Mayor's Parlour.' R.E. services are not much in request today, and none of their parapet has been knocked in by shell-fire. As we get near 'Warm Corner,' where our sector of the line ends, we hear the now familiar whistle, as a small shell comes over and pitches close to our neighbour's parapet. As it is followed by others, we decide to retrace our steps. On the way back I clamber down into a small underground gallery, oozing mud every-where, with the roof in parts permitting only a hand and knees pro-gress, with the result that there was more of me muddy than un-muddy!

"We are just in time to find our morning's working party standing easy under cover of a farm building, preparatory to returning via the communication trench. Our ears catch a few chaffing remarks at our muddy condition, not perhaps without justification. Also a voice calls out 'Play up Clifton.' I discovered that it came from an ex-Moseley Rugby Club opponent of earlier days. At this period we had in our Company R. W. Pickles and Sam Tucker who gained Rugby Inter-national caps, and E. Kibbey who was captain of Bristol Club. After consuming some hard biscuits and an apple, we meet the afternoon working-party relief, and repeat the allocation of jobs. Soon after 4 p.m. the various parties depart via the trench to keep them out of sight of prying German telescopes, as they go back over the hill. I go back with the sappers to the workshop where we load up our trestle wagon, to go up tonight with the materials required for tomorrow. 6 p.m. sees me back at our little farm drinking tea, tired with a com-fortable tiredness. Half an hour later comes dinner. Then a look at the last newspaper received, followed by a censorial reading of the love-letters of my Section. These, together with my own, will find their way to the box labelled 'censored letters,' and thence to the Army postal Department. In a few minutes I shall be dreaming probably of machine-gun positions, half-buried in a barbed-wire entanglement with a dead cow on top. And that completes my factual account of a subaltern R.E.'s day at the front.

"*22nd May 1915.* I have come through a rather dangerous experi-ence safely. Items designated 'cricket bat and ball' have reached the Company! They are not on our official equipment list! In the course of under two hours they proved almost as lethal as a Hun shell. The bowling—fast and erratic; the pitch—the less said the better. I must see if I can purloin a roller from one of our farms.

"We have been reinforced by an old friend, E. A. Sainsbury, which gives us an extra subaltern, and a very good cricketer. Yesterday I visited civilization again—the first time for about a month. I took the men to their baths at a small town about 2½ miles away [this was Nieppe]. Here they go to a factory in which there are about half a dozen large vats. They can bath 1,000 men a day, and it is very well organized. The men undress and pass their tunics and trousers through one hatch, then pass on to the vats and give up their undergarments, unless they wish to keep them. Then, in batches of about a dozen, they rush like a pack of schoolboys for the vats filled with really hot water, and in which you can just about swim. After their bath they are given a towel and clean undergarments, and finally receive back their suits after a dry steaming process. There was a most humorous R.A.M.C. fellow in charge, wearing an apron and a red jelly-bag cap with a tassel, who reminded me of a pantomime comedian. He shepherded the dallying men out of the vats in first-rate style. 'Out you get! Out you get!', and a cold stream of water from a hose-pipe was directed on to their heads, and they usually 'gat.' Everyone laughing and talking as they scampered about in their birthday suits, or coming away with a pair of pants of a ridiculous size for them. There was a small vat for officers. I got in first, and had quite a swim round it. Afterwards I rode into Armentières and devoured six fresh pâtisseries in an attractive little shop frequented by officers.''

My records of the last week of May indicate a considerable increase in gunfire both to the North of us, and on our own front. On Whit Sunday it was particularly heavy, and the area round our old billet in Plugstreet Village was badly damaged. "At one point in our new built-up fire trenches they knocked the biggest hole I have seen, and sniped through the gap all day, and at intervals turned on a machine-gun. Yet at night, when they must have known that we should be repairing the damage, never a shot came through, although there was a bright moon low down behind the trench, and a bare 200 yards between their and our trenches. They have also been doing spiteful things to part of my pet communication-trench, which they may think harbours our infantry in support. We tried the effect of putting up a few rows of sandbags and timber round a farm, already smashed to smithereens. Since then the sandbags have had heavy casualties, and no further damage to the trench.''

Our No. 1 Company were unfortunate. In the back area they had been employing Belgian civilian labour on filling wooden boxes with gunpowder contained in barrels. These boxes were designed for anti-gas-cloud protection in the front line, to cause an upward current of air, to lift the gas over the trench. One of the barrels of gunpowder exploded, probably from one of the men surreptitiously smoking. As a result there were several casualties. They also lost a G.S. wagon, which was taking the filled boxes up to the front. Luckily the driver heard a fuze sizzling, and hurled himself into the ditch seconds before the whole consignment blew up.

"*30th May 1915.* Our Brigadier seems quite pleased with our efforts on the long communication trench. We met on one of his tours of the front line. He remarked 'I have just met Major Eberle. Is he your brother?' On my replying, he snapped out 'Does he keep you in order?' To which I very gravely replied in an unqualified affirmative!

I am afraid the subaltern's impish sense was aroused a few minutes later, when he projected himself suddenly on to his stomach, as a lump of shell went singing over his head. We always seem to derive a little satisfaction when Headquarters Staffs get a share of the strafing. To give them their due, our Divisional Commander and the Brigadiers and C.R.E. set us a fine example by regular personal contact with the men, and viewing the conditions in the trenches. Our views of the higher-up commands is not so complimentary. We picture them and the base 'wallahs' as living in relative security and comfort, with very little contact with the front-line conditions. I think we are often unjust, as many have earned it by their past fighting experiences.

"*2nd June 1915.* Yesterday another of my corporals was hit in the leg, making the fifth casualty in my Section. My Section has changed over to day work, and running the Company workshop. The latter is a rough shed at the back of the farm barn which houses two of our Sections. It is mainly carpentry work of a rough nature, but we have our forge and the 'pièce de résistance,' a steam-engine. With infinite labour of six horses under cover of darkness we dragged back to the billet a rusty and battered steam-engine on wheels, which had been lying in the open only a few hundred yards behind the front line. After the plugging of a few bullet-holes, it has been successfully driving an invaluable circular saw. It had no gauge on it, but one was found at a farm. Unfortunately we could not identify the scale of the units marked on it. However, in spite of heavy stoking, the engine is still there, and turning out large quantities of cut timber for trench-boards and pickets for wiring.

"A pleasant feature of back-area life is that I can ride round the jobs on my blue roan mare. I meet envious glances from the perspiring, footslogging infantry. She is very lovely, and has just walked quite unconcernedly into the dining room. When I called her she came in quietly and asked for an apple. In going out she was a bit clumsy and knocked over a chair. It was pardonable for her perhaps to take our mess for a stable; outwardly and inwardly there is not much difference.

"The past week has seen the completion of our pet communication-trench, now over 1½ miles in length, in all its luxuriance of trench-boards, and almost upright walking. The latter part as it neared the front line entailed all-night work. We start at 8.30 p.m. and get back to our billet between 5 and 6 a.m. Midway we have a break before the second relief of the Infantry digging-party arrive, and we make tea in a dixie in a ruined farm behind our front line. When we get back we are pretty hungry, but not sure whether we are eating our supper or breakfast.

"Also my Section has been engaged in finishing off the revetting of

30

a new fire-trench, mainly carried out under a **Regular R.E.** Company. This is a trench which has been pushed forward on the right of our normal sector, and it brings the distance between the trench where the Boches are living and our trench to a bare 140 yards. It is not nearly as bad as it sounds, as very often the nearer you are the less 'windy' it is. The worst part of the job was to get the materials there. A line of 50 men carrying a number of long white planks is rather apt to be visible if there is a moon, but we were on slightly lower ground, and thereby not silhouetted. The longer one stays out here the more wonderful seems the cover of darkness, if you use it properly. Up to the last night I had almost a clean sheet, and then, by sheer bad luck, the only shot that came over finished one poor chap—not a sapper.

"In the future our casualties from stray shots ought to be considerably reduced if we stay here. Picture the difference—walking up a trench-boarded communication trench, in which I have not yet heard of a man being hit, as against stumbling along muddy tracks full of shell-holes, with stray shots whistling merrily alongside.

"Normally the men wander about the trenches as freely as taking a stroll in their home town, unless there is—as they express it—'something doing.' It is a bit different for us when we have large parties to control in the open, owing to the sense of responsibility. We are responsible for deciding where they work, and the routes they take to it. One has to decide on the spur of the moment whether the conditions, or the necessity for continuing the work, under shell- or machine-gun-fire, justify running the particular risks for the men. That is where the rather wearing nature of our work comes in, more so than any physical tiredness."

5   Our New Sector "(Plugstreet)"

June 1915

In the first half of June two changes occurred in our normal routine. One was the arrival from Bristol of another complete South Midland Field Company, to which our Second in Command, Captain E. Briggs, was transferred as O.C., 2nd Lieutenant G. T. Hollingworth being posted to our Company. The new Company took over from the 9th Field Company R.E., who had been attached to the Division, so that there is now a 48th Division Field Company working with each of our Brigades. The other was a rearrangement whereby the Divisional Front was held by two Brigades instead of three, the third being held in reserve; the attached Field Companies followed the same pattern of reliefs.

"We have been told that the Brigadier of our 143rd Brigade asked that our Company should remain attached to them in the shuffle taking place. I think that the Infantrymen have quite a wholesome regard for us, although they do not love us, regarding us as taskmasters. Our relationship with their officers is normally a very friendly and happy one.

"*11th June 1915*.   The Company has taken over an additional area of the front line, in conjunction with our Brigade. The idea seems to be that when the latter goes into reserve we do likewise, and concentrate on back-area work, and also have a general wash-and-brush-up. This means that we should have time to find out if we remember anything about pontoon and trestle bridging, forming fours respectably, and suchlike activities in what now seem far-off days. The betting is that our 'relief' days will mean merely a few extra hours *per diem* on top of normal activity. For the last few days my Section have been feverishly turning out huts and dug-out materials. The O.C. usually waves a magic wand about 10 p.m., and after studying a chit from the C.R.E.'s Office says 'you will make ten huts to be ready by tomorrow evening, etc., etc.' Probably about mid-day we get some idea of the pattern required. Of course this does not take into consideration trying to satisfy the demand for trench-boards, pit-props for dug-outs, pointed pickets for wiring, and suchlike trivialities."

"We see from the newspapers received that we have again appeared in 'dispatches from the front.' This particular effort was the sending sky-high of some 20 yards of German trench, followed by a rigorous bombardment last Sunday morning. I believe it was a question of only a few feet separating our gallery from a counter-mine, so it had to be popped off quickly. A couple of mornings ago, as I was coming back to breakfast about 7 a.m., I heard a big pop, followed by a burst of artillery fire, plus machine-guns and rapid rifle-fire. It turned out that the Germans had exploded a mine they were known to be making, but it was short of our line, and only disturbed the men's morning rest. Neither were on the part of the line we have been responsible for, and the trenches concerned will be a little healthier for at least the next few weeks.

"An inter-section cricket match last evening was a great success. We were successful in beating No. 4 Section by 107 runs to 62. An extra ball proved useful, as we were continually hitting into the farm pond. It was a curious game, or one might term it unusual, with shells pitching in a big field on the other side of the road, about 300 yards away. They were probably searching for one of our batteries. While I was batting several big fellows came over. It is apt to make one take one's eye off the ball, if you happen to hear the long-drawn whistle of a shell, just as the ball leaves the bowler's arm. However, the pitch had been improved, and I managed to collect ten runs before being caught in the long field. It was a pleasant relaxation!"

The period of our being "in reserve" with our Brigade lasted four days. When they returned to occupation of the front line they took over the new sector. This lay to the East and South-East of Plugstreet Wood. Two small hamlets, completely ruined by shell-fire on the Eastern fringe of the wood, were included in the sector. These were St Yves and Le Gheer. Up to this date we had been very parochial, and all our work confined to our allotted sector. Now we had to reconnoitre and learn all about another trench system, which differed markedly in many respects.

"*19th June 1915.* I have been struggling to write up my records for several days, but the only spare moments I have had seem to have been swallowed up completely by eating and sleeping. Today I have put in nearly fifteen hours already 'doing summat.' The day started badly by the alarm-clock, set for 2.45 a.m., failing to do its duty, apparently sleeping on its post, with the result that Hollingworth and

I did not wake till 3.30. However, getting up and dressing is only a matter of a few minutes. Also, I can get up to the most advanced point of our new-front line trenches in twenty-five minutes, with the aid of a bicycle.

"Back about 8 a.m. for breakfast, covered with mud, and my toes swimming in my waders, owing to the water, after heavy rain, having risen above the level of their tops in a badly drained trench. The cussedness of it all out here is that where we want to find water there is none, and where we don't want it, it appears in flood-like abundance. A quick breakfast is followed by a shave and clean-up. Here again we have to economize with our pond, which is dropping in level rapidly, and, incidentally, has to satisfy the thirst of the young heifers.

"My Section are engaged mainly in the workshop, but I have been detailed to guide a party of R.E. from a 'Kitchener Division,' who are attached to us for four or five days' training. 'Personally conducted tours for emigrants from England! Boche trenches and frightfulness supplied to order.' They are here to gain experience in the kind of work required in front-line trenches. It was interesting to watch the reactions of a R.E. Unit of the 'New Army,' the first time of their doing this. They are full of enthusiasm, but I do not think they liked being shown the tricks of the trade by a Territorial unit. They are supremely confident that the 'New Army' will finish off the war, whereas we have been the stop-gap till they could come out. This attitude is rather different from that of the Regular Army units. They have helped and treated us as if we were younger brothers. These fellows, however, were unlucky in having one of their number hit a few minutes after arriving on the job for the first time, and a couple more later on, at a spot which is usually quite healthy.

"About 2.30 p.m. the party departed, and I retired to eat my lunch at our bungalow, a new summer residence which we have taken over in Plugstreet Wood, and from which Sainsbury claims we can get rid of our empty jam-tins by throwing them at the Germans. This, I should add, is an outrageous exaggeration, but sounds well. Being already late for meeting Jack Wright here, I am allowed only a few minutes to consume biscuits and an apple. For the next two hours we wander round the front-line trenches map-making. To be more exact, marking in our large-scale maps their positions, communication trenches, supporting-points, etc., on our side, and on the German side. The latter could not be carried out so thoroughly, as we had not received any invitation to visit them. However, by dint of squinting through periscopes, and disguising ourselves as features of the land-scape, from vantage points behind the line, we got a very fair impression of them.

"Back in time to hand out pay to my Section, and arrange details for the next day's work, we returned to the billet thirsting for tea soon after 6 p.m. Thereafter for some reason the junior members of the Mess became more than usually hilarious, in spite of shortened hours of sleep. The result was a riotous period, such that the O.C., coming in later, wanted to know if all his officers had been touched by the sun. About 8 p.m. a cyclist orderly comes in, doubtless having ridden at break-neck speed over the rough roads, and hands the O.C. a sealed envelope marked 'urgent.' Everyone gazes anxiously at the O.C.'s face as he slowly opens it. Is it to say that there will be an attack at dawn, or that a baths parade is cancelled? With tensed voice he reads out the message 'The direction of the wind at Divisional Head-quarters tonight at 19 hours was towards South-East'—*ergo* a gas attack is unlikely. We suppress a cheer. We are getting used to these little attentions which O.C. Signals sends us."

"The O.C. also produces a long questionaire, which has come from some faraway headquarters. It asks for answers, under eleven heads, as to the advisability of an issue of flypapers. The last one reads 'How often will the flypapers be required to be renewed?' Great are the workings of the official mind hard at work at the base! Or is it the first-fruits of the new Coalition Cabinet?"

Reference has been made to Plugstreet Wood. It was situated about ¾ mile North-East of Plugstreet Village. It was thickly wooded with tall and large trees, and extended to over 2,000 yards West to East, and about 1,300 from North to South. It gave an easy and well-screened approach to a point close to the front-line trenches. Severe fighting, especially for Le Gheer on its Eastern edge had taken place in the previous October.

"*22nd to 25th June* 1915.   The bungalow is in a small clearing close to one of the wood corduroy tracks running through the wood. It was 'discovered' by me, untenanted, and Sainsbury and I share it, as our two sections are working on the front line just East of the wood. I have a few sappers living in it for emergency jobs in the trenches, and I am finding it very useful for getting a quick sleep during the day or night. I can bicycle down most of the corduroy tracks, made up of logs, but there are numerous holes. I am becoming quite expert in jumping them, and the bicycle is Government property! It is quite a pretty spot, several hundred yards from the German lines, and the bunga-low is sandbagged on the enemy side to make it shrapnel- and bullet-proof. On the other side there is a rustic seat and table, and a lean-to cook-house, all beautifully shaded, and concealed from overhead observation. Sitting outside in the evening is like being on a summer holiday, honeysuckle in profusion, and the sinking sun glinting through the trees. Unfortunately the trees are not always allowed to remain in peace, several big branches having come down in the 'garden.' It is an awe-inspiring sight to see large branches, or the top half of a tall tree, sliced cleanly off by a shell and fall crashing to the ground.

"Inside the bungalow, which bears the name 'Himalaya,' we have an officers' room, with two bunks made with revetting canvas, a table and chairs—doubtless taken from a derelict house—rough cupboards, with rusty old French rifles and long bayonets hung on the walls. Such trophies are not hard to find, relics of the October fighting. There are graves of several nationalities round us—sometimes a simple cross with the inscription such as '18 Soldiers of the 64th Saxon Regiment lie buried underneath' or 'Here lies a French Soldier.' Others are mere mounds with nothing else to guide you as to what they represent. Nearby a man has been buried on top of a previously made dugout. A short distance away from the hut is the grave of Ronald Poulton-Palmer, who was killed here recently by a chance bullet. An old Oxford Blue and Harlequin, he was one of the finest centre three-quarters to play for England just before the War. I had known him, both on and off the football field, when he was still at Rugby School and at Oxford. I had a very great admiration for his personal qualities as a man and officer.

"At one part of our sector our fire-trench has been pushed forward, forming almost a rectangle in front of the general line—it is always referred to as the 'Birdcage.' The distance between the German and our trench here is a bare 100 yards, and most of our new front is considerably closer to the German line, compared with that previously held. The trenches are so close that they are normally free from being shelled, but the Infantry get rifle-grenades fired on them. It is a case of keeping heads down also, and it is not advisable to hold a periscope in the same position over the trench parapet for more than a few seconds. The German snipers lie in carefully screened nests just behind the trench, and are good marksmen! In a ruined building about 200 yards behind our line, the top of the wall has been blown in, leaving a metal down-pipe projecting above it. I counted over 70 bullet holes in the pipe, which they probably thought was being used as a periscope.

"One of my Section's jobs was to dig a narrow 2-foot 6-inch wide trench to a newly formed crater about 25 yards out from our front trench. The crater was about 8 feet across, and over 6 feet deep. It was decided to utilize it as a listening-post against enemy underground mining, which was believed to be in progress. With the enemy trench less than 100 yards away it was advisable to employ a minimum number of sappers. As a result the work was only partially completed in the short hours of darkness. In the morning I wanted to see by daylight what sandbagging was required in the crater. From about half-way the trench was a bare 2 feet in depth, and at one point had a muddy hump sticking up in the middle. A little scratching disclosed that this was a pair of boots, toes up and with a pair of legs attached. It was a case of having to flatten myself crawling over another hump about 3 feet further on, which wobbled under pressure of my weight. I tried to convince myself that it had no connection with the boots, and hoped that my posterior would not be spotted by a sharp-eyed Boche rifleman!"

Later on, when digging new trenches in the Hebuterne/Fonque-villers area, we were faced not infrequently with the problem of dealing with human bodies lying in, or partly protruding into, the line of the trench.

My notes record the little comedy episode of the "Lost House" on our new sector front. I received instructions from the Major to find out "if a house in no-man's-land is occupied at night by the Germans." The request came via the C.R.E. from Divisional Staff. The latter had not actually seen it, but the house and its name were clearly marked on one of their maps. Its exact map reference placed it a short distance in front of the German wire, and the impression of the Staff was that it "dominated parts of our front."

"On consulting the Infantry Company Commander in the front trench I was met by a complete ignorance of its existence, and we could see no sign of it through our periscopes. The ground in front of us was rough, and had received some upheavals. I duly reported to the O.C. 'No house visible.' He was thoroughly dissatisfied with my failure to find an 'unmistakable house' sufficiently prominent to be named on the map. Accordingly, that night an Infantry Officer and I went out to find it. A low hedge gave some cover, and then we lay in the long grass and waited for flares to go up, as there was no moon visible. After changing position several times a flare disclosed, about 25 yards from the German wire, a large heap of rubble in a small depression. It was by now partly hidden by long grass, but on top of it lay the recognizable remains of a shattered wooden door. The 'lost house' was found. The explanation—the Germans had availed themselves of all the wood and brick materials for the betterment of their trenches, probably after it had been knocked about by shelling.

"I duly reported again to the Major, but he obviously considered that the honour of our Corps for giving reliable information was at stake. He refused to allay the fears of the Divisional Staff until he had personally inspected the site. After erecting periscopes along about a quarter of a mile of our trench, with Infantry officers, sergeants and sentries joining in, he was satisfied. Now if we want to pull his leg a dreamy reference to the 'lost house' is a winner!"

I recorded a rather pathetic incident on another night. "I was called by one of the sappers who were digging a trench through the back gardens of a ruined hamlet just behind the front line [this was St Yves]. He had struck his pick into a big chest buried about a foot below the surface. With visions of its containing the family jewellery, or the contents of the cellar, I thought it best to dig it out, as it would only be rifled and wasted by the next comers. I told my Corporal to take it under cover of one of the ruined houses, where a torch could be used, and to make a list of the contents. On my return from a nearby job I asked the Corporal 'Have we found the family jewels?' His somewhat glumly spoken reply was 'Oh sir, we found a second chest, but they'm nowt but linen and feminine underwear.' His list included 31 good blankets and sheets, quilts, baby clothes, shirts, ladies' vests and other garments, over 120 items in all. The damp was just beginning to affect them, so I shall hand them over to the 'Maison Communale,' for the benefit of Belgian refugees, if the owners cannot be traced.

"I believe today is Wednesday, but I am not at all sure, as there is nothing to make one day different from another. [It was in fact a Tuesday, the 22nd June.] It is 2 p.m. and I have been trying to get some sleep in the bungalow. The continual sniping attack of battalions of flies, mosquitoes and the like, have made it impossible, and my hands are swollen lumps of itching. I need a wash, but have reached the stage of believing that it can be overdone. With the water available I am not surprised if washing has the effect of making one dirtier in appearance. As somebody in the Mess remarked recently, washing a towel seems to consist of scratching it with soap, in order merely to distribute the dirt over a larger area. One has become thoroughly accustomed to not taking off any garments, other than a tunic, over several days.

"My wandering about these trenches brings daily reminders of Bristol, as they have been occupied previously by a Bristol battalion. [The 4th and 6th Gloster Battalions formed part of our 144th Brigade.] Among the names marked up on boards are 'Tramways Centre,' 'Bristol Hippodrome'—a big dugout, 'Wine Street'—a very narrow stretch—and 'Gloucester Lane,' the last named being a most unhealthy short communication-trench."

In the concluding period of our stay in the Plugstreet area we were also involved in tunnelling operations, to a very minor extent, but giving us useful experience. The Sector in which we were working was suitable for tunnelling, as the German and our trenches were separated only by about 100 yards. It was well known on both sides that underground tunnels were being made, and mines had been previously exploded. On our side the work was being carried out by a specialist

"Tunnelling" Company R.E., recruited mainly from ex-coalmine workers. Secrecy as to the position of the tunnels was of course of the utmost importance. The knowledge that the enemy were tunnelling had an adverse moral effect on those garrisoning the trench area most likely to be the target. It induced a mental strain and tension, and I always nursed an uncomfortable feeling that at any moment the whole trench might be blown sky-high when I was in it, and was glad when I passed away from it.

It happened that, early one morning when on my round of the front line, I was told that a sentry had noticed wisps of vapour rising, just after dawn, at a spot in front of our wire. It was deduced that this was warmer air escaping from a tunnel underneath. We received hurried orders to start a listening gallery with inclined shaft from our trench opposite the spot indicated, and a second one a little distance away. This involves putting in wooden frames as the burrowing work progresses, to prevent falls of earth. All the earth removed has to be sandbagged, and carried or hauled into the trench. It must be disposed of without being detected by the enemy. Apart from the actual digging by our sappers, it was dirty and hard work for the infantry party detailed for carrying up the inclined slope. As I was standing by the entrance I heard a voice from behind me; "Eberle, I hope you will use all your ingenuity in devising means of lessening the labour work required of my Infantry." It came from our Divisional General, Sir Robert Fanshawe, or "Fanny" as we all called him. This was just one of the many examples we had of the way in which he personally kept in touch, and looked after the interests of those under his command.

Progress on both galleries was slower than we had anticipated, quicksand being encountered in one of them. We were, however, not to know what further developments took place, as on 25th June we handed over to the 87th Field Company R.E., and never returned to the Plugstreet area.

Two days later I wrote: "Our last ten days in the Plugstreet trenches were rather more exciting, both actually, and in expectation of what might happen. We were working at night very close to the Germans. On one night, out in front of our wire, one fellow was whistling softly to us, and then called out 'English born.' He could not have been more than a dozen or so yards from us, as we lay very flat on the ground in the tall grass. Another one made me jump by loosing off his rifle just in front, the flash seeming very close, but I do not think it was intended for us."

On our last afternoon I showed an R.E. officer round the front-line trenches which he was taking over from us. I felt quite sorry in some respects to say goodbye to Plugstreet, where we had worked and schemed for nearly three months. As I came back through the village a thunderstorm broke out. It was the time when the daily shelling usually took place. Instead, I bicycled, under a borrowed ground sheet, to the accompaniment of a louder artillery from the skies, and a complete soaking.

In retrospect our Division was exceptionally fortunate in having an initial period of nearly three months in which to gain experience of a static trench war, and of being under enemy fire, particularly shell-fire. By later standards which we were to experience, the latter was very moderate in its intensity. Even so it was continually in our thoughts and conversations, and it exceeded in quantity the normal ration allowed to be fired by our Gunners.

The Infantry had not been called on to take part in any large-scale frontal attack, and as yet the policy of frequent harassing night raids had not been developed. Hence their casualties had been relatively light. They had gained confidence in themselves, and with it came an almost light-hearted acceptance of the conditions under which they lived. This found humorous and often inquisitive expression in many ways. One symptom which did not survive much longer was the desire to acquire as souvenirs the nose-caps of enemy shells from the craters they made. An occasion is recalled when one subaltern, in a race to outstrip competitors, tripped and disappeared head first into a 5·9 shell-hole just behind our billet, leaving his gum-booted legs waving in the air above the crater top, to the accompaniment of a murky stream of imprecations.

The same officer, accompanied by a mounted orderly, was riding, in our early days at Plugstreet, along a road, when he noticed an un-exploded German shell, about 3 inch, lying on the grass verge. He remembered a notice in Divisional routine orders to the effect that un-exploded shells should be notified to the Gunners. They might obtain helpful information, from the range-setting on the shell, as to the locality of the enemy battery. Therewith he picked up the shell, not knowing the cause of its failure to explode, which might well have been a slight sticking of a spring. He pushed it into one of his saddle wallets, and trotted merrily off to the nearest battery site. Walking into the Gunners' Mess he plumped it on their table. From his own account his reception was not cordial, and he was told in no uncertain terms to take the adjectival object away.

To sum up our experience, the Division had learned many lessons of trench warfare. Inevitably there was a daily attrition number of casualties, but I cannot recall any cases of men breaking down, or suffering unduly from mental strain from enemy shell-fire, although for nearly three months few of us had spent more than a few hours, in total, outside the ranging area of the enemy's daily dose of shells.

Whether out in no-man's-land or under shell-fire, the resulting effect was exciting rather than frightening. Perhaps the strangest feature was that, at this period, it had been a war with an almost invisible enemy. Only rarely did anyone get glimpses of the men against whom we were fighting, either in the daylight or at night.

6   We Move Southward (Loos)

July 1915

On the evening of 25th June we set out at dusk on the first stage of a trek southward, which was to take us to Cauchy La Tour, a small village about 10 miles West of Béthune.

"The heavy rain had stopped before we started, and the march by moonlight to our first billet, South of Bailleul, was a pleasant one. Four hours after settling down to sleep on a concrete floor, some one woke us all up, and we had a 'mad breakfast.' Spirits were high, any feelings of tension which existed in the shelled area had vanished, and we were on holiday.

"The O.C., after an inspection by daylight of our transport, says we look like a travelling circus. We found three mascots had been smuggled on the wagons, a grown dog, a puppy about 6 inches high, and a little nanny-goat, which the men have had for about six weeks. It follows them about like a dog. The vehicles also carried many acquired, or home-made comforts—items which are *not* listed under our mobilization equipment. We marched off again at night to near Vieux Berquin, and the following night about 18 miles, via Nerville St Venant, to Berguette, where we arrived about 5.30 a.m. Leaving here 12 hours later, we reached our Cauchy billet at 9.30 that evening. Only one man out of the Company fell out in the course of this trek.

"*29th June 1915.*   We have been on the trek, in Brigade formation, for 26 hours in the last two days. But—wonder of wonders—last night I slept on a bed, after turning off the electric light. It is three months since I have done that, and I can sit in a quasi-armchair and wash out of a porcelain basin.

"The first hour of the 28th after midnight I was trudging alongside my brother, as my Section happened to be leading the Company, and we were giving our horses a rest from our weight. We had left our previous resting point at 8 p.m., and through the night rumbled through quaint little villages and small towns by the light of the moon. It was a trying march owing to frequent checks. Gunner transport were ahead of us and behind the Infantry, the whole forming a column stretching along three miles of the road. Inasmuch as each vehicle takes about five to ten seconds to move off after the one in front, after the hourly halt, the leading unit will have been on the move for over ten minutes before the tail end can re-start. One obtains a better realization of what it means to move a whole Division by road, unless good march discipline and exact time-keeping is observed.

"As dawn broke we could see how the countryside through which we were passing had changed. It more closely resembled that of England, but the little towns were essentially French. As we near the twentieth mile of our march, we find ones and twos of the troops in front, who have fallen out, sitting by the roadside. Trench life has entailed some loss of marching practice. About 4.30 a.m. we pass some of the Infantry units bivouacking in the fields, and know we are nearing our own resting place. A short distance further on Sainsbury was waiting to guide us to it. For an hour and a half he had been watching the tired troops passing. Even then they would have their little jokes, and he was greeted with the remark, among others, 'Blimey! If it isn't the Sappers here again, looking for a working party!' We are fortunate in finding that there are barns, and a room in the farm house, available for the Company; the horses are tethered to ropes stretched between wagons, feeds prepared; the farmer's wife bustles round and produces coffee and a big omelette for us. Boots are taken off, and we slide into our valises, what time the clock should be striking 7 a.m. We expected a rest till the evening, but at 3.30 p.m. orders arrived for us to move at 5.0 p.m.—the time we had ordered dinners. We hurriedly consumed more food and packed up. There is no arriving ten minutes late when you have to join the column in your allotted position. As we drew out from the farm the driver of the 'barbed wire'-cart, an addition to our mobilization transport, drove too near the open edge of a rough bridge over the farm ditch. The result was that the cart took up a half-submerged position in stinking water, with one wheel spinning in the air. We watched the unloading of the barbed-wire contents with some anxiety. Our Mess box of drinks had been illicitly stowed away in it; hence the true inwardness of the vials of our wrath heaped upon the head of the driver.

"The march, this time by daylight, was the most interesting one we have had up to now. We were back to a land of good houses and shops, of prosperous-looking people who greeted us with smiles and a wave of the hand. On the night marches it had been through deserted streets, and past long lines of stationary lorries. It has been amusing to hear the spontaneous cheer that went up when we first saw a moving train again. It seemed home-like and cheerful to see the glow from the engine. Now in the streets of an industrial town—this was Lillers— there was movement and bustle, and a fleet of khaki-coloured London buses for troop transport. We came under the critical eye of big-boned British Guardsmen, sloppy-trousered Poilus, a party of Turcos. A couple of bright-eyed French girls tossed flowers to the passing troops, who are not slow with their 'Bonjour, Mam'selles,' or more endearing terms in English. For most of them it was their first experience of the moving panorama of a busy French town untouched by war damage."

Arrived at Cauchy La Tour we were most comfortably installed in a house on the estate of an old château. Here we had a large room for messing, and three rooms upstairs with beds. For twelve days we lived in luxury, carrying out light training, including pontooning, and practice operations with the Infantry, and overhauling our equipment. We heard only the low rumble of war in the distance. At the end of it I commented: "What a difference the trained eye would see and find in the Company now, compared even with when we left England. Such a difference too in their looks as the result of the open-air life. As a Section Officer one has gained an intimate insight into the differing temperaments of each man in the Section, and of his likely reactions in times of stress or responsibility. To pick the right man for a job is often the most important factor for a satisfactory result."

"12th July 1915. I was half dozing in the saddle last evening when I heard a voice 'Two or three lengths interval between wagons along this road, please, sir!' 'Why?' I asked, waking up. 'This road is liable to observation, sir.' Then we knew that we were back in the war picture once more. Curiously, we nearly all seemed pleased. The marching Sappers seemed to forget that they were tired, and bandied the well-worn jokes about Jerry's shells, in terms that were not complimentary to him. No-one is anxious to poke his head into the lion's mouth, but there is a hankering for getting on with the job we came out to do."

Our destination was a barren stretch of country on the North-East side of Noeux Les Mines, one of the small towns in a coal-mining district. No billets were available. Our bivouac site was low-lying fields, with a large clump of tall trees in a hollow, under which we had to conceal horses and wagons from enemy observation from balloons. In front of us was a long bare ridge of chalky soil, which stretched from West of Loos to Hulluch, 2 miles to the North. In a few weeks' time this portion of the British front was to be the centre of the British attack, known as the Battle of Loos. Historians have pointed out that it was the greatest battle, both as to numbers engaged, and losses incurred, which had ever been fought by our Army up to that date.

Our casualties in the two and a half weeks, before the battle petered out, are quoted as being over 52,000. The sudden withdrawal of our Division, as recorded in extracts following, is attributed to the decision by the Commander-in-Chief to aid the French by taking over from them a further long section of the front forthwith. As a result we were not committed to take part in the battle, as was originally intended.

"*Tuesday, 13th July 1915.* The evening of last Sunday, when we arrived at this soggy site was bitterly cold. Half a gale blowing, and ugly-looking clouds presaged heavy rain as being imminent. There was no cover other than the clump of trees and hedges. The men's bivouacs were spread along the latter on slightly higher ground. The O.C. favoured a tiny island, round which a 2-inch deep trench was dug. I preferred a position under a cart, which produced various offers of 'would I like a lifebelt?' By 8 a.m. following we were off to the chalky ridge in front of us to dig trenches on the reverse side from the Germans. We had just reached the appointed place, when the familiar whistle-cum-bang showed the un-wisdom of being in sizeable parties. Another party about 300 yards away had been spotted. They scattered rapidly as the ranging which must have been at least 9,000 yards, was uncomfortably accurate. We sat tight while some 20 shells came over. Then a message came, shortly afterwards, recalling us to our bivouac site, and for the Company to move forward by 2 p.m.

"We made our move for what was intended to be taking over the front-line area. Seven hours later we were back in the field from which we had set out. Our present views of the gyrations of faraway Staff would not be flattering to them. Yesterday's programme of orders received was as follows:

"No. 1.   Works parade at 8 a.m. till 4.30 p.m., cancelled soon after reaching the job.

"No. 2.   Company to move forward at 2 p.m.; cancelled at 1 p.m. for

"No. 3.   Move at 7 p.m.; cancelled at 7 p.m. by

"No. 4.   Move at 8 p.m.; cancelled at 7.30 p.m. for Move at 8.30 p.m. or at discretion of O.C. when sufficiently dark."

We duly arrived at the billet in Mazingarbe of a Field Company of a London Division, and prepared to take over. After some delay we gathered that their move out had been cancelled, and we were to take over the billet of another half company in a small school in Les Brebis. We did so, and just before 1 a.m. were in possession for fifteen minutes, just sufficient time to unhook and unload blankets and rations. Then came the order to return to our bivouac site. We had a big hustle to get back over the ridge before dawn. The road from Mazingarbe was

45

under direct observation, and subject to heavy shelling of any troops seen on it. Hooked in and away in fifteen minutes, we were only just clear before daylight, the Sappers swinging back at a rattling pace without a break, and the drivers keeping their horses moving at a fast pace. We have not even had the consolation of confusing the German Intelligence by our so-called relief, although from where I am writing in our camp I can see half-a-dozen German observation balloons, or sausages as we term them.

"Saturday, 17th July 1915. Just before 4 a.m. this morning we were back in our old comfortable billet, with a real bed and electric light—this was Cauchy—and now I am waiting my turn for the pit-manager's hot bath, after 'hogging it' in bed till midday. Think of the joy of climbing into one's sleeping-bag laid on a real mattress after six nights of heavy rain and wind spent in a marshy stubble field. We have only put a foot under a roof once for about ten minutes in the past week, when we made our abortive takeover. We have since learned that two men were killed by a shell in that billet which we were to have occupied on Monday night.

"Last Wednesday was the worst night since we came to France. We were digging trenches on the ridge not far from our camp. I had spent several hours of daylight in pegging out tapes and preparing for the night work, and showing what was wanted to a couple of Infantry officers. Then from 7.15 p.m. till after 3 a.m. our Sappers and 1,400 wretched Infantry, the latter in two reliefs, did their best to dig in the chalky soil. The darkness made it almost impossible to see what they were doing. The gale blew the rain as it came down in sheets. Trench macs were like sodden paper. The rain ran down our necks and every garment seemed wet and clammy. It was difficult even to guide the relieving party up the slippery slope, which was intersected by narrow paths, transformed into rivulets, with a top layer of greasy chalk and mud everywhere. Apparently the work was considered urgent, and the two infantry parties carried on with the job, working steadily the full quota of time. E.A.S. remarked to me later that he would have cheerfully welcomed a shell to wipe him out. Fortunately the rain stopped just after dawn, and we could open our sleeping-bags and find some drier clothes, and we did our best to dry out the sappers. It seems rather unfair that because we have commissioned rank we are entitled to have with us a bigger weight (35 pounds) of personal belongings. When we are in the front line, or under fire, we are all equally naked, in the defensive sense. The only requisite which marks out one man from another is what we term 'guts.'

"We have been reading the newspapers telling us of the coal strike. When will the people at home understand what we are up against?

We would like the miners to see a large village near us here, in this French coal-mining district. It was the scene of a prolonged attack a short time earlier on, with hand-to-hand fighting, not only from house to house, but from room to room. The whole area was a grim mess of ruined buildings. Apart from being shelled, a number had to be blown up by tunnelling under them to evict the Germans. [This village was Vermelles.] I wish, too, that the miners could read some of the men's letters going home, expressive of what those out here think of them, and what they would like to do to them.

"On our return march to Cauchy the rainy weather continued for most of the night. Our route was largely country lanes with some bad hills, but the drivers came through splendidly, including some tricky handling when we had to get past a pontoon wagon belonging to one of the other Companies. It had got completely bogged down on the soft part of the road edge. It was rather remarkable to note that, on a very dark night like this, the flares going up from the front line up to 5 miles away were sufficiently powerful to light up the road."

The following night we started off again at 1 a.m. on a 10-mile trek. It took us back to Berguette, about 4 miles North of Lillers. Here we entrained, a slow process, with only side loading on to the open trucks available for our wagons. Our destination proved to be Doullens, a market town about 35 miles to the South. From here we marched to Courcelles, bivouacking for one night on the way. Here we were about $2\frac{1}{2}$ miles behind the front line at Hébuterne, almost the most northerly point of the initial attack of the Somme battle in the following July. Our Division remained in the Somme River area for the next twenty-three months, with various recuperating periods away from the front line

"*22nd July 1915.* We are bivouacking for the present in an orchard, but the weather has turned fine and sunny, which makes all the difference I have even been able to change into khaki pyjamas for the night, a distinct comfort after a sweating day. When it is pouring with rain various problems arise. Your rolled-up sleeping-bag is covered by an already wet ground-sheet. The top clothes you are wearing are also wet. The sleeping-bag contains all your present possessions in the way of clothes, spare boots, torch, spurs, a few essential books and such like, all the heavier articles being in the pillow end. You insinuate yourself into the bag all right, but you do not want to bring in also your wet clothes. The answer is to wrap the latter in a small feather-weight oiled sheet, and leave them outside. In the morning they usually seem wetter than when you took them off! Perhaps the real answer is that I was too comfortably nurtured in my youth!

"There is often a certain amount of hazard from horses breaking away from their picket line—a not uncommon occurrence. One night recently Sainsbury was woken up by a horse apparently nibbling his pillow. He 'shooed' it on to the O.C., who had fastened one end of a ground-sheet over him to a rickety wire fence. Number One horse knocked it down, Number Two tried to jump the fence in the dark, with the same result, and a Number Three careered round the field at a hand gallop, and alarmed him sufficiently to make him knock it down himself. Moral—don't attach your ground-sheet covering to a wire fence if there are horses running loose and pursued by a stable picket.''

7   Hébuterne and Warnimont Wood

August 1915

"*24th July 1915*.   The French troops have moved out, and we
have taken over from them. We are installed in a comfortable billet in
part of what is called a small château, also occupied by a caretaker
couple. It is in Courcelles village. We have a large mess-room, furnished with a table, sofa, two easy chairs and sundry other items—all
very civilized.

"We were escorted round the trenches of our Sector by a French
Engineer officer. Earlier on, in this area, the French attacked, successfully capturing the German front and second lines, and dug in just
beyond the latter. Thus the present trench system is a mixture of
French and German work. It is interesting to compare them with
those which we occupied around Plugstreet. It is a mistake to think
that we have nothing to learn from the French. Inadequate attempts
to get rid of water in the trenches, are noticeable, as also sanitation
and cleanliness in general. The fighting seems to have been conducted
in a different style. The French go into a carefully prepared attack
with great gallantry. But in the periods when no attack is contempla-
ted, it is a case of 'live and let live as comfortably as possible,' so far as
the infantry are concerned. Hence there is hardly any rifle-shooting
from either side in the trenches, but both sides indulge in shelling one
another daily. Also the width of no-man's-land between the opposite
trenches is much greater. When taken on our tour, I must confess that
I was far from happy at being expected to project my head well above
the parapet, and remain gazing steadily at the Boche trench in front
of me. In parts of the Plugstreet area it would have meant moral
suicide. When, however, the French officer escorting us did this with
complete sangfroid, honour compelled us to do likewise. When he
came to the end of our part of the front line he suddenly mounted the
fire-step, and with a wave of his hand towards the Boches, exclaimed
'Voilà! C'est chic,' a somewhat surprising epithet to apply, from our

49

past experience. This is borne out by the story circulating, to the effect that the French General, who was showing our Brigadier round for the first time, *sat* on top of the parapet, remarking 'Vieu de petite guerre.' From our point of view there is much to be said for a principle of live and let live between battles, but I hardly think we shall allow it to continue."

There was also a minor sequel to our tour. "The three other subalterns and I bicycled back from our tour to the billet. Feeling tired and thirsty, as the day was scorchingly hot, we stopped at the first village where there were signs of civilian life, to consume a bottle of wine. [This was Sailly-au-Bois.] As our hearts became more cheered, we began to speak well of our foes in these parts, what nice gentlemanly fellows they appeared to be. We had warmed to our subject, when they spoiled it all. First we heard a shell or two drop nearby, accompanied by a running of inhabitants. One had got used to that sort of thing. We were still thirsty, and the bottle only half empty, and we did not move. A few minutes later they dropped a shell on to the adjoining roof, and sent the window-pane near which we were sitting flying all over the place. It was a tactless act on their part, and we have now returned to our former conception of hate.

"*30th July 1915.* On Sunday last I was preparing to spend the next twenty-four hours in the Hébuterne trenches, as we are now working on the principle of having one of our Company officers, and a few sappers, always up in the line, which we can reach at any time of the day. Instead, an order came for the left half of the Company, comprising Sainsbury's and my Sections, to move back at 2 p.m. to cut timber in a wood about four miles away. [This was the Bois de Warnimont, a large wood extending over a mile along a high ridge.] When we reached the area indicated, we found no-one apparently wanting us, and no instructions as to what was required. Accordingly I found a charming spot in a clearing in the wood, high up on the hill, for our bivouac camp, and prepared to take a holiday. Unfortunately just before bed-time a dispatch rider found us, and brought an order for me to report back to the C.R.E.'s Headquarters for instructions. Our prospective idea of a quiet employment with just our own Sappers is turning out rather differently."

At this point it seems desirable to give some further explanation of what follows. Commanders at all levels, from those of small units upwards, have differing views as to where, and how protected, those under their command should be located. This was accentuated by the fact that we were taking over from units of a different nationality. Thus we quickly discovered that practically every unit in the area was crying out for rough timber in some form or other. A priority need came from the Divisional Gunner Batteries, who were digging new emplacements, and nearby dugouts, in the open plain behind Hébuterne and Fonquevillers. They required logs from 8 to 15 feet long, and 8 to 14 inches average diameter.

Our job at once assumed the proportions of a sizeable productive undertaking, for which we were given excellent support by the Division. We were given a daily reinforcement of 250 Infantry and/or Gunners, and on some days were giving employment to up to 130 horses. On the last day of cutting timber we were swamped by the Division sending us 800 men. The Gunner Adjutant promised me that he would send up to the wood daily as many wagons as we could fill with cut timber logs for the batteries.

Our stay in the Wood lasted three weeks, during which we bivouacked under conditions alternating between very hot sun and heavy downpours of rain. We all worked hard and it was one of the most pleasant, and in some respect satisfying periods spent by us during the war. Sainsbury, older than myself but slightly junior in seniority, was a capable and delightful companion. We both enjoyed developing our organization, and running our own show. Our seniors in the Company were fully occupied in coping with numerous works proposed in the forward area. Such instructions as we received and priorities for supplying timber were short-circuited directly to us from the C.R.E.

The following extracts, mainly from letters, may give a small picture of incidents in this phase of the varied activities required of a Field Company R.E. A charitable interpretation must be placed on the obvious colouring of "self-importance" and "look what we have done," as being attributable to a pride in the first semi-independent command, and task overseas, of a one-pip subaltern, operating some distance away from senior parental officers.

"In most respects we are located in a charming, sylvan situation on our high hill. We found a small brushwood shelter, about 7 by 6 feet, made by the French foresters in a clearing. We have fixed some canvas over the top, and although by no means weatherproof, it serves as our office, and E.A.S. sleeps in it. I have a little pen at the back, with a waterproof sheet stretched from a hurdle over my head. [I was to discover later that with heavy rain it became a temporary bathing pool.] E.A.S. undertook furnishing arrangements for the hut, and proudly produced a rustic table and two chairs, one of which I unfortunately demolished the first time I sat on it heavily.

"On our first day we felled only about 60 trees. They are previously marked by us as being suitable for sizes required, and in an orderly progression through the wood. There are two good Somerset lads with experience of tree-felling in my Section. They know that the first essential is to keep the blades of the felling axes very, very sharp.

51

[Man-powered saws, axes and bill-hooks were the only tools available to us.] Our daily quota of trees felled has been rising rapidly, as the other sappers have learned the knack of felling with speed and safety. When the trees are cut down the stouter branches are cut up into lengths, suitable for high and low wire entanglements, others for revetting posts and brushwood hurdles. The remainder is collected into dumps which are thankfully taken by the A.S.C. and other Units, so we do not waste much except the leaves, and we keep the wood tidy.

"2nd August 1915. Today is Bank Holiday Monday. We have just polished off our supper of soup and so-called toast, followed by cheese and gingerbreads. About 8 p.m. I was seeing off the evening convoy of 13 pontoon and G.S. wagons, loaded up for the infantry in the front-line area. The pontoon wagons each have a good 4 tons of logs on them, and a very steep hill to go down. Outside it is raining heavily, and inside the hut we are plagued by flies and spiders.

"Normally the cooking for the Company officers is perpetrated by one of the batmen. Up here we share the meals cooked in dixies by our Sections' cooks from rations, which are sent up daily. Supplementary parcels from home are also just catching up with us after our recent travels.

"We do our utmost to see that the Sappers get the best feeding possible out of the rations issued. The cooking has to be done out in the open, in large dixies supported on two lengths of iron laid on stones. All our water for drinking, cooking or washing has to be fetched from over half a mile away, other than rain-water collected in buckets and improvised receptacles.

"The Sappers thoroughly deserve and need plenty of good food, with all the hard physical work they are doing. They are splendidly cheerful, and seem to enjoy the felling. We do not allow the other working party units to do any actual tree-felling. There are about twenty sappers in each of the two Sections, available for cutting and supervision. They keep 100 men of the working parties, and five teams of horses, employed on carrying and hauling the logs to the wagon loading dump from 8 a.m. to 4.30 p.m. daily. The remainder of the working parties are employed chiefly on stripping and cutting up the branches. So far we have had no untoward accidents. I was rather amused at a little episode yesterday, of which I was a spectator, unseen by the men concerned. Eight of the working party had been carrying a heavy log, but dropped it about a dozen yards away from a waiting wagon, and sat down exhausted. Thereupon two rather brawny sappers, accustomed to lifting the pontoons on and off the wagons, picked it up from the ground and put it straight on to the wagon. I think our fellows did it partly for swank, but it was effective, and the carrying party goggled.''

The following day I added this note: "Another day of thunder-storms and torrents of rain, followed by bursts of sunshine. I am glad I slept last night with most of me in the hut, as I have been using my usual bedroom as a washing pond. However, I think our work is going well. Our Adjutant rode over from the C.R.E.'s office, and studied our system of operations, and he has not suggested any amendments.''

Five days later: "Today, a Sunday, has been almost a real peace-time day of rest. Since lunch-time, or rather dinner, which reverted to bully beef and cheese, we have done nothing except tidy up, sleep and read. It has been the more appreciated as it was unexpected. For the first time our 250 working party failed to put in an appearance. Our sappers had felled 173 trees by one o'clock, and we decided to knock off any further work for the day—the first break they have had since coming to the wood. I had some orders to read out to them before they broke off, and directly they were dismissed they ran whooping to their little bivies. Later in the afternoon the sappers' contentment was increased when our forage cart arrived with rations. Seeing them crowded round it, I investigated, and found that a large gift case of Woodbines was included. It looks as if it works out at about 250 cigarettes to each man. A consignment of new tunics and shirts also arrived, and I have been trying to dole them out adequately. Un-fortunately the Base seem to have thought that we were all giants, supermen or Aldermen. Some of the tunics, when tried on, looked more like dressing-gowns.

"Now E.A.S. and I are relaxing outside our hut, and he has just remarked, 'If only our people at home could see us now!' It is a perfect summer evening, the fading glow in the West showing up through the trees. A lantern on our tree-stump table, ourselves in British warms and slippers, lights dotted around from the Sappers' bivouacs, and a fire round which a number of them are singing merrily.''

A week later: "For the past week I do not seem to have had a spare minute for any writing. Apart from meals it has been a case of 'on the job' from 8 a.m. to 9.30 p.m. or later. The evenings are fully occupied in collating output records against orders issued by the C.R.E. or otherwise, making out stock-lists, and listing requirements for the following day, and how to allocate the Sappers and other parties. We have become unwelcomely popular, as the demand for supplies has been intensified. Headquarters' Staffs, Gunners, Infantry, A.S.C., Signals, besides our own three Field Companies, are all clamouring. As a result we have personal visits from Staff Officers, Colonels, Quartermasters down to Cooks' Mates, all trying to wangle extra supplies for their respective units. We issue a certain amount at our discretion, but we have to regard all applicants as 'throwing their weight about,' 'potential liars' or at least 'tellers of fairy-stories,' according to their heights in the military hierarchy. We counter this by insisting on receipts for everything, and recording all issues to each unit. Specious requests to be allowed to send 'a few men' to cut on their own are flatly turned down. Also we have been honoured by the G.O.C. of our Division riding over to see us one evening. I was in shirt-sleeves, outside the hut, wrestling with out-turn figures, when I suddenly realized that 'Fanny' was beaming down on me from his horse. He chatted very happily, and no complaints.

"We have had another very heavy thunderstorm with torrential rain breaking over our heads. The evening convoy of 15 wagons had just started down our steep and rough track. I was fearful for the horse teams, as the vivid lightning was right over them, accompanied by peals of thunder, but they went down with perfect steadiness. Then I spent a damp half-hour trying to rescue our belongings. Both the inside of the hut and my bed site, just big pools at first, became merged into a river-bed. E.A.S. missed it all, having gone over to the C.R.E.'s Headquarters.

"*22nd August 1915.* Alas! The axe has fallen, this time not on the trees, but on us. The French owners or authorities decided that no more felling of the trees could be allowed. On Friday evening I received a copy of a Signals message from Corps H.Q. to the C.R.E. It stated that permission for cutting was being withdrawn by the French, with the added advice from Corps 'pending actual receipt of cancellation cut all you can.' Underneath this our Adjutant wrote 'Fell like blazes.' The result was that yesterday we concentrated on felling, and cut down 346 minimum 8-inch diameter trees, and sent away 33 full wagon-loads, and could have filled more. It has seemed in some respects rather a shame to have cut down so many fine trees. It is, however, part of the price of war, and we shall never know how many lives they may save, in the protective use to which they are being put. There was some balm when the Gunner Adjutant, who had promised to supply as many wagons as we could fill, came over and apologized: 'Eberle, you've beaten me, although I have sent you every wagon I could lay my hands on.'"

On the 21st August we returned regretfully to Courcelles, and the following day took over normal front-line work, with billets in cellars in semi-ruined Hébuterne. The torrential rainstorms had caused heavy flooding and damage in some of the trenches, with water standing 2 feet or more in them. My terse comment at the time reads: "The trenches are in a 'lovely' state. For the last week our sappers have been going up to them without wearing their trousers!" Much damage was also done to the unrevetted sides, which fell in, partly as the result of the French occupants having been allowed to scoop out holes as shelters under the parapet.

I learned that my name had appeared in the Gazette as being exalted to the rank of a Lieutenant; also that my turn for a six days' leave to England was imminent. I duly found myself enjoying a real bath in Jermyn Street precincts, in the very early hours of the morning of 27th August.

"At the end of my six days' leave I left Victoria Station at 6.30 p.m., and was back in the Company rear billet at Courcelles by 10.30 the following morning. I foolishly ran into the R.T.O. at the station, through not spotting him quickly enough, and was designated as one of the three Duty Officers for the journey. At vantage points along the railway line to Folkestone groups of local inhabitants were gathered to cheer and wave a farewell hand to the daily batch of men returning to the 'Front.' This heartening gesture was appreciated by those returning probably more fully than they realized. The last part of our journey was an 8-mile ride on top of an old London bus, which brought us to our Division's Headquarters. Here I found 'Girls' awaiting me. She was full of life, and apparently had been enjoying herself with the lighter weight of my batman on her back."

The following week the Company Headquarters and two Sections moved to a new billet nearer the front line. This was at Sailly-au-Bois, where we had stopped for refreshment on our way back from our first inspection of the trenches. Sailly was about 8 miles due North of Albert. From it one road led due Eastwards to Hébuterne about 2,600 yards away, the other in a North-Easterly direction to Fonque-villers—usually abbreviated to 'Fonkie.' Most of the 3,500 yards of the latter was under direct observation by the Germans, and liable to be shelled promptly, at a range of under 1,200 yards, if any transport, or sizeable parties used it by daylight. The Divisional front line ran North and South in front of Hébuterne and Fonquevillers, and was extensively overlooked by the Germans on the hill in front of Gomme-court Wood.

8   Fonquevillers

During August the Company had received a draft of 33 men to replace our casualties.

Our work was now switched to the Fonquevillers sector, the village itself being mostly in ruins. "In the church all the roof has fallen in. Only one wall of the big square tower stands precariously. The central part is merely a pile of stones and rubble, but a more than life-size crucifix, almost undamaged, leans against one wall."

The back billet was a very good one in a small house, where normally the Curé lived, and adjoining the church. The Curé had been called up for service with the French Army. Apart from one locked room, we had the full use of the house. Although heavy fighting had taken place, when the Germans were driven out of Hébuterne in the previous autumn, the little Sailly Church had not been hit by shell-fire. For the next five and a half months, the Company retained its headquarters and billets for two Sapper sections in Sailly. The other two sections lived in the forward billets at Fonquevillers, interchanging with the Sailly sections every twelve days. The Company's transport and R.E. Stores and workshop were located at Rossignol Farm, one and a half miles behind Sailly.

During this period the principal tasks allocated to us were maintenance and improvements of the trenches, particularly in regard to drainage, construction of deeper and better protected dug-outs, strengthening the defence in depth, and water supply. Included in these were 'battle positions' for Divisional and Brigade Staffs, behind Fonquevillers, and smaller observation posts—always referred to as "O.P.s"—for various units nearer the front line. What was known as the "Report Centre," represented the biggest dug-out provision we had so far carried out. It was the "nerve-centre" from which a future advance attack would be controlled. A 14-foot-long room was reached by two 20-foot burrowed passages. The weight of overhead was some 38 tons, and on book formula I reckoned it would stand another 60 tons. Round this were a number of minor dug-outs for the Divisional satellite Staffs. This needed a daily party of 50, in addition to the Sappers. Somewhat regretfully we had to include work on relatively eyewash features. We had a strong suspicion that with some of the 'high-ups' an ornamental stone or brick fireplace, with overmantel, in a Staff dug-out, was given a higher rating than a properly organized rescue job on the front-line trenches, with water up to or over the men's knees.

The Lloyd George stimulus to shell production was marked by an increased shelling by our Gunners, and in return by the Germans. The latter was spread over a wide area, including that of our back billet. The Company's war diary records some of these, such as "12 5·9 and incendiaries near billet, but without material damage; five hours of bombardment by our guns on enemy trenches, enemy reply brought 21 5·9 shells in Sailly." On 17th October "180 shells fired into Sailly, and considerable damage done. 60 large minenwerfer fired on sector in front of Fonquevillers, which, followed by heavy rain, caused considerable collapse of trenches." In December on four days over 230 shells dropped on Sailly.

The following are extracts from my notes written at the time.

"16th September 1915. Perry's No. 1 Section and mine took over the forward area work yesterday from the other two Sections. We have all got good billets with cellars. Perry and I reside in a house which is quite spacious, near the entrance to the village. A barn fronting the road has a wide central archway, which leads into a small paved yard in front of the house. There are two big rooms, one the kitchen, the other our combined dining and drawing room, and leading out of it two very small rooms where Perry and I sleep. At one side of the yard a shed, originally the bakery, contains a full-size ancient zinc bath. Our predecessors were French Engineers, and had collected two good tables and several chairs, two looking-glasses and some crockery; also one large bedstead. Perry, having examined it first, wisely but with apparent generosity insisted that my seniority entitled me to it. It consists of an ancient wooden frame filled with horrible large spiral springs about a foot high. With a proper mattress on top I expect it might be reasonably comfortable, but with only a slack mesh of wire netting, and my canvas sleeping-bag, between me and the springs all sorts of unexpected happenings occur. If I turn over and release my weight on one of the springs it shoots up, and hits me in some unexpected part of my anatomy. Alternatively I slide off one spring into a sort of abyss, before I am hit by another spring at a lower level. We are not lonely at night—rats and mice have the attic above us to themselves,

and at times they sound more like elephants playing a game of Tom Tiddler's Ground. Underneath our tiled flooring is a large cellar to which we can retreat. Fortunately, although we are well within rifle-range of the German line, bullets cannot hit us below the level of the roof eaves, owing to the contour of the ground between us.

"We have with us Perry's batman to cook for us, while my batman takes charge of our two horses, back at the transport lines. He is a remarkable character. An ex-Canadian rancher, he volunteered as a driver at the outbreak of the war under the name of J. Smith, but is invariably called 'Broncho Bill.' He has been much in request for dealing with bucking or refractory horses and mules. He has not previously been in the forward area. An hour or two after his arrival here he distinguished himself by telling us 'I've a dinky little shell that I found in one of the houses up the street. She hasn't gone off yet.' I found he had deposited it on our front-door-step, where I should probably fall over it. I did not attend its burial rites. Our billet is what the house agents would describe as 'very conveniently situated.' We can walk down to the front-line trenches, take a peep through a periscope at the Boche trench opposite, and imagine we can smell their breakfast bacon, and return to our own breakfast in the billet in under half an hour. There is also a great advantage in being able to walk about freely in the village, as it is screened from view other than a long-distance one from Gommecourt Wood. There is hardly a building left undamaged, but the ruins give added cover, and now the German Gunners apparently do not waste their shells on them. Thus we get only the smacks of bullets hitting roof slates. *Ergo*, no-one occupies rooms on floors above ground-level.

"*Sunday, 19th September 1915.*   Friday last was another tiring day. I felt slack, and the day got off with a bad start. I had postponed my Section's parade till 8.45 as our Infantry working party was not due till 9 o'clock. At 8 a.m. I was caught napping by a fussy Major, whom I had to address from the steps of our dwelling in pyjamas, and with very rumpled hair. Unfortunately he had decided that the morning was misty, and wanted to put a hundred of his battalion to work on a communication trench at the far end of our sector, which usually would have been done at night. I had only by chance seen the intended siting of the beastly trench once, and knew practically nothing about the reasons for which it was wanted. He had been given the job to do but knew less. He wanted it taped and pegged on the instant, as his men were due there at 9 o'clock. Result—a hurried toilet, a swallowed biscuit and a mile tramp with a couple of Sappers.

"When I got back to the billet I found a message that the C.O. of another battalion wanted me the moment I came in. I sat down for a minute to have a drink and biscuit, when he strolled into the room. 'Did I know that he wanted me?' This was brick number two. Would I take him round the inner defence areas of the village, which were just being started, and make a report on what was to be done. He had been designated to take over command of the village in the event of an attack. This proved to be a tiring and interesting tramp."

The principle had been laid down for three or four 'Keeps,' as they were termed, to be prepared. These were defensive islands with perimeters of about 400 yards, and an all-round defence and wire, the garrisons of which would be expected to hold out independently.

"Our experience out here has taught us to size up the weak points and requirements of each position quickly, to go for the essentials first all round the position, and add the refinements later if time allows. Thus we make rough sketches and notes in our service notebooks: A cottage here to be pulled down to clear the field of fire; the back-garden walls here to be loopholed; the orchard to be well wired; a trench dug along a hedge; a demolition charge prepared for a building up the street; examination and provision of pumps for wells. Time goes quickly and the C.O. does not believe in delays. 'I will let you have 40 men at 2 o'clock. We must have all this side wired by tonight.'

"There is no need for seeking anyone's permission up here for what we propose, and I trudge off to collect three or four sappers to mark out positions, and arrange for tools and wire from our nearby forward store. Back at the billet I find an impatient Captain Wright, who had been trying to find me, and 'What the devil had I been doing all the morning?' He brings up various instructions that have come through the Company, and takes a note of the various stores we want sent up. After getting the 40 men on the wiring job I make my first contact of the day with my Section, who are working on half a dozen different jobs. One of them is at the bottom of a deep well, where the air is so foul, apart from the ascending language, that it is only possible to work in it when a fan consisting of an old winnowing machine and piping is fixed up. The Section N.C.O.s and sappers take on responsibilities, collecting working parties, and going on with their jobs in a way we hardly dreamed of in the early days. I could not wish for a better or more dependable lot."

A few days later it was arranged that I should show another Battalion C.O. round the village defence areas. I wrote: "This was one of the most amusing mornings. The Brigadier also turned up, and the two parties merged into one. The Brigadier was in a 'telling-off' mood, and his Brigade Major whispered in my ear 'We are going to have some fun this morning!' A battery of a New Army unit, who were just behind the village, had allowed their habitation to get into a thoroughly dirty condition. It brought forth the finest flow of 'uncomfortable' remarks I ever remember listening to. It was quite an addition to my military education. After strafing various other units almost as effectively he arrived at my Section's billet. 'Now, Eberle, we'll see what the Engineers are like!' Thanks be to heaven our billet had been thoroughly cleansed and swept out, and brought forth 'Well! Your men do seem to have *tried* to keep their place clean.' The state of the village when the British took over was almost indescribable, and pathetically so. The straw bedding left in houses used as billets was alive with lice everywhere. Actually our billets had been well sluiced with Cresol disinfectant and washed, and every bit of straw and sacking burnt when we took over. Rats and mice abounded, and there are still a number of semi-wild cats in the village."

Certain cryptic entries in my diary indicate that around this date there were strong rumours of an imminent German attack on our front. It did not materialize.

"*27th September 1915.* Yesterday—Sunday—I was confronted with an unusual request. After we had returned from work my Section Sergeant, W. H. Sainsbury, came up to me. He is a most dependable soldier, and first-class shot. 'Please sir, the Section want to know if they can have a Service tonight, and they want you to take it.' In one way I was pleased at their wanting one, but wished they had chosen a place where parsons were more available. Almost all the Section turned up, and were thoroughly in earnest about it. Luckily I had some of *The Times* Service Broadsheets, which had been sent to me. The story of David and Goliath for the Lesson, hymns, a few prayers from the Prayer Book produced by one of the Sappers, and a briefly expressed 'thought,' which included those we had left at home, comprised our first Service within the rifle-fire zone. The singing was very hearty, and, as darkness was falling, probably penetrated to German ears. At night-time our men in the front line can hear clearly words addressed to their horses by our drivers, bringing up rations and stores to the village.

"I have just been censoring my Section's letters. One of the Sappers informs the lady of his love that 'our Service was most impressive' and that 'our Lieutenant took it.' I must find out what he is wanting from me. I am compelled to learn much about the numerous girl-friends of some of the Section, in Bristol and Essex. Also of the progeny of the older ones, including their maladies, prizes won, etc., but more often their blemishes and iniquities. Quaint ways of expression sometimes occur, e.g. one with 'P.S. remembrances to Ma.' Another finished up with 'God bless you and keep you from your loving cousin Tom.'"

During our next spell in the forward billet (9th October) my notes include the following:

"We have made our forward billet very comfortable. We even get fresh milk sent up to us, and also have improved the heating arrangements. It is probably the best in the village, and only two of us occupying it. We have reached the stage of entertaining guests to evening dinner. Perry and I were invited to mess with four Machine-Gunners near us. I have often been asked to bring my own grub with me, not to mention knives and forks. I have not previously been asked to bring my own chair with me. Picture, therefore, Perry and I sallying forth down the street, and, feeling rather like criminals, each carrying his chair. We had a merry party, but I had to leave early as the result of a call to a damaged trench.

"We now have a 'Commandant' to look after the village, but we are responsible for all demolition work. There is still a large demand for timber of all kinds, and for bricks, for which the badly ruined buildings are an obvious source of supply. Indiscriminate taking away by units can be both dangerous and perhaps unwittingly interfere with our defence areas. Hence we allot a small area from which material can be taken, and run a wire round it so that there can be no mistake or excuse for pilfering elsewhere. Woe betide the men we find sneaking material in forbidden areas. They are 'for it'.

"*12th October 1915.* This morning the O.C. arrived about midday on one of his regular 'look-around' visits, and to give us any new orders. It has been a typical day of the busy type. By 8 a.m. Perry and I had left the billet to decide where exactly to site the wire entanglement round part of one of the 'keeps' on which both of our Sections are working. At 8.30 I pack off some of the Sappers with their working parties. Allowing for cooks and other details, I find there are only 21 left to be split up on seven or eight jobs. Luckily these are all near at hand in the village. On the way I meet the village Commandant, who wants another house earmarked for pulling down, or would it be better to use explosives? At ten o'clock there is an appointment to be kept with the Brigade Machine-Gun Officer. Together we visit two positions. He sites where he wants his guns, and we have to plan how best to provide shell-proof protection, and the all-important concealment of the guns' positions. The answer seems to lie in a concrete roof for the gun, and connecting up with a cellar which can have its roof strengthened. Back to the billet to work out details of materials required, and instruct a corporal to take on the job of having tools ready for a working party the same afternoon.

"The O.C. brings with him, also, details of a new communication-trench which will be about 600 yards long. We are to expect 100 men at a certain rendezvous to start on it at nightfall. After lunch I was taping it out with a couple of sappers, when I suddenly heard a loud buzzing noise, like that of a huge swarm of bees. On looking up I saw fourteen of our aeroplanes in a bunch, the biggest number I have seen. Then they spread out and went over the German trenches. At once the German 'Archies' and front-line machine-guns and rifles, opened up on them. At the same moment about half a dozen of our batteries plastered the Boche lines. The enemy guns would not reply with our aeroplanes over them, and the latter circled round and returned. We wondered when the retaliation would come.

"The answer came about an hour after darkness, when they probably guessed that our ration and other parties would be on the move in the front area. Batteries and machine-guns simultaneously sprayed over our sector. The latter must have fired thousands of rounds in a fifteen-minute 'hate.' One of the first shell salvos burst about a dozen yards behind our digging party. In less than five seconds our hundred men were flattened out in the 9 inches or so depth of trench, which they had dug, as if they were being tucked up in their little cots. I think my head was burrowing into an infantryman's tummy, and my boot found the face of another. The muffled remarks from the recumbent figures were just as humorous as the British soldier is always capable of expressing. We were advised later that over 150 shells had come over on a narrow bit of our front.

"The day ended up with a little lighter occurrence. Back at the billet I was eating a late supper and the Sergeant came in. 'I am afraid, sir, we've got a casualty tonight!' I must have looked rather puzzled, as I had called at the men's billet on my way back. The Sergeant burst out laughing. It appears that most of the men were lying down when a loud explosion occurred, with the sound of breaking glass, in the kitchen of their billet. Thinking it was a shell they made a dash for the cellar. The true explanation was that they had been in the habit of putting jam and other food items into the unlit kitchen stove, to keep them from flies and mice. The men returning late and feeling cold lit the stove, forgetting what it contained. A McConnochie ration-tin exploded with the heat, blowing out the side of the stove, and damaging one man's arm. The victim seems, however, to have laughed as much as the others, and the R.A.M.C. Corporal has patched him up."

Under date Sunday, 17th October, an entry in my diary reads: "Heavy shelling in the morning. Collect a bit of 'Woofer' on my right foot." This is a reference to the only occasion on which I was hit during the four years I served overseas. I was standing in the open some little distance behind the front line when I felt a sharp blow on the side of my boot. I looked up first to see if someone had thrown a stone. Then I looked down, and picked up a jagged piece of shell-casing, about 4 inches long, only to drop it quickly as it was almost red-hot and burned my hand. A "Woofer," I may explain, was our pet name for a minenwerfer projectile, which contained a very heavy explosive charge.

Four days later my Section were relieved and returned to the more restful Sailly billets. "A surprise, which I am sure the Sappers have appreciated, was an entry in the O.C.'s Company Orders, on the evening of our return, congratulating Numbers 1 and 3 Sections on the work done by them in the forward area during their twelve days' period."

At Sailly I wrote: "I can now safely record the apparent urgency of some of our work a month ago, particularly the ten days prior to the opening of the Battle of Loos, on the 25th September. During that period we were on the tip-toe of expectancy. We knew that big operations on the British front were likely to start any day, but we did not know where. Although it was clear that our Divisional Sector was not intended for a main attack, everything was being made ready, as far as possible, for any eventuality. If the attack was to be made on either flank, and not far away from us, we should soon be involved, provided its initial phase was successful. Then came the time when a heavy bombardment of the enemy trenches opposite to us started. For about three days we poured shells on the German trenches and wire. We were not allowed to do much of our normal work. This was partly to keep the men under cover during expected reprisal shelling, partly so that they would be fit and ready for any action required of them. In our forward billet, some 800 yards from the front trenches, with only the two of us in occupation, the expectant waiting for something to happen made us very restless. In view of a possible diversionary attack on us, we were to be manning part of the defence system within five minutes of being warned, by day or night. That meant being ready dressed, with arms at hand always. Everyone had to sleep in cellars or dugouts in the village, the enemy shelling having been switched more intensively to the early dawn period. The latter part of our twelve days was to the accompaniment of a constant banging from our guns behind us. The retaliation was not very heavy. At our billet the shelling removed a large part of our bathroom roof, and uprooted an apple-tree in the orchard at the back. We were not sorry when we were relieved and returned to the relatively quieter area of the back billet. We were not unmindful, also, of the narrow margin by which we missed taking part in the initial attack between Loos and Hulluch, and of the fact that there were simultaneous costly attacks on other sectors of the front.

9 Winter Trenches (Fonquevillers)

November–December 1915

"*7th November 1915.* The day we moved up again to the forward billet was very wet, and also full of hate from the Germans on our neighbours. This winter rain brings far worse conditions in the trenches. We are learning new lessons on trench maintenance, but oh! the mud and water! The latter has been over the top of my rubber thigh-waders, and at times we become immovable in the mud, having slipped off the bottom trench-boards. It meant a lurid cry for help from the wretched Infantry in the front line, and we have been hard at work trying to cope with the conditions. We have available only a few lift-and-force pumps, and these have to be kept mobile. I sent some of my Section sappers to scour the village for anything that looked like a pump, and others to make wooden chutes. As there is no piped-water supply in the village, a large number of the inhabitants had wells with antiquated hand-pumps. As a result our store has looked more like an old metal-dealer's shop. These pumps are re-appearing now, however, rigged up in front-line trench sumps. Unfortunately we cannot pass our surplus water on to the Boches, as there is a dip in the ground between us.

"Last Friday was the 5th November, and provided the most exciting firework display since Catherine wheels delighted me, many years ago, in our back garden. A special 'hate' had been laid on for the occasion just after the evening 'stand-to,' Gunners and Infantry joining in. I made advances to our friendly Machine-Gunners, and bartered some of our timber stock in exchange for firing one of their heavy Vickers guns. After suffering from numerous occasions on which the Boches have attempted to upset our nerves, there is a distinct satisfaction in being able to indulge in a little personal retaliation. To press a button and 'spit' back some 300 rounds in short bursts on the Gommecourt area quite cured me of bad temper.

"Our activity along the front made the Boches suspicious of what we were up to, and they contributed generously to the show by sending up large numbers of flares. Our 'set piece' was provided by a battalion on the right of our Brigade sector. They had erected, the previous night, in front of our wire, a big gallows. From it was suspended a life-size stuffed effigy, hanging by a rope. It was embellished with an outsize iron cross on its chest, with other decorations, and another one in a hand. A large sheet of white cardboard at the base bore inscribed in big letters 'Your B—— Kaiser.' The effigy was sprinkled with paraffin, and a few rockets disposed about his person. The oracle was worked by a fuse-lighter attached to a wire. The Boches had been potting at him all day, but did not upset him. When he lit up they sent over a few 'pip-squeaks' in his vicinity, and our 18-pounders pip-squeaked back. We had a grandstand side view of the show, which pleased the troops and took their thoughts off mud and water.''

I have made earlier references in these notes to the German minenwerfer projectiles, or Minnies as they were un-affectionately called. At this period they were an unwelcome source of casualties, damage to nerve morale, and to trenches. In principle the minenwerfer may date back to the day of the Roman "ballista," designed to hurl a missile at an enemy's fortifications. In its 1915 form it was a crude form of glorified trench-mortar, and, like our Stokes mortar and Mills-bomb, was a product of the semi-static trench warfare. The missiles varied in size from that of a 5-gallon drum up to a torpedo-shaped projective $3\frac{1}{2}$ feet long by about 9 to 12 inch calibre. The metal casing was thin and filled with high explosive, producing a tremendous blast effect. The maximum range appeared to be about 800 to 1,000 yards. When fired, from a position just in rear of the German trench, it sailed slowly in a high arc, often turning over and over in its flight. At the time I wrote: "Anything close to the point of its impact may migrate about 300 yards before coming down to earth again. Yesterday I measured the crater of one which came over. It was 20 feet across and 9 feet deep. If someone were to say that they had heard its crump back in England I could almost believe them. The Minnies are usually aimed at the front-line trenches. Luckily the projectile travels slowly, and when a warning shout comes we have a few seconds to make up our mind as to its direction, and so whether to run to the right or the left.''

Our own trench-mortar exponents were most unpopular with the front-line infantry, who often had to bear prompt reprisals, whereas the trench-mortar team, having sent over their quota from just behind the trench, could decamp to another site. Probably the German Minnies, for the same reason, operated what we termed the "Travelling Circus." This travelled up and down a considerable length of the front, such that our turn seemed to come about every eight days. Unfortunately in October and November they broke the rules of the game and stayed for several days. I shall not easily forget the scene after a big Minnie landed in a forward sap occupied by three infantry-men; nor the shell-shock effect on two of my good Sappers, who were completely broken down by the blast of the explosion of one, although physically untouched.

Later on, during our offensive, I came across a crudely made form of German Minnie, which had been fired. It consisted of a tree trunk hollowed out, and the outside tightly bound round with hoop-iron—a crude weapon by even 1915 standards.

In mid-November my brother went on leave. It was slightly over-lapped by that of the Company Second in Command, who had preceded him. On his return he was evacuated to a base hospital and subsequently to England. In consequence I became acting O.C. of the Company. I found it hard to believe that it was under seventeen months since I was the latest-joined, carefree recruit in the rank of Sapper in the Company.

Throughout November and December heavy rains with an occa-sional frost entailed continual repair work on all the trenches. The Company's War Diary, under 11th November, recorded "Unrevetted trenches falling in everywhere. Many French-built dugouts have fallen in or become water-logged. Trenches, if unrevetted, require a slope of one-in-one on each side".

The daily shelling continued, varying only in intensity, both on the front line and on the villages behind it. The Minnies appeared now to be established permanently. On one day I recorded: "About 130 Minnies of all sorts fired into our F.23 Sector. No-one hurt, and blasted sections of trench found again at night!" On another: "Just missed by a Minnie, but only six came over today on our front line," and later: "Heavy retaliation by our 6-inch guns on enemy front trench."

"*26th November 1915.* The C.R.E. came up yesterday to our for-ward billet in a most cheery mood. He had received an unusual and complimentary report on the Division's R.E. Field Companies from the Corps Commander. 'The following messages have been published in Orders tonight, and copies may be sent home:

" '(1) To G.O.C. 48th Dvn. It has been brought to the notice of the Corps Commander that the Engineer services of your Division are particularly well carried out. He has directed me to ask you to inform Col. Marshall and those under his command that this report of their efficiency has given him much pleasure.

Signed: F. Lyon, Bgd. General (Corps.).

" '(2) To Col. Marshall. This report is I consider a result of your own and your assistants' untiring work, carried out often under very great difficulties.

Signed: R. Fanshawe. Cmdg. 48th Divn.'"

Five-days before Christmas my Section started a sixteen-day spell of duty in the forward Fonquevillers billets. Our tasks included the construction of five new sap-heads in front of our Brigade's front trenches. This was our first Christmas to be spent overseas, and all Units were imbued with the desire to provide traditional fare, and to make conditions as cheerful as possible for all ranks. In 1914 on Christmas Day there had been cases of fraternization between the opposing occupants of the front trenches. It was instilled into us that this was not to be repeated in 1915. Mental and physical "hate" was the order of the day.

"27th December 1915. On Friday morning—Christmas Eve—I was in our front trenches as soon as it was light, to see whether any parts were cut off by the heavy night rain causing flooding. 'You can't get further round this next bit, sir, without going in up to your waist. I am wet through!' said one of the infantry N.C.O.s. It was said with a grin and amazing cheerfulness, considering it was after a night's duty in the trench, and this is December not August. However, the two Sappers and I, by slow movement, got through with a bare inch to spare at the top of our thigh waders. We found two of our well-pumps out of action due to being clogged with mud, but the Sappers soon got them working again. On the way back we found a cavity in the main road near the entrance to the village. The timbering where the French had made a tunnel under the road had collapsed owing to the heavy rains. Luckily I met the C.O. of the Battalion stationed in the village, and he at once got an infantry party to help the Sappers in re-timbering and repairing the road, to enable our night transport with rations to get through.

"After a quiet morning there was a heavy strafing by our guns on the enemy front line. Only a few big Minnies came in response, but the concussion from one nearly blew me back up the two steps of a Battalion forward Headquarters. Unfortunately it caught the Infantry Sergeant-Major—a very good soldier whom I knew well—but otherwise doing very little damage. The rain had been coming down again in torrents, and the Battalion Adjutant later came over with an S.O.S. message that one part of the front line had become impassable, and the ground all round waterlogged. We prepared some more long wooden chutes, and directly it was dark carried them down, with extra lift-and-force pumps. From 5 p.m. to 1 a.m. sappers and infantry worked on pumping several thousands of gallons down the slope in front of our trench. By 1 a.m. communication had been re-established all along our front. I had gone back for half an hour about 9 p.m. to collect a fresh party of infantry for pumping. The rain had then ceased, and it turned into a clear night with a bright moon and stars. When standing on the parapet in bright moonlight one still has the feeling that our figures must be visible to the Boches opposite us, but hardly a shot came in our direction. Then unexpectedly there came a burst of rapid fire from a Battalion on our right. I glanced at my watch and saw that it was just midnight—the beginning of Christmas Day, and our neighbours' first instalment of Christmas presents for the Boches. It was with conflicting thoughts that I watched the spurting rifle-flashes, curving away on our right, and gradually extending all along our line. All the time the shadowy outlines of the enemy trenches opposite were clearly visible. The only reply from them was that from a couple of machine-guns.

"As I had not got back to the billet till about 2 a.m. I took an extra two hours in bed in the morning, having arranged that there should be no works parades for the Sappers unless an emergency arose. The O.C. came up later and visited the men in their billets, and wished them good luck.

"After lunch I went over to the Headquarters of the Battalion in the village to fix up parties for the following day. I found the C.O., Adjutant and three or four other Officers sitting round the room with paper caps on their heads, as the result of the gift of a box of crackers. They were very merry, and I soon found myself, with a paper bib tucked under my chin, munching for luck one of Mrs Colonel's excellent mince pies. In competition with the crackers our Gunners' shells went whistling overhead every few minutes. This was kept up while daylight lasted, so it was by no means a noiseless Christmas. At 'stand-to' time in the late afternoon I went round our Brigade front line to see if pumps and chutes were in working order, and found there was not more than a foot of water anywhere.

"We had handed over the use of Perry's and my billet in Fonquevillers for my Section's Christmas dinner. When I got back they had just finished, and were enjoying a sing-song. They had a jolly good dinner, and presents from Bristol. There is plenty of rough talent in the Section, and with the help of a gramophone they all seemed very happy and cheerful, and grateful for their tobacco and other presents. Perry and I left them about 7.30 to join up with our Machine-Gun friends in a nearby billet. Here is our menu—and all beautifully cooked—Tomato Soup, Sweetbreads, Stuffed Turkey with Peas and Potatoes, Plum Pudding. Anchovies and Sardines for a savoury, followed by dessert, coffee and port. A gramophone provided music while the plates were being washed for the next course. Not a bad effort for tradition, considering that the Boches were only about 800 yards distant from us. Every now and then a bullet would hit the roof, or a shell go whining overhead, and our M.G. humorist host would turn round with a very grave face and 'Gentlemen, I apologize, but I believe there is a war on!' With it all, our thoughts were for our families at home, especially when we honoured the toast of Our Mothers.''

There was one other event of an unusual character on Christmas Day. We were still under orders that everyone in Fonquevillers should sleep below ground-level. We had intended transferring all our sappers to certain subterranean grottoes under the cemetery. Their origin was stated to be quarrying for stone, when the church adjoining was built. When the French earlier in the war made a local attack here, they made a wide sloping entrance, and used them for assembling a large number of troops prior to the attack. To provide ventilation and more light, they constructed an open shaft, with heavily timbered sides and about 7 feet square, from the cemetery level to the grotto, where it was supported by strong props.

"The sappers had been building a big kitchen range containing two ovens and two stoves from derelict houses, at the foot of the shaft, which would serve as a chimney. The original intention was to transfer our two Sections before Christmas, so that they would have their Christmas dinner there, but it had not been possible to complete the cooking arrangements in the time available, and only about a dozen men were living there.

"Two days earlier a Minnie had landed in the graveyard about ten feet away from the shaft, and must have loosened the earth around it. The heavy rain further loosened it with the result that on the afternoon of Christmas Day the shaft timbering collapsed and fell with about 50 tons of earth on top of our kitchen range some 40 feet below. Our first intimation at the billet came from an excited and breathless sapper who blurted out that tons and tons of earth, and corpses and coffins were lying all around. This proved to be somewhat exaggerated. We found, on investigation, a strange medly of earth, chalk, corpses, broken bits of coffins and tombstones piled up on top of our kitchen range, after the 40-foot drop. There was a lady with long flaxen hair, and one poor gentleman, who has been turned out of his coffin, lies with his skull just visible under the earth, and the broken coffin a few feet away. It seems rather a shame to have a fall like that after a period that might be anything up to 200 years peaceful rest." The church was built in 1683. "We do not know what to do with a gentleman, or may be lady, whose remains are partly protruding in the shaft space some 7 feet below the surface. I gather that at least one sapper who has been sleeping in a part leading off from our kitchen has pronounced qualms about continuing to sleep there.''

10   Offensive Preparations (Fonquevillers)

January–March 1916

"*2nd January 1916.* Perry and I celebrated the opening of the New Year with a little dinner party to our M.G. friends at our billet. Unfortunately the Brigade turned us all out on a practice alarm, but we got back in time to save our dinner. The Boches celebrated it with the delivery at midnight of two large Minnies, conjointly on the edge of the village. Rumour has it that about half of the remaining roofs were lifted up. I woke up with the impression that the billet had received a direct hit from a shell.

"We sleep now in the cellar. We had been nearly caught out by the Brigadier, who called in one day and spotted our beds on the ground floor. The faithful 'Broncho Bill' apparently saved the situation by explaining that he had only brought them up for an airing!

"The cellar has its disadvantages. Recently, in the middle of the night, I was awakened by a stream of vituperation from Perry. A rat had the insolence to bite him on the hand, drawing blood. The sight of Perry sitting up with tousled hair and bulging eyes, alternately sucking the back of his hand, and sweeping his torch round, as if he expected the rat to be listening to his language, had its humorous aspect.

"*4th January 1916.* Last night I came back with my Section to our back billets. [This was in Sailly.] Pyjamas are not a wonderful subject over which to gloat, but when you have just spent sixteen days on end without fully taking off your uniform, night or day, it is a godsend to have a proper wash and don pyjamas. It was one of the hardest spells we have experienced, and nearly all our work was on the front line trenches. Water—mud—winter cold—Minnies galore—I hardly know which was the worst. The daily ration of shells sent over nowadays is considerably more than that of an average week when we were in the Plugstreet area. We were, however, very lucky as regards

70

casualties to the Sappers. Apart from the normal puncturing of the roof of the billet from rifle-fire, it only suffered from the arrival in the kitchen of the nose-cap of a small shell, to the detriment of some of our crockery. We had just finished our lunch, and the batmen were starting theirs, when it came through the open window, breaking some plates and ending up on a chair. Their comment: 'What a pity it didn't hit the beef. I would like to have seen summ'at what would make an impression on it!' As for the water—our latest trench story runs thus: First Infantryman (standing in trench with water over his knees), 'Say, Bill! Have you heard the news, how as we're a'going to be relieved?' Second Infantryman, 'Noow! Who by?' 'Why! By the blinking Royal Nivy, o'coursc!'

"Here at the back billet I have a pukka mattress to sleep on, and a shell through the roof is a less likely happening. It all helps to support the theory that life is worth living."

This optimism was, perhaps, not altogether justified by events, but in wartime present conditions are apt to be considered as relative to those immediately preceding them. On the evening of my Section's return from Fonquevillers I received orders to hand over the Section to another Subaltern, and to take charge of the Divisional R.E. Store, then located in Sailly. I promptly advised my family that I was now 'on a safe, soft job.' We looked on the duties of Officer i/c Stores as being nearly half-way to becoming a 'Base Wallah.'

The following morning I went to take over the Stores Office, which was a small wooden shanty alongside the road. There were obvious visible signs of disruption and casualty. I learned that two days previously one of a salvo of four shells had pitched in the road outside the hut. A man standing inside by the table I was to use had been killed, and 2 nearby Sappers seriously wounded, and 2 horses killed outside. The Company's war diary also records 220 shells falling in Sailly on 8th January. On the tenth I recorded "Village shelled four times today. Large hole knocked in Section's tool-cart." A further comment reads: "This is the Army's idea of a rest billet."

To our surprise, a memorandum was issued by our 143 Brigade to the effect that the time had come for the Infantry to maintain their trenches, and carry out the simple forms of field engineering, such as revetting and drainage without R.E. assistance. Consequently Sappers would not be used in the front trenches, although R.E. Officers and N.C.O.s would be available to give advice as required.

The reason for this became apparent later. It stemmed from the decision of the High Command to launch a large-scale offensive by the British and French in the early summer. The area eventually selected stretched from the high ground of Gommecourt Wood, opposite Fonquevillers, to South of the River Somme. Constructional works

71

were to be carried out on a far larger scale. These entailed deep dug-outs for command posts, O.P.s and bomb-stores, and other assembly preparations, on which our sapper work was to be concentrated. Presumably it was realized that there would be an increased demand for heavy materials, and that the existing site of the Store was too vulnerable. A week after I had taken over I was ordered to reconstitute the Store on a new site at Courcelles, about 1½ miles South-West of Sailly. I enjoyed organizing it, with about 2 acres of ground available, and some useful covered buildings. Before transferring stocks from the old store we constructed rough roads or brushwood tracks to give access to all the various dumps. Freedom from mud makes a vast difference, and the planned spacing enabled us to deal with about thirty wagons in the same time as ten at the old site. Within a fortnight we had "a happy little colony of 40 men living on the site in two big wooden huts made by us, with a cook-house, ablution-shed and office hut. The men are quite 'cosy,' and have our patent collapsible beds, guaranteed to collapse only when so desired. After sleeping for a time in the office hut I have wangled a small Armstrong type hut about 12 × 6 feet, covered by rainproof(?) canvas. The only drawback is that it has become intensely cold. Our emporium has become a twenty-four hours a day service.

"I mess with one of the two Battalions' officers in the reserve billets nearby, who kindly treat me as one of their family."

While at the Store I sent home a parcel of unwanted belongings enclosed in a sandbag. I was rather amused at receiving the return of the sandbag, obviously washed, from my parents. In acknowledging it I wrote back: "Many thanks for the two parcels including the returned sandbag. You need not trouble to return the latter in future, as we have several here!" Out of curiosity I looked up the figures in my stock book. I found that in the last three weeks we had issued over 130,000 sandbags from our Store, and had over 60,000 in stock. These issues were solely for use in our own Divisional area.

Among a number of visitors the Chief Engineer, 3rd Army, arrived one day. After asking a large number of questions, and making a close inspection of the Store, the great man expressed his approval, with no adverse comments.

Our Company's Second-in-Command having been evacuated to England a month previously, and no replacement made, I had to return to Company duties after six weeks at the Store. The O.C. also having started a new round of seven-days'-leave, I had to function temporarily at a two-step-higher level. This called for a little brushing-up of my knowledge of the powers of temporary commanding officers on active service, when exercised by a two-pip subaltern. Fortunately our crime sheets were light. Perhaps this could be accounted for by the men being worked long hours, and by being in a battle area where there were few opportunities of getting into mischief. Also, not being "old soldiers," the culprits to whom we doled out what was meant to be justice knew even less about their rights under military law.

On the return of the O.C. on 22nd February, in view of the increase in the call for dug-out and constructional work, I returned once more to work in the forward Fonquevillers area for a sixteen-day period of duty. Two reinforcement subalterns from England had been posted to the Company, one of whom remained with one Section in the back area. There were thus five of us available with the other three Sections, concentrating on preparations for an offensive, and also strengthening the defences of the village.

The new conception, compared with that of 1915 operations, of the need for deeper dugout protection had been brought about by the increased intensity of shell-fire. The number of guns employed, particularly the increase in those of heavier calibre, and the provision of vastly greater quantities of shells, by the enemy and ourselves, set a new pattern for battles between two strongly entrenched enemies. We were soon to learn that the Germans had realized this earlier than we had, and had taken remedial action. The principal tasks on which we were now employed included the Divisional Report Centre, Command Posts for Brigade and Battalion Headquarters, O.P.s for Artillery and Infantry, and bomb stores. Also more Infantry dugouts, dressing-stations, new artillery and machine-gun emplacements and dugouts, shrapnel-proof assembly-shelters for attacking troops, new forward communication-trenches; and, further back, screened approach-tracks. These had to be designed and constructed, under the supervision of the R.E. Field Companies, in accordance with the general instructions from the C.R.E. The provision of the necessary materials, and arrangements for their transport to the site remained the R.E. reponsibility, the bulk of the labour being provided by the Infantry in Brigade or Divisional Reserve. Our Company's tasks also included the laying of 4,700 yards of a trench tram-line for carrying ammunition and stores into the forward area.

At the same time the defences of Fonquevillers village were further strengthened on the principle of "keep" areas and subsidiary "strong-points." Work could be carried out by day at the main Divisional Report Centre at La Haie Château, which was about 2,500 yards behind our front line. This represented the "nerve-centre" for operations, and comprised a number of heavily protected dugouts to accommodate the various Headquarters Staffs. A reserve bomb-store dugout was constructed to hold 30,000 grenades, with a separate detonating chamber.

The other works were mainly in the forward rifle-zone area. Over

20 protected O.P.s were built for the Divisional Gunner Forward Observing Officers and the Infantry. They were of many varied types. One took the form of a square concrete tower 30 feet high, built inside a house known as the Notary's House, and renamed Artillery House. Another consisted of a shaft 15-feet deep with a long gallery leading to an 8 by 6 foot shelter, with an upward shaft to the O.P. A thick tree-stump above ground-level, previously photographed, was cut down one night, and a hollow steel replica substituted. The latter was painted and camouflaged to look exactly like the original tree-stump by the Army back-area workshops, and was provided with screened slots for observation.

Our Company's nightly convoy bringing up R.E. materials usually comprised up to fifteen G.S. or pontoon wagon loads. A typical indent taken from my army service notebook in March, making up 13 wagon-loads, included 90 six-foot slatted trench boards, 34 9-foot girders, 19 pre-fabricated dugout frames 7 by 6½ foot, 70 coils barbed wire, 300 foot scantling and boarding timber, 4 Dunkerque pumps, 3 hundredweight nails and sundries.

The task of the drivers from all units was not always an enviable one. It involved driving their teams on dark nights, without lights, over rough roads or tracks, often pitted by fresh shell-holes, and subject to occasional bursts of shell-fire. These journeys were their nearest points of contact with the enemy, but they were inveterate souvenir-hunters, as well as retailers of news and rumours, culled from the back areas.

The Transport Officer of one of the battalions, seeking a souvenir, removed the figured metal weather-vane on the roof of the Brasserie, a Battalion Headquarters in Fonquevillers, on the night his Battalion was being relieved. It took the cut-out shape of a man trundling a wheelbarrow, and was punctured by several bullet-holes. The following morning the C.O. of the relieving battalion took his accustomed look at the weather vane to see whether the wind was favourable for an enemy gas attack. Filled with indignation at its disappearance, he made inquiries, and as a result sent a stiff note to the offending battalion, demanding the immediate replacement by the offender. The latter, not wishing to be deprived of his treasure, placed the original on top of one side of a large stout tin container, and neatly cut out a replica, punctured a few holes and rubbed dirt over it. Having been sent up by his C.O. to replace the vane on the following night he substituted the replica, and humbly apologized to the indignant C.O. The latter is said to have emerged at daylight and seeing the vane from ground-level in its customary position high up on the roof, remarked to his Adjutant: "That'll teach those thieving blighters of the blank battalion!" Clearly a case where all parties concerned were satisfied.

After a sixteen-day period in the forward area, involving somewhat strenuous employment, accompanied by much noise, I returned on 12th March to the Company Headquarters, which had been moved to Souastre. The weather in March had turned very cold with snowstorms. In spite of the conditions night raids on opposing front-line trenches were becoming much more frequent. On two occasions we had gas-attack alarms, which proved to be false.

For over three months the Company had been without its 2nd in Command, whose duties normally included responsibility for the Company's Headquarters and Mounted Sections, comprising about 65 men and 75 horses. With a full numerical strength of officers the O.C., who had borne the brunt of the work, could now be relieved. I took over the duties, and a few weeks later received an official gazetting as Temporary Captain and 2nd in Command. The horses had come through the winter conditions well, but the heavy work had left its mark on vehicles and harness. A number of big mules had replaced the original light draught-horse teams for our tool- and forage-carts.

The Company had one Sapper Section in the back billet area, where there were numerous tasks to be supervised, principally in hutting and water supply. They included converting a large barn for use as a cinema. It served, also, alternately for Church Services, lecture room and music hall. Officially known as the Theatre, it was packed every night for performances by the "Barn Owls," or by another Troupe called the "Orfhinds"; in both cases they were men who took their places in the trenches, or were with other units in the Division. They helped to keep up the spirits of the troops in their periods out of the forward area.

We had just settled down to the prospect of a more peaceable existence, with only occasional visits by day to the forward area, when an unexpected call was made on our energies.

11   Bangalore Torpedoes (Fonquevillers)

April 1916

It was the 25th March 1916. The C.R.E. had come into our Mess. "I want the Companies to carry out experiments in making up Bangalore Torpedoes." The name denoted a weapon of which I had not heard previously, nor had I seen it mentioned in our R.E. text-books. The C.R.E. explained that it denoted a device, such as a plank or tube, carrying a length of explosive, which could be pushed into a belt of enemy wire entanglements, to blow a gap, enabling the attacking infantry to pass through it. The experiments were to be made in close consultation with our Brigade Infantry, who would have to operate the Bangalores. The O.C. looked at me and remarked "A job for you, I think." From this there developed unexpectedly for me, a new interest and an experience of Army tactical weapon techniques.

It should be remembered that, in this long battle-line of trenches sited in the open country, barbed-wire entanglements had become one of the principal defensive elements. Our Sappers were trained in rapid wire-drill, as being one of the first essentials after the capture of an enemy trench. Normally a typical belt of wire was between 6 to 12 feet in depth. Lines of stout wooden posts, not less than 3 feet above ground-level in rows, were connected up laterally and diagonally by barbed wire. Loose concertina wire could be placed in the middle, and a barbed-wire criss-crossed apron added in front, connected to pickets about a foot high. Corkscrew-type iron posts were also employed in place of wood posts.

Up to this period the Higher Commands appeared to have only two methods for overcoming the obstacle presented by a belt of wire. The development of the "Tank" was still in the future. The two methods were the manual use of long-handled wire-cutters or artillery bombardment. In daylight the former method in the face of well-placed, enfilading, machine-guns had proved suicidal. With artillery fire even the most accurate shooting failed to ensure a clear passage through the belt. After a heavy expenditure of shells the tangled mass could remain a difficult and delaying obstacle. The bombardment had to be carried out by daylight, and nullified any prospect of surprise, or concealing an area to be attacked. Recalling the stories of our heavy casualties, when attacking at Neuve-Chapelle and Loos, by men being held up and mown down at the wire, my imagination was fired by the potential possibilities of the Bangalore.

The morning following the C.R.E.'s visit, I went forward to Brigade Headquarters. Here it was arranged that Lieutenant Geoffrey Walker, Bombing Officer in the Warwickshire Brigade, should collaborate with us. He was a most likeable, keen, and very quick-witted young officer, whose ideas and assistance proved most helpful. We learned that the Army Grenade School operating in France had worked on the idea of the Bangalore, but as far as we were concerned we had to start experimenting from scratch, and without any information. Also that other Divisional R.E. were making similar experiments. One such, on which I was detailed to report, proved to be in the form of a 60-foot length of iron 1-inch-diameter water-pipe, filled by hauling up one end to the top of a church tower. The handling and carrying up of such a weapon seemed impracticable. Lightness and ease of carrying up in the dark were essential aims. Blastine, guncotton, cordite and ammonal were considered as possible explosives. We decided on using ammonal, a relatively safe explosive, easy to handle, and available in the form of a grey powder.

Our various tests behind the line to ascertain the best form of container, and the quantity of explosive required to produce an adequate passage, and its detonation, were sufficiently advanced for a trial use in a raid by a Warwick Battalion. Two torpedoes, made up by our sappers were carried up. Each took the form of 3-inch diameter tubes made of light tin in two sections, each 6 foot long. They had an overlapping sleeve for connecting up, or for a pointed wooden plug in the front section. Firing was by a Nobel lighter and fuse, which was led into a detonator and guncotton primer projecting into the ammonal. The raiding party also carried up a Bangalore sent direct to the Brigade from the Army Grenade School. It transpired, subsequently, that it had been made up about six months previously, and was sent up for practice purposes, and should not have been used in a raid. We sent a 6-page report to the C.R.E. with recommendations, based on information from members of the raiding party. It showed that the night was wet and misty. The Bangalore first used was successful in blowing a gap, approximately 12 by 12 feet, through the wire, after considerable difficulty in getting the fuse to light. The Grenade School type, which contained Blastine was also fired. Only a small explosion followed. For some seconds part of the explosive burned with a bright orange flame, but the sticks in the front portion were not detonated. The second one made by our sappers was also brought forward, but the man holding the rear section either dropped it, or else pulled it back, with the result that the two sections came apart. There should have been no difficulty in sliding it in again, and slightly crimping the joining sleeve, but it was not required, as successful entry had been made into the enemy trench by the other gap.

From these results a number of valuable lessons were learned. The outstanding one was that Nobel lighters and trailing unprotected fuse were uncertain of action in the prevailing conditions, with the torpedoes dragged through wet grass, when close to the enemy wire. Successful detonation of number one was achieved only after three Nobels and a cigarette-lighter had failed to ignite the fuse. A fresh end was then cut in the latter, and full detonation took place. It was clear that the Infantry could not be expected to have confidence in prompt and reliable detonation unless assured of a damp-proof ignition device. Firing by an electric detonator and exploder was impracticable in darkness. We then hit on the idea of a device based on the mechanism used in the Mills hand-grenade, recently issued. Pending workshop manufacture of such an igniter, it was possible to adapt a Mills-bomb for the purpose, after removing the explosive, fuse and base portion.

Thus by 31st March my scale drawings of the adaptation, and of the igniter device in an improved form, if made for the purpose, were sent to the C.R.E., with a request, supported by the Brigade, that supplies might be made available from Army Workshops. These were forwarded to Fourth Army H.Q.

Two days later my turn for short home-leave came round. On arrival, with the C.R.E.'s permission, I took a copy of my scale drawings to the head of a well-known Bristol Engineering Company, a close friend of my father's. Under conditions of secrecy as to the purpose, I was able to take back to France at the end of the week a number of igniter tubes, ready for charging and fusing. They were excellently turned out in gunmetal and brass tubing. They could well be made in cheaper metals.

Thus in its final form the Bangalore consisted of a rear and one or more front sections of 3-inch tin tubing, each 6 foot long, containing the explosive, and a separate small igniter tube, approximately 10 by 1 inches, with a projecting hand-grip at the rear end. The rear ends of the sections were sealed with tin discs, and after filling with the explosive an overlapping sleeve with a disc in the middle was soldered on the outside of the front part of the tubes, making the contents damp-proof. The open ends of the protruding sleeves enabled a front section to be slid into it, or in the leading section to take a pointed wooden plug. The sealing disc at the rear end of the rear section comprised a tin tube, open at the rear end, and a flange at the other end, so made that the thinner igniter tube could slide into it.

The igniter mechanism comprised a strongly compressed spring round a metal striker-pin. When the latter was released by a hand-grip lever, the striker, actuated by the spring, shot forward and set off a percussion cap which lit the fuse. The latter (normally about 8½ inches) could be cut for a timing of 10 to 15 seconds or longer, and in turn set off a standard-type fulminate of mercury detonator, surrounded by ammonal at the forward end of the igniter tube. Complete detonation of the whole length of torpedo was obtained, without the need for a guncotton primer. In all the tests and demonstrations given by us there was not a single failure in detonating at the first attempt.

This was not quite the end of our little team's collaborations. A further use for the Bangalore was suggested, and further experiments initiated. It arose from recent Infantry training for the attack on an enemy trench, based on successful infiltration at a given point. The Infantry then worked their way up the trench by lobbing Mills-bombs over the traverse in the trench into the next bay, followed immediately by a bayonet attack round the traverse. But if it was intended to hold the trench the almost inevitable counter-attack could do the same. Hence the need for what was termed a "bomb-stop," in other words to have a clear field of fire beyond bomb-throwing range up the trench. Experiments showed that the protection given by a traverse could be quickly removed by inserting a Bangalore tube to demolish the upper part. It only needed a stout picket slightly wider than the torpedo, which could be driven into the side of the traverse at the required height, to make a hole. There were always plenty of pointed pickets near a fire-trench. It could equally well be used for other quick demolition.

Our Brigade took a keen interest, and I found myself having to adopt the role of "showman." The first general demonstration was at the request of our Brigadier, when his Battalion C.O.s and a number of other officers were present. It took place near La Haie Château on Good Friday morning, 20th April. In the demolition of a traverse I took refuge behind another traverse about 20 yards away. It seemed as if half of the countryside was pattering round my back. As one of my Sappers put it to me, "It fair shifted some, sir!" Afterwards I was summoned to the Mess to meet a Major-General of a nearby Division, who had come over to the demonstration. He began with "I am very interested in this idea of yours. Please explain carefully to me how it all works." Having noted down particulars, he said he would be sending his C.R.E. to interview me!

Three days later, on Easter Monday, at short notice, I received a message from Brigade that the Corps Commander, Sir Aylmer

Hunter Weston, was coming at 6 p.m. to their Headquarters, and they wanted a Bangalore demonstration staged for him to see. There was a fairly large muster from all ranks. At the time I wrote: "Luckily I had prepared some more Bangalores, and charged them, and this time used an igniter made out of a Mills-bomb, and adapted by one of my sappers. We demonstrated it on a big traverse, but it fairly shifted it." In my notes I added somewhat irreverently: "I got the old man a good distance away, but the explosion and upheaval was a fine one. However, nothing hit the old man in the eye." Afterwards he told me that he was very pleased with the demonstration, and considered it most successful. Having made his Aide take down some particulars, he asked me about our Company, and finally shook hands in the most affable manner. Walker, the Grenade Officer who has been so very helpful in co-operating, overheard a remark made by one of the Infantrymen who was watching: "A blankety fine thing I calls it, when a blankety Corpse Commander [his pronounciation] 'as to come and learn 'ow to fight from a blankety lootenant."

"The following Friday evening I received a message to the effect that our Divisional General wanted a demonstration the next day, in conjunction with a pre-arranged demonstration by our Army Command of a captured German Flammenwerfer, or Flamethrower. It took place near Authie in the presence of the G.O.C. and several hundred representatives of all Units in the Division. The open field in which it was held did not provide us with a very suitable site, and there was no cover, or convenient shell-hole to which I could retire hurriedly after triggering off the Bangalore. The igniter was fitted with only a ten-seconds fuse. My rapid retirement, before going prostrate on the grass, was to the accompaniment of cheers and cat-calls from the troops seated round the field, a safe distance away. I felt more as if I had just made a dash down the touch-line to score a try, and afterwards I had some leg-pulling congratulations on fleetness of foot.

"Colonel Howard, our G.S.O.1, came over and spent some time in asking for full details about our experiments." I was subsequently shown the copy of a letter to higher authority by General Fanshawe requesting that supplies, based on our type of Bangalore Torpedoes, be made forthwith in England and issued to his Division.

The final episode in our Company's part in producing a Bangalore came three weeks later. Our Division had then been taken out of the line for three weeks for a refit and training, and our Company were at Hem. On 22nd May I received a copy of a telegram from Divisional H.Q. to the C.R.E.: "Army H.Q. wants Officer inventor of igniter for Bangalore Torpedo to attend there at 10 a.m. tomorrow Tuesday to discuss the question. AAA. Can you arrange?" Also copy of reply

"Captain Eberle detailed to attend. AAA. Will Army supply a car at Mairie, Hem, at 8.30 a.m."

The next morning I had a long lonesome ride in the back of a very large staff car to Fourth Army H.Q. On arrival I was taken out to a small party headed by General Buckland of Army Command, and including the C.R.E. of another Division with satellite officers. After the C.R.E. had fully explained his type to the General, my solitary presence from our Division was remembered, and I was called on to do likewise. I was able to indicate several points in which our type was lighter (about 20 pounds), more easily handled, damp-proof and fool-proof both as regards the igniter and the sections containing the explosive. I used the Bristol-made pattern for the former, and the sections (uncharged) had been made up by one of our sappers in the early hours of that morning.

The General and C.R.E. generously admitted that our Division's type was the better one, but I recorded at the time that I did not think the C.R.E. liked the somewhat brusque way in which the General brushed aside his proposed type. In the upshot we were both thanked, and the General said that he would put in an order for 1,000 igniters and 4,000 tube sections to be made at Army Workshops from my drawings.

The foregoing account of just one phase of our Company's activities may well seem to be over-full in detail. I have done this purposely, including the quoting of actual expressions indicating interest and approval from responsible Senior Officers at the front in making use of the Bangalore. So far as I am aware there are few references to it by those who have written the story of the war. I know little as to the extent to which experiments or use were made of it by other Divisions. But in all the accounts of battles up to this date there are constantly recurring references to our Infantry being held up, and mown down, by enemy machine-guns as they struggled at uncut or only partially cut wire. I know that one Divisional R.E. Company had 5 casualties in their experiments. I have a five-sheet report printed and circulated by the Engineer-in-Chief 1st Army to units under his command. It contains description, drawings and results of tests on the Bangalore Torpedo, referring mainly to the type made in 1st Army Workshops. It was heavier and more cumbersome, made of 22 gauge iron sheeting with 10-foot long sections. The ignition was by an exposed Nobel lighter and fuse, fitted into a wooden plug in the rear section. The fuse and lighter were thus subject to dampness, and the detonating tube had to be screwed into a wooden plug in the rear section, and waxed round *before* it was taken on the operation.

Why was the Bangalore Torpedo not used to a greater extent? That is a question which I have often asked myself. From close contact with the semi-static conditions at the front I was convinced, in that Spring of 1916, that it could have been a major factor in reducing casualties in the 1915 attacks on enemy trenches, and in bringing greater success to the operations. I still hold that conviction. Also that its use was by no means outdated subsequently in 1916 and 1917. The need for it was reduced by the vastly greater expenditure of shell-fire in the major battles, by the advent of the tank and by the German "pill-box" defence at Passchendaele.

In night raids such as those for securing identifications of the opposing troops, where surprise was the important element, the Bangalore could clear the way for a quick penetration and for the return. In major attacks at early dawn, gaps in the wire could be made under cover of darkness, in conjunction with a co-ordinated light shelling to mask the Bangalore explosion. The tendency for the attackers to bunch is obvious, but the important aim in raids must be to ensure a quick entry into the trench at one or more points. I believe that the British Infantryman's fears immediately before an attack—and who could truthfully say he had none?—were not in regard to close-contact fighting, but of being trapped in front of the wire, unable to make contact with his enemy, and exposed to M.G. fire.

One answer to my question above was given to me more than two years after the end of the war. Only those who took part in the 1915 and 1916 battles can rightly judge the correctness of the views then expressed. I was in correspondence regarding the Bangalore with the War Office, and the Royal Commission which considered inventions during the war. A letter from the former in June 1921 stated: "The Bangalore Torpedo is not, and never has been officially adopted as an article of store, but it would appear from correspondence that a number were manufactured in France by G.H.Q. Workshops. . . . A report shows that an original design was considered by G.H.Q. France early in 1915, and that the destruction of barbed-wire entanglements, etc., by this means *was not considered to be practicable.* The experience gained at that time, through the use of H.E. shell, showed that obstacles *could be easily removed* by means of a systematic bombardment with such shell, and this without loss of personnel. [The italics are mine.] Supplies of this device from home were not therefore required." Would the thousands of our Infantrymen who were called on to face and surmount those wire entanglements in 1915 and 1916 have endorsed that view?

One other question seems pertinent. If this decision was later reversed by Army Commands at the front, as is clearly shown by the above records, why was its design left to hasty improvisations at the front? It may well be that the result was that those who should have used it felt too little confidence in its reliability in action.

As a fitting postscript to this chapter, I briefly record some impressions on the support given us by the various Supply Services.

In most respects the organization of supplies was wonderfully efficient. In four years at the front in Belgium, France and Italy I can only recall two occasions on which my Unit's rations for the day failed to materialize in time, and one of these was when we had penetrated rapidly into enemy territory. This applied also to the provision of the vast quantities of R.E. equipment and materials needed at the front. Such criticism as we made was mainly regarding offensive weapons, compared with our enemy's. A truer comparison should perhaps have made allowances for the fact that they had been preparing for a war, whereas we were relatively unprepared for a major conflict. The outstanding deficiency of shells in the earlier part of the war was made good by the efforts of those in the Home Country, when the facts were made known to them. In 1915 we talked scornfully among ourselves about our Gunners' daily ration of six shells bringing a retaliation of three times that number. In addition to a lack of heavy-calibre artillery, we were relatively inferior in machine-guns and light automatics. Criticism, such as it was, devolved on the feeling that there had been a lack of foresight, prior to the war, in not appreciating their full potentialities in providing fire-power. The British recruit had been taught "The rifle is your best friend." In the 1914–1918 War the rifle was not his worst enemy. Nine months after war was declared, and when the Germans were well provided with stick-throwing-bombs, our Company was employed on making hand-throwing-bombs consisting of old jam-tins filled with odd scraps of metal. They had a projecting fuse, which had to be lit by a fusee match, scratched on a roughened pad strapped on the thrower's arm. Another type made by us, and known as the "hair-brush," consisted of a slab of guncotton wired on to a thin piece of wood, shaped like the back of a hair brush.

Such deficiencies were our teething troubles, and we chafed at delays in remedying them. As time went on the British genius, and the spirit of the people behind it, made us a Nation fully armed for war. But let us not forget that we had paid a heavy price in the manhood of the Nation for our unpreparedness.

As an anti-climax: instructions were issued that our swords, so brightly sharpened for us before we embarked for overseas, could be taken back to England on our next leave and could remain there. I gladly obeyed the permissive instruction!

12   Somme Battle Preparations (Hébuterne)

May–June 1916

At the beginning of May the Division was relieved, and moved into the back area for rest, combined with training and refit. The Company's destination proved to be Hem, a small village about two miles West of Doullens. Appreciation of a return to civilized surroundings, and the creature comforts that go with it, were very apparent in my letters. "I am sleeping again in a real bed, between sheets of a whitish colour. Apart from my short home-leave, the last time such a thing occurred was more than nine months ago." Once more the Company officers could all mess together in a large farm, and our number was increased by two additional subalterns sent out to us from England. We fared well, being able to make purchases in Doullens. Our French interpreter took charge of the buying, and we engaged a lady cook of somewhat ample proportions, so that our batman cook would be available for brushing up his military duties. Supervision of the Sappers' and Drivers' messing had now become one of my general duties. I wrote: "I could hardly keep a straight face in front of one of the Sections' cooks this morning. I was strafing him for leaving old food-tins scattered about and for not burying them. His reply was "Well, sir, it's as 'ow they're building an 'Insinuator,' and I was going to put 'em in it.''

"*22nd May 1916.*   We have been thrown into gloom tonight by a sad accident to Driver 'Broncho Smith.' He was drowned in a nearby stream, after falling off a crazy raft, which he had made out of petrol tins and some old farm timber. Two other drivers who saw him fall off, and like Broncho could not swim, ran up to a barn where a Corporal and I were checking stores. We raced across a field and at the spot indicated there was no sign of him, but bubbles were coming up to the surface. The stream was deep, and running fast after heavy rain. There were long reeds at the sides. The weight of army field-boots made

84

it difficult to keep swimming deeply under water, and, although other men quickly arrived and stripped, it was an hour before we found him lower down the stream. Broncho was an individualist, a rolling stone who had hastened to volunteer on the outbreak of war. We never knew his real name. He had brought with him the atmosphere and spirit of his native Canada. Whether he was called on to subdue an unmanageable kicking remount, or, as batman devoted to his officer, in producing some unexpected accessory to our comfort, he was always alert and active. This single casualty left with us a peculiar sense of revolt. For long months we had known and seen the hand of death beside us in the fighting area—it was to be expected. Here, in these peaceful country surroundings that hand seemed out of place."

Our three weeks out of the line were spent in all phases of R.E. work, including pontoon and trestle bridging, route marching and reconnaissance. By this time a considerable proportion of the Sappers were reinforcements who had replaced our casualties. Our working hours were from 6 a.m. to dinner-time, so that the men were free for the rest of the day. Sports and matches with other units were arranged, and all ranks entered keenly into the various games. In the officers' sprint race all our officers competed, including the O.C., who was an ex-English Trials and Oxford wing three-quarter. Rumour said that he was not far beyond the halfway line at the finish, whereas he stoutly declared that he was only a few yards behind the winner, who had similar past claims as a three-quarter.

After three weeks in our peaceful hamlet we took our place in the front-line area, taking over the sector in front of Hébuterne. As previously, two Sapper sections were billeted in the Hébuterne forward area, and the remainder of the Company at Rossignol Farm near Coigneux. In the middle of June the latter were moved back to bivouacs about 1,000 yards West of Sailly, and remained there till after the opening of the Somme Battle on 1st July.

By this time all ranks knew that a big offensive was likely in the very near future. We had no idea as to the extent of the front on which it would be made, nor of the date. As a matter of history it appears that the latter was open to last-minute changes, and was postponed for a couple of days or more from the earlier anticipated date.

The O.C. was away from the Company for a week prior to the 19th June, and in his absence I had the experience of being called in his place to various Brigade and Divisional Conferences. Information as to the exact state of completion of preparations in our area was a principal subject. Thus in my diary: "Quizzings today from four of the five Generals in the Division. Thank heaven we wear the R.E. badge. As a result they seem to think that we know more about what is going on in the area than they or anyone else, and accept our statements." It may be noted that in those days Brigadiers were designated Brigadier-Generals. That the day fixed for the attack was close had become evident from orders received to work continuous night and day shifts on certain dugouts, and to fill up forward dumps of materials likely to be required in an advance.

Earlier in the month we had been instructed to make in our workshop a large number of semi-open wooden cases, 4 foot 6 inches in height and width. These were to be referred to as "special boxes," the real purpose for them being kept secret as long as possible. These cases were to be built into a part of our Brigade's front-line trenches to house cylinders containing gas, which was to be discharged in conjunction with a smoke-cloud. Arrangements for the provision of the cylinders and smoke candles were in the hands of an Officer from the Chemical Section R.E. On the 13th June the Senior Subaltern and I accompanied the latter in selecting positions in the bays of the front-line trenches for the emplacements to hold the cases. The task of getting the heavy gas-cylinders from the back area into the cases was left to us, and involved a long manpower carrying from Hébuterne village. It was not a job that I cared for. Work on digging out the emplacements started that night. As a clue to the imminence of an attack my instructions were that they were to be completed by the 17th June, which gave us a day in hand only on specified time, and it was stressed that this was of the utmost importance.

For carrying up the cylinders it was decreed that the operation should be carried out in one movement, and a party of 800 men was allotted for the purpose. Use of the Serre road from Hébuterne was ruled out owing to its being a well-registered target for enemy night shelling. This left us a choice of using the winding communication trenches with the protection they gave, or going overland on open ground. The advantages of the latter seemed to me to outweigh the former. The route was carefully marked by short pickets painted white on one side, and in places by a strand of wire. It followed the general line of Knox Street, Jean Bart and Valentine trenches. The first-named was so called after the C.O. of the 7th Warwickshire Battalion, a very fine officer who was killed two years later in Italy. It had been arranged that no raid or shelling activity on our part should provoke the enemy that night, and the task was completed without any interference by the enemy, or mishap to the large carrying party involved, but I recall a considerable feeling of relief as the tail end of the party disappeared in the darkness away from Hébuterne. On the night of the 22nd June I toured our front-line sector, and was able to report that our commitments were all practically complete. As far as we could foresee we were ready for the battle to come.

The following day orders were received to withdraw our Sappers from Hébuterne, except one officer and about 20 men. Anti-gas blankets were put in position in all dugouts and O.P.s. A steady but not heavy bombardment of the enemy trenches started at 6 a.m. How long would the bombardment prior to the actual attack last? Two days? Three days? Bets were freely exchanged in the Mess. In those last days of June all of us were gripped with a mounting sense of expectation and tension. We had less cause for this than the Infantry. For the battalions destined for the assault, not knowing what the next morning would bring forth, those last days of waiting must have been hard to bear. For two more days heavier shelling continued, but on the 26th and 27th the weather turned colder and wet. On the 28th rumour spread around that the attack had been postponed for 48 hours. Owing to the bad weather air observation by the Royal Flying Corps had been difficult, and the scheduled programme for the bombardment was in arrears. The odds seemed heavily in favour of "Z Day" being the 30th. They seemed even longer when at 10.30 p.m. on the 29th we received at our bivouacs totally unexpected orders to dig two dummy trenches in front of our fire-trench. Our three available Sapper Sections were quickly aroused from their sleep, and marched away to the front line to join a working party of 400 Infantry. This party started work at 12.40 a.m., and in two hours marked out and dug two shallow trenches, 50 yards apart, and with a total length of 1,320 yards. Presumably this was to divert enemy artillery fire from our front line to the dummy trench.

The morning of the 30th came with no signs of an assault. We remained in our bivouacs all day. Bayonets were resharpened, equipment and kit checked, and every preparation made for an immediate move forward. In my diary I recorded: "Bombardment more intense all day. Enemy reply heavily. Shelling continued at night." A little later I wrote: "The bombardments, especially when seen at night, were a fearsome yet wonderful sight. We had a small observation post on a hill close to our bivouacs. The front-line trenches were hidden from us by a ridge, but we could watch our shells bursting on the further enemy-held ridges, and the enemy bombardment on the villages behind Hébuterne—Sailly, Courcelles and Colincamps. The latter on one night seemed half in flames, but our old billet in Sailly, the Curé's house, escaped damage."

Whatever the individual tension might be, our communal life under our big mess/bedroom tarpaulin persisted with little noticeable change. Just before the battle started I wrote in a letter: "Last night I slept soundly despite the noises outside, the mosquitoes, pattering rain and occasional digs in the back from tree-roots. The Major was unlucky in that a bad leak developed in our tarpaulin roof over him.

In the morning I awoke to find him doing the oyster trick—sleeping with his bath-tub turned upside-down and propped up over his head. Now I am lying on my tummy writing this by candle-light, and the rain is beating a regular tattoo on the tarpaulin. Tonight we had a sumptuous dinner including an unexpected course. The soup was good, the beef quite tender and edible, with young potatoes and fresh vegetables. Then we opened our eyes as the Major's batman brought in a large plum pudding. 'Where did this come from?' said the Major. 'It's one we had at Christmas which you said I was to keep for a special occasion, sir!' 'Is this a special occasion?' 'Well, sir, we thought as how we'd been strafing the Boche a lot today, and that you might like it!'—And we did."

Wellington's officers may have indulged in a ballroom supper before Waterloo. We must have been unique among British units, on this near mid-summer evening, prior to the Somme Battle, in fortifying ourselves with a Christmas plum pudding.

Before the battle started Colonel Marshall, our C.R.E., received a personal letter from the Corps Commander, General Hunter Weston. It read: "Please express to the Officers, N.C.O.s and men of the 48th Division Engineers my appreciation of the splendid work which has been undertaken by them in anticipation of our attack. Our victory will be greatly due to the work that has been done by you and them in the past, and to the work that is about to be done by you during the battle that is now about to commence. The best of good luck to you and your fine command."

It is only fair to say that we had our reservations, regarding the probability of similar encomiums having been distributed by him, on a rather lavish scale, to Units of all arms throughout the Corps.

(*Above*) All that remained of 'Villa Rozenburg' in March 1916. On 21 April 1915 Eberle was ordered to blow it up. 'Two more small charges and a landmark for miles around was gone.'

(*Below*) The Bois de Warnimont, January 2020. Eberle's and another section had to produce timber for artillery emplacements. 'Our stay in the woods lasted three weeks … one of the most pleasant and, in some respects, satisfying periods spent by us in the war.'

(*Above*) An entrance to a deep dugout under the cemetery in Foncquevillers, photographed in late 1916. On Christmas Day 1915 part of the cemetery collapsed into it, producing '… a strange medley of earth, chalk, corpses, broken bits of coffins and tombstones piled up on top of our kitchen range …'

(*Below*) The main street in Foncquevillers (Fonquevillers on British trench maps). The rebuilt church and former cemetery are in the centre rear of the photograph.

(*Above*) A staff car outside a headquarters in Foncquevillers.

(*Below*) View from near Leipzig Redoubt, across Blighty Valley (and the Nab, down in the valley) towards Ovillers and Pozières.

The Windmill Pozières Church

Approximate area of the action of 18 August 1916

OVILLERS

Just west of the Leipzig Redoubt

(*Above*) Life at the Front: loaded packhorses pass by a field kitchen near Hamel, shortly after the official end of the Battle of the Somme on 18 November 1916.

(*Below*) Moving ammunition to the Front, near Flers, November 1916. 'It is almost heartbreaking for the drivers to slog away at grooming … only to find that in the first hundred yards outside that everything is covered again with mud and slime.'

(*Above*) Infantry in the snow near Contalmaison, February 1917. 'January 1917 brought the start of one of the longest periods of extreme cold that France had experienced for many years.'

(*Below*) Clearing trees felled by the Germans in Péronne during their withdrawal to the Hindenburg Line. '[In Péronne] Churches, public and private buildings of all kinds, bridges and railways had been blown up…'

(*Above*) Amongst other tasks, Eberle's company built a number of bridges to replace those destroyed by the Germans in their withdrawal. Here members of an RE Field Company complete a small bridge over a stream, Spring 1917.

(*Below*) The scale of the support required to keep men in the field is illustrated by this transport column parked up by the sides of a road (motorised on the left, horse-drawn on the right) in the Spring of 1917.

(*Above*) Pilkem Ridge, 31 July 1917 – giving a wounded German a light for his cigarette. 'On the opening of the morning of the 31ˢᵗ July I was awakened at 3.50 a.m. by the opening barrage of our guns.'

(*Below*) Wounded men being brought in from the battlefield, Menin Road, September 1917. 'Round our new front with the CRE. Passing Genoa I saw more dead lying out in the open than I have ever seen. Ground fearfully cut up by shell-fire.'

(*Above*) Early British troop arrivals build a barricade across a road leading up to the front in Italy, late November 1917.

(*Below*) British cyclists cross the Piave by means of a lengthy pontoon bridge, 1918. The Piave was usually at its fullest after the winter snows melted.

13   The Somme Battle (Ovillers)

July–August 1916

We now entered the second phase of our war experience. In the first phase which had lasted fifteen months, we had held different parts of the long Allied front under regular shell-fire, with only sporadic raids by the Infantry into the enemy's trenches. The second phase comprised assault and contact fighting inside the enemy's heavily defended areas, extending a considerable distance in depth. The German defences included villages strongly fortified with all-round defence, and redoubts or strong points strategically sited. Large, deep underground dugouts provided protection during shell bombardment. The third phase came in the following year, in advancing over open country, and also in the final stages of the war in 1918 in Italy. Each of these three phases brought with it differing techniques and employment for the R.E. Field Companies, and also marked changes in our conception of war, and in our mental reactions to war-weariness.

On this morning of 1st July 1916, we learned at an early hour that the projected attack on a wide front had gone forward. About midday I met the first batches of prisoners. A number of them were slightly wounded. All looked tired, sullen, mud-covered, and took no interest in what they were passing.

It was two or three days before it was possible to assess the full results of the first day of the Battle. It became clear that at the northern end of the front attacked, from a little North of Gommecourt to Ovillers, about 8 miles to the Southward, our attack had failed to retain possession of any part of the German trenches. Further to the South, British and French troops had advanced their lines, but in no sense could it be called a complete break-through of the enemy defences. British casualties on this first day are quoted as being over 50,000.

The 6th and 8th Warwickshire Battalions of our 143rd Brigade had taken part in the assault, attached to the 4th Division. The latter, with the 29th and 31st Divisions and our own, formed Hunter Weston's VIIIth Corps; 29 Battalions attacking on a front of about 4 miles. The two Battalions had attacked on our right against the Serre ridge. They had penetrated a considerable depth into the enemy lines, and, in spite of heavy enemy counter-attacks, held their position until ordered to withdraw. The casualties of these two Battalions on that day, as given by Charles Carrington,[1] at that time Adjutant of the 5th Battalion, were 41 Officers and 1,005 Other Ranks. These were the officers and men we had known and worked with for fifteen months at the front. It was a sobering reflection in our inward thoughts, but one to which we did not often give expression. It brought, also, a realization of the power of the German war machine opposed to us. On our immediate left, VIIth Corps, in a pincer attack on Gommecourt, had similarly failed to retain a foothold in the enemy's trenches, although the four battalions of the 56th Division penetrated nearly 2,000 yards. Reinforcement support, bombs and ammunition had, however, failed to reach them in the face of intense artillery and machine-gun fire.

In his book, *The Somme*, describing the battle, Brigadier A. H. Farrar-Hockley refers to other Divisions of the VIIth Corps—as also in other areas of the attack—finding the wire "extensively torn in front but *indifferently gapped*. The 56th Division had made sure of having gaps by sending out parties with Bangalore torpedoes to the enemy wire on the previous night, and were *rarely stopped by the well-gapped wire*. [A footnote explains the torpedo as "being at this time an iron pipe filled with guncotton primers."] This device was *subsequently* developed into a more powerful and manageable engine." At the expense of a reiteration of what has been written in a previous chapter, why was its potentiality in aiding a frontal attack not appreciated, and its tactical use employed more widely in the 1st July and subsequent assaults? Was there any need for the delay in its production as a standard weapon? I think it is a fair statement that a proved efficient type had been evolved by our own Division in the previous April, and could be made in the field by any R.E. Company, apart from types produced by other Divisions.

There had been no frontal attack from our own front-line sector, the plan of attack being a pincer movement. Charles Carrington, who was observing from a position close behind our front line, graphically describes in his book how our gas-cylinders and smoke-candles were successfully in action at zero hour. The gas- and smoke-cloud had blown steadily away from the trench. "We had formed the curtain of smoke just where it was required, and drawn fire which might have

[1] *Soldier from the Wars Returning.*

90

been aimed at the attacking battalions, and had isolated the Gommecourt operation from the main battle.''

On the 13th July orders were received for the Company to march on the following day to Albert, about 12 miles to the South. The O.C. was on the sick list and not allowed to rejoin us until the 19th. At Albert we were placed temporarily under the direct orders of the Chief Engineer, Xth Corps, and after some difficulty in establishing contact secured billets among semi-ruined houses in the Rue de Cadran. The next afternoon I was taken by a young Staff Captain to reconnoitre the Albert–Bapaume road, on which the Company were to work that night. This was the main road linking these two important towns. It ran in a straight line in a North-East direction, gradually rising along the Northern slope of the Pozières ridge. About half a mile from the outskirts of Albert lay the village of La Boisselle, with the original German front-line trenches bulging out in front of it. Half a mile further on, Ovillers lay about 500 yards North of the road, separated from it by a shallow valley. It marked the limit of our advance at this date, and the point South of which a considerable wedge had been driven into the German defence system.

As the Staff Captain and I walked through the shattered German trenches I stopped to look at my map and asked "Where exactly is La Boisselle Village?" He grinned and replied "You are about in the middle of it now." The village had been literally levelled to the ground by our bombardment. Close by was an enormous crater where one of our biggest mines, said to have contained 60,000 pounds of explosive, had been exploded. The scene of destruction was almost unbelievable. Further on many British dead still lay out in the open, their faces blackened by the sun, so that for a moment or two I thought they were African troops. As we parted on our return, the Captain remarked casually, "Good luck to you! We had a battalion working on the road last night. They had about a hundred casualties." It may have been intended as a piece of advice, but it was not exactly a comforting one. However, our good luck held. Our four sapper sections worked steadily all night on the 1,500 yards stretch inside the old German front line, which brought us to a point opposite Ovillers, and not a single shell came near us, although there was heavy shelling by both sides.

Fortunately on the following day we came again under the wing of our own Division. For our first round period in the Battle the latter was committed to widening the wedge driven into the enemy's lines by assaults on the area around Ovillers. These attacks were made not from our old front line facing East but from the South, where we had penetrated at La Boisselle.

The Division was then relieved, and moved into the back area for a fortnight's rest from the battle zone, before returning to the Ovillers sector for our second round in the battle. While out of the line we received replacements for our casualties. These had included two officers, G. S. Perry and L. M. Watts, wounded, and my brother and I were the only two officers left in the Company out of our original complement. Four subalterns from a R.E. Fortress Company in England were sent out to join us, so that we became over our normal strength. In the R.E. Corps it was the junior officers who bore the brunt of the long periods of being under enemy fire. The duties of the two senior officers were more of a co-ordinating nature, involving intermittent but less lengthy periods in the front-line trenches. Reconnaissance and reports on newly won trenches were important duties shared by all.

In both of what I have termed our first and second rounds, the latter lasting till 28th August, the fighting consisted of localized attacks carried out by a Brigade with limited objectives. The general aim was to gain possession of the high ridge positions around Thiepval and further to the North of it.

Our Sappers were fully trained in the use of the rifle, bayonet and bomb, but were not used as assault troops. In the Somme fighting their principal tasks were to help in consolidating the ground gained. Many of the German trenches were wrecked and blocked by our shell-fire. The essential need was to put them in a state capable of defence against the enemy counter-attack as quickly as possible. Where part only of a continuous fire-trench had been captured a "bomb-stop" had to be made, and "strong-points" at selected positions ."Apart from the initial 'over-the-top' assault, much of the fighting is carried on in the trenches, where the conditions are not unlike finding oneself in the Hampton Court Maze. The Infantryman and Sapper often knows only what is happening in the tiny section of trench in which he finds himself. At times he does not know whether it may be a friend or foe on the other side of the next traverse." This applied also to the fighting in the villages where small parties of the Germans held out. At Ovillers the Prussian Guards Regiment fought among the ruins for ten days with the greatest bravery, after being subjected to intense bombardment, but by the 17th July it was entirely in our possession.

In Hutchinson's well-illustrated book on the Battle of the Somme[1] a passage reads: "Ovillers presented a horrible spectacle. Not only had it been pounded to rubbish, but the unburied dead, some of them terribly mangled by shell-fire or bombs lay about everywhere, and the whole place reeked of slaughter. The entrance to the village from the Bapaume road had been defended by two field-works. These had been entirely destroyed, but in their place had arisen another rampart— a rampart of some eight hundred corpses piled one upon another."

[1] *Sir Douglas Haig's Great Push.*

92

The Times published a description of the battlefield around La Boisselle and Ovillers, written by its Special Correspondent, who was conducted over the ground. The dispatch is dated 8th August. This was more than three weeks after our Division had been engaged in the fighting here, and by then our front had advanced northwards towards the Thiepval Ridge. In the interval the more gruesome remnants of humanity among which we moved and worked had been cleared away.

The following are extracts from the dispatch: "There is probably no more dreadful region in all this stricken battle area than that which lies about and beyond Ovillers. There are no adjectives with which to describe its hideousness. . . . La Boisselle is not more than a flat layer of pounded grey stones and mortar on the bare face of the earth. Of anything like a village or individual buildings there is of course no semblance. Ovillers is non-existent. . . . We went down across the torn and blasted earth to the white line of what was once the German front-line trench. It is a trench no more. It was pounded day and night through all the desperate fighting which went on for the possession of Ovillers. It and the ground around are littered with equipment, cartridges used and unused, and unexploded bombs, bits of shells or whole shells—duds are everywhere beneath your feet. The heat beats back on you from the baked earth, and the air is thick with the dreadful smell which belongs to battlefields, and with the buzzing of flies. . . . Ovillers is more utterly destroyed than any other village in the battle area. Undoubtedly a church once was there, because the map says so, and there is still one fragment of wall which may have been part of a church. . . . Underground it is different. It was estimated that the dugouts here could hold and did hold 2,000 Germans. It is doubtless true; one fears from the smell that they hold many yet. The entrances to most are battered in by shells. . . . And all around was heat and noise and that almost intolerable atmosphere."

In the two periods our Sappers spent four weeks working around Ovillers and the trenches North of it. My own abiding memory associated with it is that of the appalling stench which persisted there throughout this period. One difficulty which may not be generally appreciated was that of pinpointing one's exact position in the enemy trenches, and of conveying the correct position in reports sent back for the information of Brigade and Divisional Staffs. It was largely overcome by the excellent large-scale, 1/10,000, maps printed with the enemy trenches marked on them from aerial survey. These were continually brought up to date, and were divided into numbered and lettered squares. By subdividing the sides of the latter into tenths, a figured map-reference indicating any position in the square could be given, *if* it could be identified on the ground. On one occasion I received firm instructions from rear Headquarters to consolidate at once, at a point about 400 yards behind the enemy's front, and held by them continuously for many months previously.

The day following our night work on the Bapaume road was taken up by reconnaissance of the trench area in and around Ovillers, which now formed our Divisional front. Thereafter the work of the Sapper sections was mainly carried out at night. Company Headquarters and Sappers moved from the Albert billets to a wooded area close to Aveluy, a small village on the Ancre River, which lay opposite Ovillers. Our bivouac site here was somewhat marred by the German counter-battery guns' habit of sending over gas-shells. Two Sapper sections occupied forward dugouts at Donnetz Post, and a pontoon bridge constructed over the river.

In the July phase the initial attacks made by our Division were on the Eastern flank of Ovillers. They were directed in a North or North-East direction, taking advantage of the wedge previously driven into the enemy positions. As these originally faced West, we were able to attack up the four, or in some parts five, lines of trenches which constituted their front-line defences. The forward right flank of our Division was, however, separated by a wide gap of about ¾ mile from the front line of the nearest British troops on the South side of Pozières Ridge.

I recorded a somewhat unusual reconnaissance in this area which fell to my lot to carry out, and provided me with some of the worst qualms I had so far experienced. On the morning of the 25th July the C.R.E. came over to the Company. General Fanshawe wanted an R.E. Officer's reconnaissance along the Northern side of the Pozières Ridge. I gathered that the Australians and a London Division had made an assault up to Pozières village outskirts from the South side of the ridge. The fighting during the period 23rd July–3rd Sept., known as the Battle of Pozières Ridge, has been described as one of the toughest struggles in the whole course of the First World War. The position on the morning of the 25th was very obscure. The G.O.C. required immediate information as to the existence of any German trench along our Northern side of the ridge; presumably for the possibility of giving support from that side. I was instructed to take an N.C.O. with me, a sign that we had learned to recognize that they wanted two chances against one of a report getting back to them.

For about a mile there was a German communication trench running from La Boisselle, roughly parallel with the main road to Pozières, and about 300 yards above it, on the ridge. The trench having come to an end, we came under the clear observation of the enemy on the Northern slopes opposite to us. There had been heavy gunfire all the morning on the Pozières area, but I was puzzled at the time as to why the open slopes of our Northern side of the ridge were being systematically shelled. We can now read the accounts of the tremendous bombardments inflicted on the Australians, and of the Germans' determined counter-attacks on that morning of the 25th, and again in the afternoon. With their usual thoroughness the Germans were laying a curtain of shell-fire across both sides of the ridge behind the Australians to prevent reinforcement, ammunition and bomb supplies reaching them. Our concentration of fire was equally heavy, and their two counter-attacks were unsuccessful in driving back the Australians.

As it was now open ground, and two figures more likely to attract attention than one, I told my companion, Corporal Weeks, to wait in a deep shell-hole, from which he could see along the contour of the ridge. I made my way towards Pozières, progressing from one shell-hole to another. There was no lack of them. I wrote afterwards an account of what up till then had been one of my most curious, unexpected, and I may add, frightening experiences of the war. "It was a fine clear morning, and from my shell-hole O.P.s I had a magnificent panoramic view over the whole of the battlefield, North of the Albert/Bapaume road, spread out in a wide arc before me. To the North-West on the left of the arc the trenches North of Ovillers pointing up towards the high ground round Thiepval. To the right the grassy slopes leading up to Pozières, and its cemetery further to the North. Half right across the open valley below, the higher ground still held by the Germans, distant perhaps 700 or 800 yards, and forming a gap in the new British line which our Division had been steadily eroding. Where exactly the German front line opposite, or our extreme right flank, lay was only a rough guess. The curious aspect was that not a man, not an animal was visible over that wide landscape, nor even the usual tell-tale wisps of smoke. The only movement to be detected by ear or eye was the swish and bursts of the shells on the ridge. And yet one knew that within visible range there were many thousand human beings, whom modern war had driven into ant-like groups burrowed in the earth.

"There was probably no British soldier within a half-mile radius, and perhaps for the first time a feeling of loneliness came over me. In my experience of war, loneliness and inactivity under shell-fire are the greatest begetters of fear. Normally for an officer the responsibility of having men in his charge is a great dispeller of fear. He has to keep his mind active, thinking what he could or should be doing for them, whereby his own thoughts of fear are pushed on one side. If, without further endangering them, he can invent some light task he can help those with him similarly, in giving them something to do to distract their minds.

95

"The only trench on the ridge was a shallow cable-burying trench, but there was dead ground out of my view on the North side of the road. There was no visible wire between me and the position held by the Germans opposite me. Were they holding any outposts in the folds of the ground in the valley nearer the road, to deny its use against a flanking attack? I worked my way down and crossed the road. The thought came into my mind that I must be the first British soldier to have set foot on this part of the ridge and road, some 2½ miles inside the German front line of 1st July, since the Somme Battle started. Two or three nearby pings warned me that some distant (I hoped) rifleman was resenting my presence on his side of the road. I was now fairly close to the Western outskirts of Pozières, round which and across the ridge the shelling had continued on a heavy scale. It was clear that the Germans were not occupying any positions on the lower slopes North of the road, and there was no approach-trench or cover along the North side of the ridge which we could use for a supporting attack. I travelled back to Corporal Weeks considerably faster, but shortly before I reached him I realized that my revolver was no longer in its holster. I remembered making a dive to the ground about 50 yards back as a shell arrived—luckily they were for the most part H.E. and not shrapnel—and I scrambled back and found it. In reply to a query from me, Weeks' reply was to the effect that he had only been concussed three times and had to change to another shell-hole." He was a good lad, and soon afterwards went back to train for taking a Commission.

"As we hurried back after reaching the communication trench, which was well beyond the area which had been consistently shelled, we were slowed down in the narrow duck-boarded trench by a party of three or four infantrymen in front. I was following close on the heels of the last man, when there was a loud bang from just behind us. The man in front of me toppled over, and I half caught him. He had been hit in the middle of the back by a shell fragment. When I glanced back I saw the black cloud indicating the burst in the air of what we call a 'woolly bear.' It was low down and just behind us, and from our relative positions I am still wondering how that bit of shell missed my head. However, when the victim's mates called loudly for stretcher bearers, he lifted his head and joined in with his own 'Yes, stretcher-bearers!,' probably with thoughts of a 'Blighty,' so I do not think he was badly wounded. Without further incident I reported back to Division on the ground features, and the absence of any cover for a possible supporting attack by daylight along our side of the ridge."

After we had gone into the back area in September, I wrote this commentary in a letter to a male relative: "We caught it pretty hot during the past weeks, but the men came through magnificently. We were having a meal in a café a couple of evenings ago, and we heard this remark made by an Australian at the next table—"I saw more b—— shells in three b—— minutes up at Pozières than the whole b—— time in Gallipoli."

Our second round in the Battle started on 13th August. On the 18th our Brigade carried out one of the assaults with limited objectives, from a starting line approximately eight hundred yards North of Ovillers. It resulted in the capture of Leipzig Redoubt, and may be taken as typical and illustrating the procedure and nature of the Sapper contribution in this phase of the Somme fighting. Having been warned of the operation beforehand, my brother and I on the previous day had gone round the Brigade front, and checked up on the R.E. forward dumps of materials and tools, before visiting Brigade H.Q. to discuss details involved in the operation. At 11.30 a.m. the C.R.E. issued our operational orders as follows:

"1. 143rd Inf. Bde are attacking this afternoon, 1st objective X.2.b.62-20-03—X.2.a.91-81—X.2.c.39.

2nd objective $\left.\right\}$ (Similar reference numbers given.)
3rd objective

"2. O.C. 2nd Field Coy. R.E.—

"(a) Will send 2 Forward Observing Officers, each with 6 men to follow the last wave of the attack; they will assist the Infantry in putting bomb-stops, to maintain hold on the first objective and in clearing any mouths of deep dugouts that have been blocked.

"(b) If the 2nd objective is gained, it may be possible to employ R.E. on the line of the first objective. Word will be send back to the two R.E. Sections standing-by in Ovillers village [reference point given], where 4 parties, with necessary stores will be ready detailed to go forward and form strong points at [four reference points given]. Name boards for these strong points are to be prepared and erected as soon as possible."

Three further paragraphs dealt with Pioneer Battalion employment, the sending of situation reports, and a warning against carrying maps or documents useful to the enemy during the operations.

From that point our Company Officers carried on in close liaison with the Brigade Staff and Unit Commanders. The assault was made at 5 p.m. "over the top," under a creeping barrage, by the 5th and 6th Warwick Battalions on a 700-yards front. By about 8 p.m. the three objectives had been gained, and over 400 prisoners, including 9 officers, taken. About 8.30 p.m. the Germans staged a counter-attack over the top by their reserve troops, which was beaten off.

Our first R.E. Section went forward to the captured area at 7.35, and the second a little later, and assisted in repelling the counter-attack. At 3 a.m. they were relieved by our other two Sections, who were at one point consolidating within 50 yards of the German-held trench, and suffered a number of casualties. The two Warwick Battalions had fought splendidly, and I felt very proud of the way our Company's Officers and Sappers had played their part in the operation.

A few days later I recorded some details of what I had experienced on that night. "I was given a small task of siting the line for a new communication trench from the original German front line facing West—if the attack was successful—to link it directly with our pre-1st July front line trench. The obvious connecting point was at 'The Nab,' the name given to a small pointed salient in our front line, where no-man's-land was about 300 yards wide. A direct West–East line would bring it slightly in rear of the proposed final objective. We had to wait for darkness, and by 11 p.m. the shelling had died down to desultory firing. We were more liable to be shot at by our own troops holding the original front line, as we approached them from what, up till then, had been a German-held trench. With two of my old Section Sappers we soon completed the marking-out. The O.C. who was in Ovillers had been slightly gassed. As I wanted to take back a report on the consolidation carried out during the night on the captured trenches —a daily report had to reach the C.R.E. at 6 a.m.—I went forward, but there was little I could see or do until it began to dawn. Knowing by experience the value of taking any opportunity available for an hour or two of sleep, I looked out for a German dugout. I found a large one which was obviously a first-aid dressing station. By the dim light of a couple of candles it appeared to contain only two or three infantry stretcher-bearers and some wounded men. There were a number of empty rough wire beds, and I was quickly aware of the most appalling stench. As I went out in the first glimmering of dawn, after an untroubled two hour's sleep, I could see the cause. In a short narrow length of offshoot trench, alongside the dugout, German bodies had been piled on top of one another to a height of about 5 feet. They must have numbered a hundred or more.

"In making my way along the trenches, where the assault had taken place, the shattered trench and bodies presented a grim sight. The exhausted Warwicks lay stretched out on the floor of the trench, alongside the dead, British and German, so that in the half light it was difficult to know which one was stepping over. At one of the forward bomb-stops the body of the officer of the Warwicks in command at this point, who had been killed just previously, in a counter-attack, had been laid on the firestep. The Infantry Sergeant's comment to me was firmly spoken—'We're all right. If they come again we'll beat them off.' Infantry and Sappers had made a good job of rapidly building up a defensive position, and making communication trenches passable. It was just 5 a.m. when I got back to our bivouac site."

The following brief extracts from the Company's daily reports and War Diary may give an indication of the conditions under which progress was made towards capturing the high Thiepval ridge, which was eventually achieved a month later. The abbreviated references are to captured German trenches.

"15th August. One Section attached to 144 Inf. Brigade for operation at night. One sapper killed.

"17th. A reconnaissance was ordered of trench 92-71. This trench has been obliterated. One Officer and 6 O.R. wounded.

"18th/19th. Company attached to 143 Bde. for operation. (detailed above). R.E. casualties so far as known 2 O.R. killed, 2 missing believed killed, 11 wounded, 3 missing. Right Section assisted in repelling counter-attack.

"20th. The following trenches [three map references] have been practically destroyed by shell-fire. Other trenches blocked, choked with earth.

"To C.R.E. from O.C. Coy. The two forward sections are in urgent need of rest. They have lost over a third of their strength and the mental and physical powers of the remainder have been strained very nearly to breaking-point through so much work in exposed positions. I propose if possible to relieve them this afternoon, and hope to be able to utilize the other two sections only, during the next 24 hours. Both officers and men are so exhausted that their work is likely to suffer.

"21st. Work on the new Nab communication trench, this area has been very heavily shelled all night. Two Sections attached to 1/4th and 1/6th Glos. Battalions of 144 Brigade for operation. First objective gained and most of the second (R31 d 81 area). About 4 Officers and 150 prisoners taken."

In this attack on the Leipzig salient Second Lieutenant J. A. Bessant, with No. 4 Section attached to the 1/4 Glosters, taped out a 250-yards new trench from the British front line to the captured trenches. With a working party the trench was dug to a depth of 4 foot 6 inches by dawn. He organized the consolidation of the captured trenches, including construction of a small strong-point, under continual heavy shell-fire, and reconnoitred and reported on the whole of the new front reached in the attack.

"22nd. 3.30 a.m. . . . Point 64 cannot be reconnoitred yet as it is not in possession. No. 3 Section working at 31 d 81. Infantry Officer in charge ordered them back as he required the trench to be kept clear owing to enemy bombing attack up the trench. Section Officer reconnoitred to 31 a 81, but 31 c 15 is not in possession. German trench from 1 b 19 to 31 d 62 is almost entirely demolished and practically a track only.

"23rd. Bangalore prepared and sent up midday to clear complete block in communication trench due to a mass of tangled barbed wire half buried in earth. Of great importance to clear this during the day. One Section attached to 144th Brigade for small attack on x 2 a 79, which was not successful.

"24th. Yesterday afternoon after the attack for which he went forward with six sappers, Lieut. T. Barrat reconnoitred existing positions. Although he received your permission [C.R.E.'s] to return with his section he decided to remain after dark as he thought the section could do useful work. This included construction of Lewis Gun emplacement, bomb-stop and fire-bay for 20–25 rifles. The men were more or less under fire the whole time but worked splendidly and returned at 12.30 a.m. without suffering any casualties. The following four lengths of trenches taken on 18th are now in very bad condition owing to shell-fire, there being practically no trench left in parts. . . .

"25th. Heavy shelling during the day. Trenches which had been cleared the previous night again blocked. Clearing had to stop at 3.30 a.m. owing to shell-fire becoming too heavy. Casualties 2 sappers wounded, 1 killed."

Company's Diary records: "All Sections very much exhausted. 1.30 p.m. Two Sections ordered to provide two parties to follow intended infantry attack in evening, with remainder standing by to consolidate trenches gained as required. 26th/27th. Two Sections clearing and reopening forward communication trenches and support line.

"During the past three days nearly all the strong-points have ceased to exist as such owing to the very heavy shelling. Fourth Street between d 44 and b 62 is only a shallow ditch now for the greater part of its length." The latter was one of the German main defence trenches facing West. Conan Doyle in his historical account places on record that in this period "the three Brigades of the 48th Division took it in turns to surge up against the formidable German lines, showing the greatest valour and perseverance, overcoming difficulty after difficulty, and always getting slowly forward. . . . Many prisoners and a fine extension of the line were the fruits of their exertions."

14   Winter Discomforts (Mametz Wood, Bazentin)

September–December 1916

28th August 1916. The Division was relieved and we marched back with sobered thoughts to a land where civilian life existed and, perhaps even more welcome, to the unpolluted air of the countryside. To the Sappers had come the full stark realization that the war had reached a stage where they had to face a man-made whirlwind of destruction, against which they were personally helpless. Individual survival could come only by God's providence.

Man is, however, a resilient creature. After a few days of light training, physical jerks, games and route marches, mental and physical recovery was rapid. The O.C. set about the task of welding the replacements among the Officers and men into the pattern of the original Company.

In the two periods between 16th July to 28th August 48th Division's casualties were over 200 officers and 5,000 men. The casualties in the Company up to this date, including all cases of evacuation, totalled over 80, including 4 officers. Of these all but 6 were in the dismounted Sapper Sections, and represented a loss of 47 per cent of the latter. Fortunately the Company, in spite of losses, still had a nucleus of first-rate N.C.O.s, with well-tried experience. As a result, the new men had confidence in them, and the former esprit-de-corps was steadily established. Casualties among officers in all Units had been proportionately high. From our experience of the later replacements, most of them had been given little opportunity for regular command or control of even a small body of men. It was understandable that much of what now seemed to us elementary principles were new and strange to them under active-service conditions. In their home training schools it had been mainly a case of each man for himself. They might have been lectured on the duties and relationships of an officer to his men, but they had not the experience of putting them into effect. It is no

101

reflection on those who filled the gaps to say that many of them were less fitted by nature, or by having fewer opportunities of taking responsibility in their school-time lives. There were marked but perhaps subtle differences in the Officer/men relationships, when comparing the Regular, Territorial and New Army Units. So far as my experience went the original T.A. Units were more ready to learn from the Regular Army. Also they were more closely bound by local ties into a comradeship which engendered an almost family atmosphere. Having volunteered to serve alongside the Regulars they were "damned well going to put up a good show."

The War had now lasted over two years, and the question that almost inevitably arises is "What was it that enabled men to continue facing odds which were so heavily loaded against them?" It was now not so much remembrance of the initial surge of patriotism—the duty call of "Your Country needs you." The answer lies in a unity of purpose which depended on, and took its strength largely from two sources—leadership and comradeship. In every sphere of activity where men act as a team, leadership, clearly seen, and confidence in that leadership, are vital elements. Also I know of no stronger bond of comradeship between men than that which was forged on active service. Collectively it formed the strength of purpose of the Unit, with its corollary of not letting down one's pals.

The greater part of September was spent in the area behind Hébuterne. In this period we were able to arrange for all ranks to visit Doullens or Amiens. My diary again recalls the delight of seeing trams running, of looking into windows of well-stocked shops, and seeing neatly dressed people. In turn we billeted or bivouacked near the country villages of Authie, Hem, Outrebois, Bernaville and Causmenil. We were inspected and addressed by General Fanshawe, who also presented some of the immediate awards for bravery in action. Two Military Crosses and six Military Medals had by now been awarded in the Company. A note in my records refers to Sergeant E. Kibbey of my Section, who was later commissioned. He was at one time captain of Bristol Rugby Club. "At dawn one morning he saw a figure lying out in no-man's-land make a movement. Without hesitating he went over the top and brought him in, though he knew that he was in full view of the Germans about 300 yards away. To their credit they did not fire. The rescued man had been lying out in a shell-hole for six days, and that night our Sappers found three others still living."

It is worth recording an extract from a letter modestly written by a Sapper, which I noted when censoring it. He wrote: "You will be surprised to hear that they have made me a Lance-Corporal. They have also given me the M.M." Then he passed on to discussing the weather.

My own duties now lay primarily with the Mounted Section. With the crops all gathered in I could get some splendid cross-country rides on my latest remount, which I had named "Snuffles." He was easily the fastest horse in the Company. I wrote: "The only trouble about Snuffles is that he won't be tied up. He breaks every head-collar put on him. No vice about it, he just dislikes being tied up, so he breaks it and then stands by and smiles. We have to make a sort of box for him out of ropes whenever we bivouac. He has been off colour for a few days but has demonstrated his return to health by depositing my groom in the road."

At the beginning of October 1916 we returned to our old front-line area, with three Sections in Hébuterne working on dugouts and revetting front trenches, which were badly affected by rain. We then moved back to a camp near Hem for employment on urgent provision of winter huts for the Infantry. "We have fetched up in a so-called camp. To get in or out of it we have to walk through liquid mud which in places comes over the top of our boots. We occupy skeleton-framed huts of wood with old canvas stretched over it. The floor consists of greasy mud. At 4 a.m. this morning steady streams of water descended on eight recumbent forms—came snorts and cussing as they rose and gazed at the descending rivulets. Then somebody laughed and the situation was saved. Everything has become wintry and wet now; sheets of rain and all around us a sea of mud."

After reconnoitring the Fonquevillers front, with a view to taking over, our next destination proved to be, instead, a return to the Somme battlefield area further South. The Sapper sections had the unusual experience of being taken by motor-bus to Franvillers, South of Albert. I took the Company's transport to join them. Leaving at 8.30 in the morning it proved to be a long and tedious march in a long column. It was dark before we reached Talmas, and two more days before we reached our final destination—having linked up with the Company—in the old German area near Mametz. The roads were in a shocking condition and frequent diversions had to be made. On the final stage near Contalmaison several wagons became completely bogged and had to be left half a mile from the camp. I was fortunate in missing the digging-out operation. I received a message that I could have an unexpected seven-days-leave vacancy. My spirits rose again as I travelled back with lifts in a Q. Staff car, and an ambulance to Amiens, and thence to Havre by what was termed an express train.

The return journey was a painfully slow one with a very rough crossing and warnings of a supposed enemy submarine in the Channel. It took three whole days to reach the Company located in Shelter Wood, about a mile North-East of the ruins of Fricourt. The transport were located near Contalmaison. Thus all were in the devastated area of the battlefield, but we were within a few days of the closing down of the active forward operations of the battle, owing to weather conditions.

Our living conditions were described somewhat lightheartedly in a letter to my parents.

"15th November 1916. I am back with our transport which has been dumped on a spot around which houses no longer exist. Luckily we are near some old German dugouts, in which some of the men can live. The remainder are still out in the open, and it is miserably wet and cold, but I hope to get all of them into some huts in a day or two. When I arrived after leave I found Hollingworth—one of our Subalterns—in charge, and he is staying on here. I found that his accommodation suite was a half share in a hole about 7 feet by 4, which he shared with our Quartermaster-Sergeant. As this was a bit cramped for three, especially as the Q.M.S. is an unusually large size, we hunted round for fresh apartments. After exploring various holes and remains of dugouts we found one which had possibilities. Perhaps you would like a rough description of our desirable (!) residence. When first found only a small hole was discernible, but after a little clearing, it was possible to slide down on one's backside to a wooden-framed dugout entrance. The original steps have now been uncovered and a second entrance or exit also opened up. After descending about twelve feet the chin-high entrance leads into the hall-kitchen-cloak-room combined chamber, size about 5 by 3½ feet. Herein stands a stove whereon our cooking is done. The tin flue-pipe extends for about a third of the stairway, and you are likely to be met by a stream of sparks and smoke in your face as you descend. A second chamber of about the same size is the dining room. Along one side a plank forms the table, leaving just enough room to sit on a bench and lean back against the opposite wall. A shelf over the table holds our impedimenta and 'H' has already provided a picture gallery composed mainly of Kirchner drawings. The roof clears our heads by about 6 inches when we are sitting down.

"Passing on from the dining room the passage narrows. A shell appears to have damaged the timber framework on some earlier day, and a new frame has been inserted inside the original. If you are fat it is advisable not to go further, but a relatively lean person such as myself can crawl through on hands and knees, once the shoulders are past the obstruction. The passage then divides into three directions—on the right to the back exit, also not recommended for the fat; on the left our batman's cubby hole, and in front the double bedroom. The top of the doorway being only about 3½ feet above ground level, the best method is to dive head-first, thereby landing on the end of H.'s bed. From that position it is easy to roll over the four inches space to my bed. The greater danger comes from sitting up suddenly when in bed, as your head is liable to come into abrupt collision with the roof. As I had not undressed fully for a week I decided to do so last night. However, the task of lying on one's back and dressing again does not encourage frequent changes of raiment, also the bedroom walls are distinctly damp and mildewy. This is the only case I have come across where the Boche has built a dugout with such low headroom. We call it the 'Pigmy Dugout.' Still—after a long day's tramping in mud, once we have snuggled into the old flea-bag, and the 'balaclava' put over the head, the world seems kind and peaceful. Silently we bless thoughtful Fritz who built our little home for us, as also Lloyd George, by whose aid we are tenants without paying rent. Our noses at times make us wonder if a particular Fritz is still somewhere adjacent. 'H' is crowing with joy at having inserted a piece of string in a wickless candle and induced it to burn. It emits more smoke than light. Now he wants to go to bed, and if I go after him my entry is apt to leave him flat and breathless.''

A few days later I was detailed to attend a short course at a Divisional School of Instruction. The following day it was cancelled. Thereby I achieved what must have been the very rare experience of serving for four and three-quarter years between 1914 and 1919, and passing through five steps in rank without attending a single course of instruction.

In this our third round in the Somme battlefield area the Company was destined to spend the greater part of three months among the shattered remains of Mametz Wood, Bazentin, Martinpuich and Flers, in the area North of the Somme. Our advance had penetrated about 5 miles, leaving a completely devastated, shell-torn area. Protection for men and horses against the winter's weather had to be provided in addition to the maintenance and improvement of the new front-line trenches. There was thus a continuous demand for materials and Sapper labour. The small country lanes were totally unfit for the heavy traffic leading to the new front.

At the end of November I wrote: "I seem to spend most of my time coping with harassed drivers of our Mounted Section, endeavouring to keep to time schedules for delivering essential stores, and with wagons that are stuck in the mud. On the track leading to our transport lines laden wagons sink in the mud right up to their axles. In the camp in wet weather I wear a pair of thigh-high gum-boots, a fisherman's heavy oilskin coat and a sou'wester. All our living accommodation is hastily improvised. We have now managed to erect a rough mess-hut for the men, and some cover and footings for the horses. It is almost heartbreaking for the drivers to slog away at grooming and cleaning harness, only to find that in the first few hundred yards outside everything is covered again with mud and slime. There is, too, the dreary monotony of their work. It is difficult to find a way of giving the men relaxation, owing to our isolation from civilization, and the long dark nights of winter.

"Last night was one of our 'sing-song' evenings. Picture to yourself a wood-strutted erection, covered by a tarpaulin; about 50 men crowded on roughly made benches; a thick haze of tobacco smoke which the oil lamps pierce with difficulty, and a wheezy gramophone droning out the choruses."

Lest it be thought that the 'Pigmy'' dugout was typical of the accommodation provided for the Hun officers, the following gives a somewhat different picture. "H. and I have now moved into a relatively palatial dugout, probably a German Company Headquarters. It has been occupied temporarily by an undisciplined Infantry Unit, who had made no attempt at clearing it out. The atmosphere nearly knocked me down on first entering. Now we have removed and burned masses of filthy German overcoats, equipment and food litter of all sorts. Even so it was two days after we had taken up residence before we discovered that a sack, nailed across a gap in the wall panelling, contained at the bottom a dismembered human arm.

"At the bottom of about twenty broad steps a fitted doorway opens into a large mess room, with the roof supported by pillars over 6 feet high. Beyond this a passage with alcoves on each side leads to two large and two smaller rooms, and a broad secondary stairway. The walls throughout were originally panelled with wood in two tiers, and a horizontal strip half way up was embellished by a stencilled frieze depicting an iron cross in a shield, with acorns and leaves between the shields. The mess room walls were originally covered by tapestry, but only portions remain *in situ*. My chief crab is a persistent leak in the roof over my bed. We seem to share the dugout with about fifty mice. They have no fear of us, and will get on to the table, walk up to a few inches from our fingers and wink at us—one has just helped himself to a piece of bread on a plate beside my elbow!"

A little later I wrote: "The three nipper mousetraps just received are proving a godsend. I toasted some cheese in our candle and set the traps about 7 p.m. By an early bedtime the bag was eight—not bad for a start! They also effectively stunned two rats. The rats have given me a little target practice for my revolver. In my bedroom the upper part of the panelling has been torn out—probably for firewood—leaving a gap of about 4 feet on the wall opposite the foot of my bed. The rats normally scuttle about behind the panelling, and run across the gap on a horizontal strip of wood in full view. I sit up in bed with my revolver cocked, and take pot shots at them. I have not been very successful so far, nor popular with my fellow inhabitants, as the bang seems intensified in the confined space. Incidentally the bed is entirely the work of my own hands and is most comfortable. I have rigged up a ground-sheet over it, which collects about a gallon of water during the night, and leaves me no excuse for not washing when I get up."

There is this entry in my diary shortly after my return from leave— "*Her* photo comes." This was the foreteller of the biggest and happiest event of my life. On my previous home leave I had gone one morning to my tennis club, where I found a country vicar member and two ladies, all unknown to me, playing a threesome. I was asked to join them and partner the youngest, who had recently come down from Cambridge, where she had represented the University in tennis and hockey. The partnership, renewed in my last leave, was destined to develop in the widest sense, and to last for forty-six happy years. Its impact on my war service was far-reaching, and brought an overriding personal longing for the completion of the task of defeating the Germans.

For nearly four weeks I saw only occasional glimpses of the Sapper Sections' work in the forward area. For the latter part there was no other officer in our transport camp. With some 50 drivers and a heavy call on our wagons for hauling stores there was little spare time outside sleeping hours. Up at 6.30 a.m. in the darkness it was mainly out in the open air, whatever the weather, till it became dark again. Then there were transport schedules for the following day to be drawn up and many letters to be censored. With the long dark evenings many of the men turned to more frequent letter-writing. By day any spare drivers worked on making a new causeway track from the road to the camp entrance. Thus I recorded early in December: "We have completed our new causeway track and 'cheered in' the arrival of our water-cart by the new route. Unfortunately we discovered a few minutes later that our ration-wagon, arriving by the old route, was axle-deep in mud and with a broken splinter-bar."

In the middle of December I rejoined the Company Headquarters and took over from the O.C. who was detailed to attend a ten-aay Senior Officers' Course at Flexicourt. A few days later we received orders to take over the work of the 91st Field Company. With the exception of one Sapper Section, who were sent to work on hutting in the back area, we moved into a much better hutted camp near Bazentin. I wrote: "I think we are settled into our winter quarters or at least till after Christmas, and we shall not do badly unless Brer Boche makes himself unpleasant. Recently we have had very little shelling over our part, and hope our good luck continues. For the past month we have had one of our Sections engaged on a forward job of the non-cushy type. Over the period our only Sapper casualty was one man slightly wounded. The first night, after another Divisional

R.E. Company took the job over from us, they had their Captain slightly, and a Subaltern badly, wounded, four N.C.O.s and seven Sappers killed or wounded, together with an Officer and five O.R.s in their working party.''

Life in the late battle arena had been slowed down to a tempo dictated by human ability to withstand conditions imposed by weather, and the polluted and disease-ridden terrain. With it there always remained the nagging knowledge that life was still in pawn to the hostile hazard of the German daily shell-fire.

An indication of our isolation from civilized habitation occurs in a letter written to my brother: "It is now just seven weeks since I last entered a normal dwelling house, or building, other than one put up by ourselves or the Boches."

A long letter to my parents describes how we kept up the Christmas tradition for our second Christmas in France. Two Sapper Sections had been detached for back-area work. The O.C. and I visited them the previous day, and they shared in the gifts and Christmas fare. There were no parades for work and we had the joy of a late breakfast. The men had their dinner in our recreation tent. Turkeys were the gift of the O.C., and there were plum-puddings from England, and many extras in the vegetable and fruit lines. Everyone received a metal cigarette-case, and over 52,000 Woodbine and other cigarettes and pipe tobacco were distributed to all ranks of the Company. Nine of the ten officers now attached to our Mess dined sumptuously, with champagne on the wine list. "The men's concert was a great success, the O.C.'s entry, being greeted, after the 'ten-shun' command, with 'For he's a jolly good fellow.' This was promptly followed by a voice 'And three cheers for the Major's Father!'—he had been responsible for arranging the gifts of cigarette cases and smokes." Primitive as they were, our Christmas-Day celebrations brought many appreciative comments in the letters sent home. For a short period the foulness and desolation that surrounded us were forgotten. Although we were within the range of the enemy artillery, there was no shelling in our direction.

15   The Germans Withdraw (Bazentin, Péronne)

January–March 1917

January 1917 brought the start of one of the longest periods of extreme cold that France had experienced for many years. It lasted until mid-March. Instead of mud we had hard frozen ground. Digging work was slow and tiring, and snow and ice made roads very difficult for the horses. Fortunately round our camp there was an ample supply of firewood from the ruined remains of villages and the old German trenches. With the New Army Divisions available, there were now 50 British Divisions in France and Belgium and the periods of front-line trench duty were reduced considerably, compared with the previous winter. A major attack by either of the armies, involving large-scale movement of troops, was relatively improbable.

We had handed over our work in the front line, but remained in our Bazentin Camp for the greater part of January 1917. On the 5th the Chief Engineer of the Corps came over and explained that the whole Company was to come under his orders for work on a new Corps defence line. The O.C. and I then accompanied him on a long tramp in which the general lay-out instructions were given us. The work at first had to be carried out at night, as we were still under German observation, but the organization was much simplified by having all four Sapper Sections on one task.

On the occasion of the above inspection with the C.E. my brother had been present in the capacity of acting C.R.E. He had been transplanted to Divisional Headquarters while the C.R.E. was on leave to England. From the beginning of January for the next nine weeks he was almost an unseen member of the Company's Mess. On the C.R.E.'s return he went on a month's leave, having served overseas for just on two years. After rejoining the Company he vanished again to take part in a Senior Officers' course in England. At one point the Mess delicately asked me for a photo of the O.C. to remind them of

109

him. This may, however, have been dictated by their sighing for a relief from the demands made on them by his understudy. We also narrowly escaped committing a lèse-majesté type of crime, the penalty for which is not exactly laid down in Army Regulations. I recorded: "On my return to Company H.Q. yesterday about 4 p.m. I learned that a wire had been received, instructing us to send transport to railhead 'to meet one reinforcement Officer.' This had been taken as meaning the arrival of a new Subaltern, and they had despatched the cooks' cart, an open limber, in which probably the greasy remains of the Company's meat ration had not yet been washed off. 'Heavens!' I cried, 'You have sent the Cooks' cart to bring back the O.C. from leave!' The picture of the Major squatting in the back of a dirty limber about 4 feet square, with his long legs probably dangling over the tailboard was too awful to contemplate. The situation was saved by the hurried despatch of his two horses."

However in that nine weeks' spell of acting stand-in duty I became more inured to the foibles of Staff Officers, and the idiosyncracies of our Company's eight subalterns, half of whom were older than myself.

For the greater part of January the Company worked steadily on the Corps defence line. The soldier's privilege of "grousing" was now directed mainly against the extreme cold, snow and ice.

"29th January 1917.   Still arctic weather. Two inches of ice coating our water-cart. Toothbrush, sponge, shaving-brush, etc., are like pieces of iron in the mornings."

On the 26th January we had received orders to move on the following day from our Bazentin Camp to Mericourt-sur-Somme. Unfortunately we were still under Corps orders, and when Bessant and I rode over to fix up billets, nobody seemed to expect us. However, we found a fine big farm which could house most of the Company in its barns. Our trek via Meaulte was a triumph of slithering over icy roads, but unfortunately there was no sign of our rations.

The following day, as it appeared that Corps had discarded us, although our ration-wagon had found us, I rode forward to Cappy, where it was thought I might find our Divisional Headquarters. Here I ascertained that the Division were about to take over a sector from the French, but our actual dispositions were not yet disclosed. However we could now consider ourselves as having come again under the wing and orders of our Division. We learned later that Rawlinson's Fourth Army were taking over about 15 miles of the French front line, South of the Somme.

The Sappers were left for five peaceful days at Mericourt, in which a much needed "clean-up" and overhaul of equipment was combined with light drill and lectures. The officers went up in turn to reconnoitre our new front line. Our sector lay at a point below where the Somme River (with the Somme Canal running alongside on its Western bank) took a sharp bend to the West in its course, between Biaches and Frise. The Germans held the Eastern bank with the village of Halle and the town of Péronne opposite to us. They also held a bridgehead area on the Western bank at Biaches. Our Company Headquarters and two Sapper sections were at Frise, and two in the forward area fronting Biaches. We had two long days starting at 5.30 a.m., reconnoitring our new front line under the guidance of officers of the 2/7th Company of the 3rd Génie. It was noticeable that, compared with our take-over from the French at Fonquevillers, they did not expose themselves in the front line to the view of the enemy.

Throughout February and the first half of March the Company remained in this sector. Two Sapper Sections were employed in the forward area, and two on a new part of the Corps defence line, the sections interchanging at intervals. There was very little enemy shelling activity, and we had only one casualty from it during February. The work on the Corps line was interesting from the planning point of view. The actual siting of the trenches and wire, and mapping it, was done by us, subject to the C.E.'s approval. A note in my diary recorded: "Meet C.E. and Corps Staff Colonel and show him over line as proposed. He seemed rather pleased."

A number of personal incidents and reactions recorded in letters and diary in the absence of the O.C. indicated that this was an active but not unpleasant period in our campaigning. The ground conditions restricted the use of our horses. Hence almost daily I had long tramps on foot: "Out last night till 9.30 p.m. and off again this morning at 5.30 a.m. I have developed the appetite of a rhinoceros in this biting atmosphere." I think I am fitter for hard physical work than I have ever been. . . . I am not popular with our Adjutant, and, in some respects at least, an affliction to the Company subalterns. To our great regret the C.R.E. has left us and I have been trotting round all our work with the Adjutant. After about half an hour he is usually puffing like a grampus." Also: "Overheard in the Mess—No. 1 Sub., 'Are you going out to-night?' No. 2 Sub., 'Yes, with the O.C.! (Acting).' No. 1 Sub., 'Oh! That means you canter all the way!'" This did not refer to movement on horseback. However much they may have sighed for a termination of the regency, constant companionship and the guiding hand of the Major had welded them into a firm and active loyalty to the Company and its tasks. I do not believe one of them would have wished for transfer to a similar unit.

In the middle of the month I had leave from the C.R.E. for a day's visit to my second elder brother, who was an officer in the Somerset

L.I. He had been sent down from the front line to hospital at Amiens with chest complications. After a 6 a.m. start, and an hour's hard ride on Snuffles, I was taken to Amiens, by arrangement, on the Divisional H.Q. laundry lorry—obviously as part of the Staff's dirty linen. I was surprised to find that my brother had been in the line in the Combles sector, only about 5 miles distant from us. A kindly disposed nurse brought me an excellent lunch on a patient's tray, which had to fortify me till I got back to the Mess at about 9.30 p.m. Under some wartime regulation the food shops in Amiens were closed between two and five-thirty in the afternoon. After some pleasant shop-gazing I found my laundry-lorry, which dumped me, in the guise of clean linen, 12 miles from our headquarters. However I got a lift in an ambulance to a point where my two horses were waiting. The day was a very pleasant break from our normal seven-days-a-week routine.

"I have acquired a dog, or to be more exact he has acquired me. There are often wandering dogs which attach themselves to units. He is most loyal to me and nothing will induce him to be palmed off on one of the other officers. He follows me extraordinarily well, and even if I am mixed up with a big working-party he never loses touch."

"*2nd March 1917.* I was standing outside our dugout yesterday [this was at Frise] when I noticed a German aeroplane flying lower than usual, and heading in our direction. One of our observation balloons, known in the Mess familiarly as 'Rupert,' was tethered nearby. The crew manning the balloon's windlass at once started hauling it down, but it is a slow process. The balloon was still at a good height when the observer jumped out, seconds before the plane's machine-gun sent a stream of tracer bullets into it. Balloon and observer disappeared in a thick cloud of black smoke, from which the observer emerged with his parachute open, but burning with a ring of fire round the edge of it. As it burned away the pace of his drop accelerated and he hit the ground—to survive, but I believe with both legs broken."

In the latter part of February rumours reached us that the Germans were preparing for a withdrawal, and rumours became facts. At the Northern end of the Somme battlefield the Gommecourt/Serre ridge, where our attack on 1st July had cost so many lives, passed into our hands, not without stiff fighting against German rearguards. Southward the advance reached to the outskirts of Bapaume. Would the withdrawal extend to our sector, South of the Somme? Would the withdrawal be substantial in depth? Would we now experience some fighting over open country? These three questions were to be answered affirmatively over the next few weeks.

Plans for the crossing of the Somme on our Divisional front were being prepared by the higher Staffs, and called for reconnaissances and daily reports on the enemy's holding of their front. It early became clear that the initial crossing was to be on our Brigade front. Reconnaissance tours with our Adjutant, and with Colonel Giles on his arrival as our new C.R.E., were followed by explanatory tours with our Section Officers. There were also demands for reports and sketches of enemy dispositions and defences from R.E. personal observation.

We were handicapped in all our movements by Mont St Quentin, a hill lying behind Halle, from which the Germans had a wide-ranging observation over our positions. Our back dugouts were nearly 3 miles from parts of the front line, and we usually preferred reaching it above ground under cover of darkness, as against using a long and often congested communication trench. On both sides of the river the banks rose steeply, but in places there were wide areas of low-lying marshy ground in the valley bed of the river.

Entries in my diary for the week beginning 25th February indicate six consecutive nights, part of which were spent in no-man's-land. I recall vividly lying out on the steep banks, or in the low-lying reedy marshes, with my binoculars for long periods, noting the positions from which machine-gun flashes came, and other enemy dispositions. These were solitary vigils—perhaps not in strict accordance with general instructions, but it was the way I preferred. It was some satisfaction, a few weeks later to find that my resulting sketch plans had accurately pinpointed the German M.G. emplacements covering the river crossings. In a letter written on 3rd March to a friend I wrote: "I regretted my lack of knowledge of languages on a recent night. I had half lost myself till the nearby voice of a Hun gave me the required direction. Luckily he had not absorbed the golden rule that sentries should keep silent. One Boche Officer had the cheek to promenade almost under my very nose, but for my purpose silence too was golden."

"The home papers have taken the Boche retirement very calmly. Before the Somme offensive the idea of their evacuating such strongholds as Gommecourt and Serre would have been scouted. From the morale point of view I think it will open the eyes of the German people more than anything that has so far happened. The eyes of the Boche soldiers have already been opened on the Somme."

The last-quoted paragraph was written before the retirement of the Germans South of the Somme. The full extent of the retirement and its depth was not realized till another month had passed, and our advance halted at the new Hindenberg Line of defence.

The first fortnight of March passed without any recognizable change in the enemy dispositions on our front. Snowfalls had descended again on the 6th. On the 8th the O.C. returned from his course. This time the Divisional H.Q. had sent a car to bring him up to Frise. At midnight of the same evening a German 5·9 shell landed within 20 yards of our dugout, in an area which hitherto had seldom been shelled. Clearly an indication, as we expressed it to the O.C., of the efficiency and compliments of the German Intelligence.

On the 15th March two events occurred, which as far as I was concerned, indicated an early departure from Frise and moves in two opposite directions. In the morning the wonderful news reached me that I had been given a month's leave, starting on the 22nd. At 11 p.m. an order was received to "Stand by and have our pontoons ready for moving forward." A tired Sapper section was aroused from sleep, and on further orders our pontoons were taken up to Buscourt Lock. My brother and I went forward for a final reconnaissance of the proposed crossings and the approaches, returning at 7.30 a.m.

Events now moved rapidly. On the 16th March, Numbers 1 and 2 Sections during the day prepared trestles for a new bridge over the canal. These were carried up as soon as it was dark, considerable difficulty being experienced in getting all the materials to the site owing to bad road communications. By this time, in Péronne and the nearby villages numerous large fires had broken out, accompanied by demolition blasts. Our probing Infantry patrols were still coming under fire, indicating that German rearguards were still in position in their Biaches bridge-head on the West side of the river. There was also more than normal shelling of our front.

17th March.   Early in the day the West bank was cleared of enemy troops, and the 5th Battalion of the Warwicks occupied Biaches. By noon our numbers 3 and 4 Sections, after fourteen continuous hours on the site, without other units' assistance, completed the new trestle bridge over the Canal. This involved spanning a 60-foot gap, and a total length of 85 feet, with revetting and reinforcing the abutments. The latter had been blown up together with the old German bridge at the site, resulting in the bottom of the Canal being uneven and choked with debris. The height of the bridge above water-level was 15 feet. In the evening the Divisional R.E. Field Company pontoons ferried a Company of the 8th Warwicks across the main Somme River opposite Halle. From here they moved down the East bank and occupied Péronne.

18th March, Sunday.   The way was now open for bridging the main river bed of the Somme. The pontoons were again brought into use to ferry a Gunner Field Battery and two Troops of Cavalry. The Company constructed a new transport bridge over the main bed of the River and marshes on the site of an old German bridge, built on piles for the most part, which had been demolished, but some of the piles and other material were able to be re-used. This bridging involved a total length of 280 feet, covering the river and adjoining marshes. The depth of water varied from 5 to 15 feet. Over the main river bed, approximately 65 feet wide, the new bridge was supported on our floating pontoons. The remainder was supported on trestles and piles at intervals, to form about twenty bays. The 10-foot wide roadway could carry all normal Infantry transport and light field-guns. Using largely salvaged material, and with a carrying-party of fifty Infantry for part of the time, the bridge was made available for transport vehicles in slightly under thirty hours, a time much shorter than we had estimated in view of the length to be bridged. Starting on the site at 10 a.m. Number 4 Section worked continuously till past midnight, when they were relieved by Number 3, who completed the task by 3.30 p.m. A light Infantry foot-bridge was also completed. Two days later the pontoons were replaced in six hours by made-up trestles.

Under date 20th March, Divisional Headquarters sent the following message to the C.R.E.: "G.O.C. wishes you to convey to Major Eberle, and all ranks of the 475 Field Company his thanks and appreciation of hard work they have put in on Bridges at Halle, and excellent results achieved. AAA. This work will not only be of value to the Division, but to the Army by materially assisting the advance. AAA. He wishes a strong repair party under an experienced officer left to maintain the good work already done to the bridge."

By the 24th March the three Divisional Field Companies, in addition to work on Bristol Bridge, had completed three horse-transport bridges and six foot-bridges across the Somme.

The German withdrawal on our front, at this stage, had been skilfully carried out from the tactical point of view, but the ability of a few light machine-guns, manned by the rearguards, to slow up our advance must be taken into consideration. The whole operation of our taking possession of the West bank was in fact carried out at a very small cost in casualties. Had a decision been taken by our higher command to force an earlier assault, the cost is likely to have been out of all proportion to that inflicted on the enemy. So far as our Company was concerned, after three days and nights of strenuous effort we were a very tired but elated body of men.

On the 20th March I rode with two of our officers across the river and down the East side to Péronne to look for billets for the Sappers. "All the inhabitants had been removed. Churches, public and private buildings of all kinds, bridges and roadways had been blown up; water-supply sources and communications destroyed. There are few signs of the town being shelled by the French or British. The almost complete ruination of the buildings in the principal streets has been brought about by the Germans blowing out the fronts or setting fire to them. The underlying mentality of the Hun is boastfully shown by a large sign-board, high up on the wall of the ruined Hôtel de Ville—a Renaissance building on a fine corner site, 'Nicht ärgern, nur wundern' (Do not grow angry, only wonder). Fires were still burning in many directions, with occasional explosions as booby-traps and delayed-action mines exploded.'' We quickly learned that the most innocent-looking object, such as an apparently discarded steel helmet on the ground, might cover a bomb arranged to explode if the helmet were picked up. Everywhere the debris of war and discarded equipment lay around. For any souvenir-hunter the choice was unlimited. For my part, with my promised leave so far holding good, I watched my steps with the utmost circumspection and took no risks. I permitted myself one reminder of Péronne. It was a prominent notice posted on a wall, and printed in French and German. Translated it reads: "It is forbidden to throw sweepings, kitchen refuse, or any other rubbish into the stream. Offenders will be punished—Péronne—24.5.1915. Military Command—Von Krupka." My father had it framed, and it still hangs on one of the walls in my house.

On the morrow I set out for England. After a short ride on Snuffles with a farewell exchange of an apple and a nuzzle, and a lorry-lift to Amiens, a train deposited me at Boulogne shortly before midnight. The foretasting luxury of a bed in the Hotel de Calais, a smooth channel passage, and four weeks of expectant carefree joy! Life was tinged with rosy spectacles once more.

A few days after reaching home I received a letter from my brother. On the day of my leaving the Company, one of our young subalterns, Harry Lambert, who had succeeded me in charge of No. 3 Section, had been killed instantly by a German booby-trap mine. He had gone on one of two German light bridges across the river to their bridge-head. They had been partly demolished and preliminary reconnaissance indicated that they might be mined. After warning two sappers with him he passed a plank across a wide gap in the centre of the bridge. Directly he stepped on it a mine in the water exploded, and two others, one on each side of the gap. The two sappers were blown into the water. They were rescued by an N.C.O. diving into the river, but one had to suffer the loss of an arm by subsequent amputation.

The Company's searchlight-wagon, with driver and four mules, had plunged over the edge of the new bridge on its way to the billets in Péronne. The mules had suddenly shied at the water. Although it entailed a 20-foot drop neither driver nor mules were seriously hurt. The Major's and my kits with our Headquarters papers and books were recovered and dried out, but we had lost much of our Mess provisions, and the Company's stamp for censoring letters. The letter concluded with "Don (the dog) refused to take any interest in the Company after your departure—he disappeared almost at once. Y—— saw him later, and tried to get him to follow, but he went off, and has not been seen since, though I left Sapper H—— behind for three days at the old place." I determined to "acquire" no more dogs while on army service.

My application for leave in England had been fortified by reference to the requirements of the family business, due in part to the illness of the other executive director. I must admit that there was not much I could do in the short period, and that there was a more impelling motive. Midway through this leave I became engaged to my future wife. Together we drove in the little family car round the unspoiled countryside, in the glory of its Spring revival. Thus the entry in my diary for the last day of my leave reads—"Packing up and saying good-bye before catching the London midnight train. Oh so hard!"

I was in Etaples by 4 o'clock the following day. Here I was held up at a "rest camp" for three days. On two of these I went to Paris Plage. Its seaside resort atmosphere was positively gay, and it was crowded with officers of different nationalities, including promenading Portuguese officers in smart uniforms. A good military band played outside the Duchess of Westminster's Hospital. The war seemed very far away.

On the fourth day, after a fourteen-and-a-half hours' train journey starting at 5.30 a.m., I reached Péronne, and spent the night at the R.E. Store, where I found G.T.H. in charge, and the following day rode on to Company H.Q. near St Emilie. The Division were now operating about ten miles North-East of Péronne.

I learned that the Company after moving into Péronne had carried out its most outstanding engineering work of the war. This was the construction of a timber plate girder bridge over the canal, to take vehicular loads of 12 tons. It was designed by our C.R.E. The total gap was 97 feet. The central part over the canal was carried on two built-up wooden girders each 40 feet long, resting on crib piers, the remainder on trestles. The web of the girders consisted of 1-inch planking nailed diagonally, and involved the driving of 1,600 6-inch nails in each girder. The bridge, officially named the "Bristol Bridge," was completed in four and a half days, and was the only heavy-traffic bridge available for many miles on either side of Péronne. It continued in use for several years after the war.

An indication of the various operations carried out under the Divisional R.E. supervision, as the result of the German destruction and delaying tactics, is given in a tabulated document prepared by the C.R.E. Altogether 13 new or repaired bridges over the Somme and the Canal were made available. The total man-hours expended, between the 16th and 30th March, were: R.E. 15,200, other Units 18,200.

The roads leading Eastwards had been blocked by blowing them up at road junctions and other selected points, and by felling across them the trees lining the verge. On one main road 300 trees of substantial girth had to be cleared away. The filling-in of craters and removing obstructions, or making diversions in the first five days after crossing the Somme took approximately 2,500 and 7,500 man-hours expended by the R.E. and other units respectively. Fortunately these works could be carried out by daylight, and without the men being subject to enemy shell-fire.

16   Open Warfare (Ronnsoy, Lebucquière)

April–June 1917

After Péronne the Company had moved up from Villers-Faucon to bivouacs in the railway cutting behind St Emilie, in the middle of April. From this point the German resistance had stiffened. Villages and large individual farms were strongly defended. In turn our Infantry had to dig in, and the Sappers were utilized in wiring and forming strong points against counter attack. It was realized that we were near to the Germans' new prepared withdrawal positions— the Hindenburg Line. In its final stage the withdrawal extended over the front between Arras and Soissons, distant approximately 70 miles, but varying in depth. Thereby the Germans considerably shortened their line, releasing about twelve Divisions for offensive or mobile defensive operations. By local attacks our front had been advanced between the 23rd and 28th April to the Ronnsoy area, the fighting for possession of Gillemont Farm being particularly severe.

My first experience of what may be termed a fluid fighting front was not a happy one. Owing to injuries and sickness only three of the Company's Sulbalterns were available. It was arranged, therefore, that I should take temporary charge of No. 2 Section. On the 27th April I went up with the Section in the afternoon to the left sector of our Divisional front, which I had not previously seen. The trenches were only of the hurried "dig-in" type. The Brigadier wanted us to dig a short outpost trench that night at an estimated 300 to 500 yards in front of the position where our Infantry had dug in. This latter was on a slight reverse slope, and the enemy trenches were out of sight on the other side. He wanted a position giving observation over a shallow valley which our maps indicated. The Company Commander pointed out to me that there were some German rifle-pits near the site of the intended trench. One of these, capable of holding two or three men, had been reported that morning as being occupied by the enemy, presumably as an observation-post.

Thus about an hour after sunset I was given an Infantry N.C.O.

and three riflemen to remove them. Approaching from a flank we crawled slowly through the long grass—my first experience of enemy stalking with intent to attack. My signal for a final rush on the post was not required. Our enemy had departed under cover of darkness, and my heart-beats returned to normal. There were obvious signs in the pit of recent occupation.

Having collected No. 2 Section and an Infantry covering party, we went forward, only to find that the contours made the position pointed out to me for the trench quite useless for the purpose required. It had to be sited a considerable distance further forward. The work went well and just after midnight I went back with a Sapper as escort to report to the Company Commander. When I set out to return to the digging party I found that very heavy black clouds had come up and completely obscured the moon and stars. I had taken particular notice as a guide to my route that I should keep to the right of a farm track which ran diagonally across our front. In the darkness, however, we crossed this track without realizing it. For nearly three-quarters of an hour we wandered over unhedged open country. There was no sound of a digging party, only occasional Vérey lights in the far distance. The Sappers had learned by experience the need for a minimum of noise when out in no-man's land. I had not brought my prismatic compass, as I had expected our work to be only in the trenches; we did not know how near the German trenches or their patrols might be. Eventually there came a murmur of voices, and the outline of a trench facing us. I crawled forward—was it German or British? I could not be sure, the sound was muffled by the trench. There were no recognizable ground features in front. To approach either might be equally unpleasant. We withdrew and turned left-handed in what I hoped was a Westerly direction. After going a short distance there came a stroke of luck. I half-stumbled over the body of a dead German. The body was lying face downwards with both arms outstretched over his head. I remembered at once having noticed it during daylight, owing to its peculiar attitude. It was lying just beyond the extreme left of our Brigade trench and *behind* it. We had in fact been lucky enough to walk back unchallenged through a gap between our Brigade trench and that of the Division on our left. Our course from where we set out must have been that of a semicircle in an an anti-clockwise direction, which had brought us on to the front of our neighbouring Division, luckily without their spotting us. We set out again, and this time we made no mistake in finding our Sappers. A further two hours were sufficient to complete our task of digging and wiring without any interference from the enemy. I trudged back with the Sappers a wiser man, resolved never again to be without my compass in open warfare operations. Our Infantry held the trench until the Division was relieved, but I heard later that it was lost by the relieving Division in a German counter-attack.

There was one unpleasant role which the R.E. had to fulfil during this advance. It was the searching for booby-trap mines in houses that had been left standing. There were a number of casualties from them, including the C.O. of the 6th Glosters and 5 other officers killed in a farm at Villers-Faucon where they were billeted. As a result units were forbidden to occupy buildings until they had been searched and passed as safe by the R.E. This task exercised no mean strain on the strength of our nerves. The booby-traps were of two types. They might be set off by hidden wires attached to movable objects such as a chair or cupboard door, or by pressure on a board. Secondly there were the delay-action mines which might not explode for two weeks or more. One of our other Field Companies first discovered how these were operated. The device used was based on a wire which at one point passed through an acid solution. The acid slowly corroded the wire according to the strength of the acid used, and when the wire broke the mine was exploded.

At the beginning of May we were relieved in the front line and moved our Headquarters to Péronne. At 10 p.m. on the evening of the 11th orders were received for the whole Company to trek northwards at 8.30 the following morning. After a very hot march over part of the old Somme battlefield we bivouacked for the night in an orchard, near Le Mesnil, about six miles S.E. of Bapaume, which was now in our possession. The next night was spent at Fremicourt, and then forward to Beugny and Lebucquière.

At Beugny we took over a sector of the front line close to the Albert–Bapaume–Cambrai road, which had provided our first night's active work in the Somme Battle. For the second half of May and the whole of June we worked in this sector. It proved to be a very quiet one, and during the period we lost only one Sapper, killed by shell-fire.

We learned that we had ceased to form part of the 4th Army. On the 22nd May General Rawlinson sent the following to General Fanshawe for publication to all units of the Division: "I cannot allow the 48th Division to leave the 4th Army after seven months strenuous service without expressing to all ranks my appreciation and warm thanks for the valuable services they have rendered.

"After a winter of unexampled severity in indifferent trenches the change to open warfare in March and April found them in a high state of efficiency. The skilful leadership and dash displayed in the capture of Péronne, St Emilie, Epehy, Basse, Boulogne, and Tombois and Gillemont Farms are deserving of the highest praise, and show that the standard of efficiency that has been reached, more especially in the close combination of Artillery and Infantry, is an exceedingly high one.

"I congratulate all ranks on the successes that they have attained, and I shall look forward to some future date when I trust I may have the good fortune to find the Division once more under my command."

The six weeks spent in this sector were uneventful, and made no heavy demands on the Sappers or our transport. The O.C. had undergone a particularly heavy demand on his energies during the advance in the previous month, involving continual night work with personal reconnaissance. It entailed organization of numerous working parties operating separately, and of materials for consolidating new positions gained in successive attacks. The C.R.E. decided that the opportunity should be taken for him to be attached for a month to his Headquarters, partly as a Staff Course, and as a temporary relief from Company commitments. Thus for the whole of June I was deputizing for him in charge of the Company's work. With practically no active operations on our front, General Fanshawe seized every opportunity for training the Division, with its large replacements of Somme casualties, in offensive and defensive operations, and making it "fighting fit" for its next battle experience.

Describing our bivouac camp at Lebucquière I wrote: "We occupy a charming garden, with the rest of the Company, including horses and transport in the field adjoining. This makes administration much simpler. Our rations have been very good of late and we get fresh bread every day. Altogether we are living most comfortably. For a short time our rations came through an Australian Supply Point. They were the best we ever had. By orthodox or non-orthodox methods they got what they wanted. No continual plum-and-apple jam for them. It was also advisable if they were quartered near you to make sure that you did not lose one of your best horses. The open-air life at this time of the year is delightful, and again I have hardly known what it is like to go inside a house for several weeks on end."

On the last day of June my brother returned to the Company's fold, and I made my last tour of the front line in this sector with the O.C. of the 458 Field Company, to whom we handed over our work. Two days later the Company marched back some 8 miles in the direction of Hébuterne to the Achiet-le-petit area. Here we rested for two days. On one afternoon several of us rode to Fonquevillers and Hébuterne, now 6 miles further back. My diary records: "Most interesting to re-visit our old billets and O.P.s. Civilians were moving about in the villages. Still more interesting to ride over the battered area held by the Germans around Serre and Gommecourt, and to appreciate the strength of their positions, as we gazed back at our old front line."

On the 5th July we marched to Achiet-le-grand, and entrained for the Ypres front.

17   The Salient (Ypres)

July 1917

After a fourteen-hour journey we detrained the following morning at Hopoutre. Needless, perhaps, to say the place name, divided into three syllables, was the subject of appropriate comments from our more cheerful would-be humourists. After cooking breakfasts we marched to bivouacs on the N.E. side of Poperinghe.

Our movements at first were dictated directly by the Corps Staff, and our initial reception in the Ypres area was an unpleasant one. Under the guidance of a young Staff Officer we moved forward to a small clearing in a wood where we pitched camp. Officers and men were given leave to go into Poperinghe, situated due West of Ypres. It was the first opportunity for a long time that many of them had of going into a town where civilian life existed, and shops and cafés were open. Only about 10 men including the stable picket with myself were left in the camp. Our 70 horses were picketed along the West edge of the clearing. Shortly after mid-day I was half dozing in my little bivy on the other side of the clearing when a salvo of four shells burst right on top of the horses, quickly followed by another salvo. We all rushed to lead the horses away. It was a beastly sight of plunging horses with blooded flanks, and others lying and kicking on the ground. Each of us grabbed the halters of several horses and ran them away from the clearing. Included in my second batch was a heavy-draught horse, known to all as the "Dolly mare," of whom we were particularly proud and fond. She had a long cream tail and mane, and had been with the Company since mobilization; she was previously with a well-known firm of Bristol millers. For about 50 yards she trotted alongside me, then without warning crumpled in a heap and lay still. We found afterwards that a piece of shrapnel had penetrated to the brain.

After a few more salvos the shelling ceased. The cost to us of those few minutes of enemy shell-fire on a well-taped target was five men wounded, including a very good N.C.O. and three drivers of the mounted section, and over 30 of the horses and mules hit. Eleven of them were killed, 7 were badly wounded and evacuated to mobile hospital. The remainder were more lightly wounded, and we were able to treat and keep them with the unit. Our anger rose to a high pitch when we were told in effect by units in the area, "It was only to be expected! That clearing is in what is known round here as 'Slaughter Wood.' It is shelled regularly every day by a German battery, which has the exact range. Several Units have been dumped in it— all with the same result." Rightly or wrongly, we blamed the Corps Staff for putting freshly arrived troops, without any warning, into a back-area camp site, which they should have known was a regular target of the German gunners. The same day the O.C. left the Company under orders to go to England for a month's Senior Officer promotion course.

We moved away from Slaughter Wood, making four changes of location in the next five days. First a night in tents in "E" Camp, then to "L" Camp, and one on the "Chemin Militaire," which again was not a healthy resort, and finally settled down in what had been a D.A.C. Camp, as our back billet. From here it was not difficult to ride into Poperinghe, where Toc H. and an Officers' Club and restaurants provided us with a reading room and a rare change from our normal rations. In the same period we reconnoitred our new front, and fixed forward dugout billets for two Sapper sections, who moved up for work mainly on communications.

We had our first view of a shattered Ypres, once the capital and wealthiest town of Flanders, with a population said to have been around 200,000. We were accustomed by now to the sight of battered villages, but the revelation of the vicious destruction of the magnificent, centuries-old buildings in Ypres filled us anew with anger and hatred. The ruined façade and central tower of the early Gothic Cloth Hall still held a poignant but majestic beauty, especially when seen by moonlight. It had been built about 1300, and restored a few years previous to the war. Close to it was the shattered Cathedral Church of St Martin, and around the Grande Place other historic buildings had been wantonly reduced to rubble. Who could blame us for the upsurging feeling that we were fighting an evil and soul-less enemy?

The opening assault phase of the battle for the Passchendaele Ridges on our front was three weeks ahead, but its imminence was obvious from the preparations on our side. The Germans were fully aware of them and daily expended a heavy weight of shell-fire over the whole area behind the front line. Our Company's casualties, in the three weeks before the battle opened, amounted to 42, a large proportion being due to gas-shells. The other two Companies also had heavy casualties, including a subaltern killed. My old fellow-subaltern, E. A.

Sainsbury, was wounded. Over the past year he had been attached to the C.R.E.'s Staff, and a few weeks previously had taken over the duties of our Regular Army R.E. Adjutant, on the latter's leaving the Division. There was also a change in our 475 Field Company Command. As it was anticipated that my brother would be appointed to a senior command on the conclusion of his course in England, Captain J. R. M. Crawford, a senior pre-war Officer in the South Midland R.E., who had come out later in 1915, was appointed to command the Company.

The battle known to history as the "Third Battle of Ypres," or as "Passchendaele," lasted slightly over three months. Including the three and a half weeks preceding the opening phase our Field Companies remained in the battle zone fourteen weeks. The 48th Division was one of four initially forming General Maxse's XVIIIth Corps, which was part of General Gough's Fifth Army. The Corps normally operated with two Divisions in the front line alternating with two in reserve in the back area. The sector of the battle in which we took part throughout the period lay to the North-East of Ypres, facing the village of St Julien in the opening phase.

The Passchendaele battles, designed to capture the N. to S. ridge of that name, differed in many respects from that of the Somme. The difference was accounted for mainly by the weather and ground conditions, and the altered defensive tactics adopted by the enemy. The ground over which the battle was fought in our sector was low-lying, and intersected by small streams flowing through it. The month of August was exceptionally wet. The normal courses of the streams were blocked by the intensity of shell-fire, and large areas were converted into a morass of gluey mud, with shell-holes half full of water. A year earlier, on the Somme the German defence had comprised successive lines of connected trenches. In this sector the defence depended on shorter lengths of trench, and a series of "strong-points" mutually supporting one another, and in greater depth. The keynote of these were numerous strong concrete blockhouses. They were always known to the troops as "pill-boxes". Fully protected all round, they were sufficiently strong to resist direct hits from all but the heavier-weight shells. With only narrow slits for two or three machine-guns, and with protected or tunnelled entrances at the back, they were very difficult to capture, and were held by the German troops with great gallantry.

In many of the attacks made by our Infantry a steady forward movement entailing keeping pace under a creeping barrage became an impossible task. Floundering through mud they sought to edge their way forward from one shell-hole to another, in groups of twos and threes. In two other respects the Germans revised their tactics.

125

Throughout the operations they kept up heavier harassing shell-fire on the whole area in rear of the attacking troops. They also used gas-shells to a much greater extent, including the liquid-mustard type. These were responsible for a very large number of men being put out of action at least temporarily. As a small example I recall one of our orderlies having to go to hospital as the result of leaving his bicycle outside our Canal bank dugout for a few minutes. In that time a shell had sprayed the gas on to the saddle, and he remounted the bicycle without realizing it. Officially recorded as "wounded—gassed," he was unfortunate in that modesty prevented him from displaying the scars of his wound!

The individual courage and tenacity of purpose of the British and Empire Infantrymen under the appalling conditions of mud, shell-and machine-gun-fire can never be recognized adequately. In a captured trench, however badly smashed by shell-fire, as in the Somme fighting, there was some feeling of protection and mutual support. Here in the morasses of Flanders they held out against counter-attacks, wet to the skin in water-logged shell-holes. They went forward in the attack, under a tremendous concentration of enemy shell-fire, both before and during the advances, although suffering very heavy casualties.

To gain the Passchendaele Ridge entailed on our sector an advance of about 6 miles. This time there was little talk about a break-through into open warfare. It had been made clear that this was to be a battle of limited objectives, to be captured in turn after adequate preparation, until the higher ground which dominated the Salient was in our possession. It seems to have been dictated, primarily and basically, by the overall aim of bringing about attrition of the enemy's armed manpower, and forcing him to use up his reserves.

The role of the R.E. was largely one of opening up road and track communications over the deep mud and shell-torn ground as the advance went forward. Small parties followed the attacking troops, but, generally speaking, the wiring and strong-point work which had been their task on the Somme was often impracticable under the prevailing conditions. Our Company's records show that 96 per cent of their casualties in this area were from shell-fire.

A week before the battle assault started, the C.R.E. on returning from leave in England, offered me the appointment as Divisional R.E. Adjutant, subject to official confirmation. The possibility of such an offer had never occurred to me. Hitherto we had always associated the post with its being held by a senior Regular Army officer. To us he represented the training and experience of our Corps. Initially he had been the principal exponent of its technical, administrative and disciplinary requirements. I had no experience or grooming in these qualifications, and for several reasons was reluctant to break the ties which had bound me to 475 Field Company for the past three years. On the other hand I should be less exposed normally in the battle areas if attached to Divisional Headquarters, and thereby I hoped a cause of less anxiety to my parents. I accepted and took over my new duties the following day.

My ideas of a more "cushy" job were slightly modified when, on a tour of the front with the C.R.E., we met "Fanny." I received a cordial but characteristic homily from him. It was to the effect that my new job was not to sit in an office and receive reports from the three Field Companies and Pioneers. I was to make myself acquainted regularly and fully with their work, and the conditions in front-line and back areas, so that I could keep the C.R.E. and himself fully informed from my personal observation.

Two days later, with the C.R.E., I attended a high-level conference under the Chief Engineer of the Corps. From this the scope and immensity of the pending battle became clearly outlined.

18   Passchendaele Battles (Ypres)

August–October 1917

On the morning of the 31st July I was awakened at 3.50 a.m. by the opening barrage of our guns. The 48th Division were held in support of the 39th Division attacking in the low-lying valley of the Steenbeek Stream opposite St Julien. The latter was captured in the initial attack but not firmly retained in our hands till two days later. On that day I had my first reconnaissance of the conditions of the old German front line after heavy rain.

When men speak of this, the Third Battle of Ypres, or Passchendaele, what does it convey to the listener? Few of those who took part in it could give a coherent connected account of it in its entirety. The reason is that it was made up of a series of battles. In the post-war official designation of battles, the 1917 Battle of Ypres covers a period of fourteen weeks from 31st July to 10th November, during which eight separately named battles are designated. These were spread over the wide front held by five Corps Commands, which took a part in the advance. Based on an average of four Divisions in each Corps, of which two would form the attacking and two the support or reserve Divisions, the battles were fought on an attacking front of ten (plus) Divisions, but not all at the same time.

The 48th Division was engaged in four of these battles, designated Langemarck (16th–18th August), Polygon Wood (26th September–3rd October), Broodseinde (4th October); Poelcappelle (9th October); and in support on the opening battle (31st July–2nd August). Between these dates there were a number of local attacks and counter-attacks in which the Division were fighting. Their first period in the front line, after the battle started, was from the 4th to the 29th August. They were then relieved and Divisional H.Q. and the Infantry moved back to the open country behind Ypres. The three Field Companies and R.E. H.Q. remained in the Ypres shelled area for work on road and track maintenance and hutting. In the last week of September the

Infantry returned after a well-earned rest, coupled with a refit and training for the further planned advances. These included the battles of Broodseinde and Poelcappelle, after which the Division was relieved and moved away from the Ypres area. Another month was to elapse before the final objective—the Passchendaele Ridge—was firmly in our possession.

My only task in charge of Sappers was at the beginning of the battle to repair a forward road named "Admiral's Road." It was pitted with large "crump-holes," and my orders were to make it usable, in the hope that our advance might make it possible to bring forward our field batteries. Working through the night we dumped into the craters anything solid we could lay our hands on. Sandbags from near-by trenches, smashed tree trunks and a large dump of barbed-wire coils disappeared as part of our unorthodox road materials. Although enemy shelling over the whole area was persistent we had only two slightly wounded casualties. I quickly learned the soundness of "Fanny's" dictum on the need for my being fully conversant with the dispositions and work of the three Field Companies from personal observation. Without this knowledge hurried reports from them during operations could not be assessed adequately and passed on to the Brigade or Divisional Staffs. The difficulty of getting back accurate information as to the progress of an attack, or of the Companies' requirements, was far greater than that experienced on the Somme.

The casualties sustained by the 39th Division in the initial fighting for St Julien were so heavy that they were relieved on 4th August, and withdrawn from the Corps. In one Battalion every combatant officer taking part in the attack had become a casualty. Our Division took over their front, the Field Companies taking over dugouts in the Yser Canal bank. Over the four days following the opening of the battle there was persistent heavy rain. Before a further advance could be made it was essential that roads and tracks from the rear towards the new front line should be made usable. Normal movement by either vehicles or troops had become almost impossible. Of the Somme, it was said, men battled in a man-made hell of shell- and machine-gun fire. In the swamps of Passchendaele that hell was intensified, and to it was added a nature-helped hell of mud—mud that clung and sucked at every footstep. Behind the actual front line men toiled in the mud under constant shell-fire to provide wood-based tracks and duck-boards, and a light tramway, for the forward movement of men and the materials of war.

There are numerous references in my diary to the reconnaissances of the forward area. Shortly after the initial capture of St Julien, I was on a solitary tour of the valley beyond the Steenbeek Stream in mid-morning. It was quite a formidable task merely to pick one's way at leisure through the mudbath and shell-holes. Even where trench-boards had been laid progress was a matter of slithering over liquid mud. As frequently happened the Boches' artillery opened up with a minor barrage shoot without there being any obvious target. The shelling was much too close to be pleasant, but luckily there was one of our disabled tanks nearby, into which I clambered. Inside the only occupant was one dead German. I sat on the floor and wondered how he had got there. Had he been wounded and managed to climb into the tank during a German counter-attack, or had he been dumped inside by one of our stretcher-parties collecting the wounded? The shelling lasted about fifteen minutes, during which I indulged in solitary contemplation of the dead German, and of the narrow dividing-line between life and death, on which we had both stood, before we shared the protection of the tank.

Afterwards I noted: "Many tanks disabled or bogged down." I believe the number I counted was fourteen within my view from one point. In this particular area they had an almost impossible task, becoming sitting targets as they were held fast in the gluey mud.

Later on, as our advance went forward, and I had been wallowing through the morass which formed the battlefield I wrote: "It is sad to come across the old tanks which we had known rumbling along in the back area, recognizable by their painted names such as 'Smoking Willie.' Now this is lying smashed and derelict alongside a German pill-box. In these parts I have seen them in every stage from the complete tank with its crew in action to that of a mass of twisted pieces of scrap iron after it had gone up in a blaze of glory."

On the evening of the 15th August, the day prior to the Battle of Langemarck, the C.R.E. and I joined the Field Companies in the Yser Canal Bank, "dossing down in the 475 Company's Officers' dugout, ready for the battle." These well-protected dugouts were to be our home for most of the weeks during which our Division was in the line.

"*16th August.* Our attack started at 4.45 a.m. 475 Company detailed for forward strong points; 474 for roads and tracks; 477 for tramway. Progress very obscure. Final objectives not reached in entirety." On the following day (17th August) I recorded: "475 returned at 2.30 a.m. after gruelling experience in forward area, without being able to do much effective work." They had lost 4 Sappers killed and 11 wounded, all by shrapnel or machine-gun fire. In addition 3 of the Mounted Section had been wounded in leading up pack-mules on the previous day. For some parts of the line pack-animals were the only means of getting ammunition and stores to the front, and they suffered greatly in doing so. Man and beast became equally engulfed. Over the 17th and 18th we could do little, and tempers were strained as we waited impatiently trying to piece together the scanty information as to the overall result of the battle. Briefly the results had been that the XIVth Corps on the left of our XVIIIth Corps in the Langemarck area had successfully taken their objectives. Our own Division with the eleventh on its left, attacking across the Langemarck–Zonnebeke Road, had gained most of their objectives and thereby successfully covered the flank of the XIVth Corps. The two Corps attacking South of us had made only small progress.

The miserable wet weather, which had started again just prior to the battle, continued over the following fortnight period. During this period in three operations the 11th and 48th Divisions gained a further 800 yards, by local attacks. In that of the 22nd August the planned attack, on what was known as the Springfield Line, met with little success. The condition of the rain-soaked ground was so bad that the movement of the tanks was delayed, and they could not give the full co-operation anticipated.

Five days later the attack was renewed by our Division, and the heavily protected areas round Springfield and Vancouver farms successfully captured and retained. This attack went forward at the unusual hour of 1.55 p.m. We were in a position to watch our opening barrage as it crashed down on the enemy's defences. Perhaps, more than at any other time, the role of distant spectator brought with it a great wonderment at man's power of endurance, and at the follies that required it of him in the form of war. Was it only war-weariness that caused me to write down at this time some of my reactions to the War? They indicate a marked change from that early enthusiasm to "join in smashing the Boches." There was no faltering in our conviction that we were right in what we were doing. Now, that enthusiasm had given way to a grim but reluctant determination to complete at any cost a heavy task, which had been laid on us. Of the Germans I wrote in a letter shortly after this date: "I am quite sure of one thing, and it is powerfully borne out by the Boche prisoners, everyone in the German lower ranks is tired and sick of the war. Their education has reached the stage where it looks for stalemate as a possible end to the war. It has not yet reached the stage of expecting actual defeat."

Two days after the battle for Springfield the Division was relieved. The C.R.E. and our small staff quartered ourselves in a new small camp near the R.E. Divisional Stores in the back part of Ypres. In September the weather turned warmer and finer, and our camp site was relatively peaceful and pleasant. Midway in our "rest period" I was given nine days leave.

At the camp, with the Divisional H.Q. many miles away from us my work was light, and I could ride freely into the open country behind us, and walk into Poperinghe. My second horse, which I had taken over on being transferred to R.E. Headquarters, had been killed in Ypres in August, and my brother's horse was also wounded.

A reference in my diary to heavy aeroplane bombing at night recalls the fact that up to this period we had seldom been troubled by it.

On 25th September the C.R.E. and I went forward again to our old dugout H.Q. in the Canal Bank to make arrangements for relieving the Divisional R.E. in the line. Here we met Colonel Kelly and his Adjutant of the 58th London Territorial Division, R.E. We learned details of the attack five days earlier made by the 58th with the 51st Highland Division on their left. This attack was part of one carried out on an 8-mile front, and had successfully carried our line further forward. Preparations for a further advance were to be made, and called for reconnaissances of our new front. An early entry in my diary records: "Round the new front with the C.R.E. Passing Genoa I saw more dead lying out in the open than I have ever seen. Ground fearfully cut up by shell-fire."

On 28th September a grievous loss befell 474 Field Company. A Sapper group were gathered round a dugout, which they were making, when a single heavy shell burst in the midst of them. Their O.C., Major H. C. Clissold, D.S.O., and six sappers were killed, and seventeen sappers wounded. He had been my Science Master at Clifton, where he commanded the School Cadet Corps, and was much beloved by his men for his courage and leadership. He had been wounded in the August operations, but refused to be taken to hospital. My brother, who rejoined us on the 1st October after his Senior Officers' Course was posted to take over the command of the Company. Later in the month he relinquished it on being posted to the 5th Royal Sussex Battalion—our Divisional Pioneer Battalion, and shortly afterwards was gazetted to command it with the rank of Lieutenant-Colonel.

I saw little of the two battles in October in which our Division renewed the attack, that of Broodseinde on the 4th and Poelcappelle on the 9th. In this period all three Brigades attacked in turn. My diary records briefly: "Warwick Brigade advanced across the Stroombeek. Wellington and Winchester Farms reported taken and nearly all objectives gained. Good show!" Charles Carrington who commanded a Company of the 5th Warwicks in the advance, has given in his books a vivid first-hand description of what they endured, and the involved difficulties of maintaining direction and cohesion.

In the battle of Poelcappelle (9th October) the attack was carried forward by the 144th Gloucester and Worcester Brigade. Among my records is a copy of the Orders issued to the three Field Companies and Pioneer Battalion. It may be cited as typical of those received during the Passchendaele battles:

"Secret—Extracts from 48th Division Orders.
"No. 283—Ref. Sheet: Spriet 1/10,000. 7th Oct. 1917.

"1 (a) On a date which has been communicated to those concerned, and at an hour to be notified later, the XVIIIth Corps will resume the offensive.

"(b) The 49th Division of the Anzac Corps will be attacking on the Right of the 48th Division, and the 11th Division of XVIIIth Corps on our left.

"3. The attack of the 48th Division will be carried out by the 144th Bde.

"8. Strong Points (marked in blue on map) will be constructed by 144th Bde. approximately

"(a) On reaching dotted green line at Adler Farm, V26.b.56.

"(b) On reaching Green Line, between Wallemolen and Varlet Farms. V.27.c.84; Berks House V.27a.06. The retention of the Wallemolen Ridge is of special importance." (Particulars of H.Q. and O.P. locations were added.)

An Appendix scheduled the work to be carried out by the R.E. and Pioneers under C.R.E.'s orders. It comprised:

"(a) The continuation of forward trench-board tracks.

"(b) Preparing large white boards (with black letters) to be put up at Vacher Farm—Oxford Houses—Berks Houses—Inch House—Adler Farm—Varlet Farm.

"(c) Roads. All available labour will be employed on the St Julien —Triangle Farm—Genoa—Hubner—Quebec Farm Roads.

"(d) R.E. Dumps to be maintained at two points, each containing shovels, picks, 200 coils barbed wire, 1,000 screw pickets, 5,000 sandbags.

Under the Divisional Order was written a laconic "For Information," over my signature "for the C.R.E."

Did we ever pause to think of orders, such as these, as representing a death-warrant for the manhood that would, in consequence of them, be cut down by the scythe of war? I do not think we did. In the aftermath, and in the light of retrospection, they seem clothed with a cold impersonality, yet assuming, as a matter of course, the right to direct the mortal lives of those under their command. That is the concomitant of war.

It may be noted that the principal employment of the Sappers differed materially from that required of them on the Somme. Carrington, in his account of the battle of the 4th October, refers to the party of Sappers detailed to follow his attack with sign-boards to be posted on captured objectives. "We questioned more than one of their identifications, and were much amused when a Sapper marched out into no-man's-land and nailed up his notice on a tree-stump well inside the German front. I think everyone lost the way two or three times a day."

An extract from the congratulatory message of the Corps Commander, after the battle on the 4th, included: "The Infantry of the 11th and 48th Divisions gained their objectives along the whole Corps front." Another one from the Army Commander: "Captured documents make it clear that this was one of the heaviest blows which the enemy has ever received." A total of over 5,300 prisoners are reported to have been captured.

On the 9th October, in the battle of Poelcappelle, the 144th Brigade casualties were over 800. They had been over fourteen hours in getting into their forward positions for attack, under conditions of heavy rain, and trench-board tracks almost buried in mud.

The following day the Division was relieved. My diary records: "Companies hand over to 9th Divisional R.E. G.T.H. and I ride back through Ypres and survey the battered scene—I hope for the last time."

Whatever arguments may be put forward as to the underlying strategical reasons for the long-continued battle for the Passchendaele Ridge, it was clearly a battle of attrition for both armies. The British casualties are quoted as being over 240,000, of which 65,000 were killed or missing. Those of the 48th Division exceeded 3,000. The Germans are said to have employed a hundred divisions in the battle. Throughout they made constant counter-attacks.

What was it that marked out a great difference in the attitude of the British soldier on the Somme from that at Passchendaele? In both it was a case of:

> "Theirs not to reason why,
> Theirs but to do and die."

Before and during the Somme fighting there was a spirit of optimism, in spite of initial failures, a readiness for "getting to grips" with their enemy. At Passchendaele, so far as our front was concerned, one sensed from the outset only a reluctant determination, and an unspoken cry of "God help us" as the battle developed in the confusion of mud and shell-fire. On the Somme the battle casualties (killed or wounded) in our 475 Field Company were 35, all in the Sapper sections. This represented 22 per cent of our Sapper establishment strength. At Passchendaele they were 99. This represented 22 per cent of our drivers, and 55 per cent of our Sappers. For the three Field Companies and the Divisional Pioneer Battalion the total battle casualties were 541; of these 294 were R.E. and 247 Pioneer Battalion. Forty-five out of the R.E. and 64 out of the Pioneer casualties—mainly from gas-shells—rejoined their Units subsequently. When it is remembered that these Units were not assaulting troops in the actual attacks, the above figures illustrate the destructive effect of the German artillery on the supporting Units following in their wake.

The figures also take no account of the toll taken by sickness, arising from men spending days and nights in soaking wet clothing. Records show that in this period 56 R.E. and 100 Pioneers were taken off duty at some point in the battle on this account. A Division on our right, where the ground was less of a swamp, reported 1,200 men at one time under treatment for trench fever and swollen feet.

A final valedictory message from General Gough, Commanding Fifth Army, was received by our Divisional Commander: "The 48th Division have taken part in much hard fighting during the past two months, including five general engagements. Their spirit and determination on all occasions have been admirable, and temporary setbacks have in no way affected their morale. I am very sorry to bid goodbye to such a dependable Division, and feel sure that the future holds many further successes for them."

For us there were no regrets at departing from a battle area in which so many thousands of men had already laid down their lives. As to the future—we were just thankful that we still had one.[1]

Three days later (13th October) we entrained at Peselhoek in the evening and travelled southwards. At 3.30 a.m. the following morning we detrained at Maroeuil and marched to Fort George, near Neuville St Vaast, abour four miles North of Arras. Our new front was to be the Vimy Ridge area.

---

[1] There is an indication of the effects of war's attrition in the Field Company R.E. Units among the 475 Field Company records in my possession. They refer only to those of all ranks who were killed, died or were wounded in Belgium and France on active service in the period up to November 1917. The total number is 151, a figure of over 70 per cent of its establishment strength of 215. The proportion of those who lost their lives compared with those wounded was slightly over 1 to 4. The officer casualties were 4 out of its establishment of 6.

19   Vimy—Journey to Italy

October–November 1917

The Vimy Ridge had been gallantly won from the Germans in the previous April. It was now a quiet sector to which Divisions which had suffered heavy casualties in battle could be sent. The capture of the Ridge will always be associated with the successful attack by the Canadian Corps. As a result the Allied Forces had the advantage of holding the high ground on the Ridge.

In making the usual reconnaissances of our new front with the C.R.E., we were most hospitably received by the 2nd Canadian Divisional R.E., from whom we were taking over on 18th October. There was nothing of a Spartan nature in their standard of messing. Our Headquarters were located in comfortable huts in Fort George. There were relatively small demands for Sapper work in the front line, and in consequence more time could be devoted to training our replacements of Passchendaele casualties. Hitherto, over the past three months, my own job as Adjutant had been mainly under battle conditions. For better or worse I settled down to tackling the duties as Adjutant under conditions of a semi-static trench war. I found them varied, interesting, ideally demanding considerable patience, tact and the ability to give firm unequivocal instructions. To a somewhat surprising and to me alarming extent an R.E. Adjutant appeared to be also the repository of many other men's difficulties and aspirations.

One requisite was clearly to relieve the C.R.E. of the more humdrum chores of administration. Fortunately we had an experienced Sergeant Clerk to deal with the routine returns to various Army administrative branches. From a list made at this period there were four daily returns (e.g. ration indent, casualties), sixteen weekly and over a dozen monthly.

I recorded: "It is now thirteen months since the Sappers of the Division had more than brief rests out of gunfire range, and everyone

136

is a bit 'edgy.' The Colonel has been down with a bad chill. He has had a very trying time during the past four months.''

The only active operation which I saw while we were in this sector was on 8th November. From an excellent O.P. on Vimy Ridge we watched a successful raid by the 31st Division on Acheville.

I learned three days later that the Division was to make an early move to Italy. The strictest secrecy was to be maintained in regard to the move, apart from those concerned on the Divisional Staff. I was to form one of a small advance party who were to travel ahead of the Division and prepare for its arrival. It was to comprise our 2 Senior Staff Officers, Colonel H. C. L. Howard, G.S.O.1., and Lieut.-Colonel G. H. Barnett, A.A. & Q.M.G., with 3 other officers on the Divisional Staff, and about 4 O.R.s. Our only information was that about 5 British and 7 French Divisions were being sent to the aid of Italy, as the result of the heavy defeat of the Italian Army at Caporetto. The Austrian Army aided by 9 German Divisions had swept down from the mountains in the North-East of Italy on a wide front. The question of the day was—could they be stopped before overrunning the important industrial towns in the northern area?

On the 16th November our party travelled from Amiens by train to Paris and stayed for the night at the Edward VII Hotel. After revelling in a glorious bath I joined the others of the party in dining at the Café de Paris, where we ordered the best dinner we could get. Afterwards we split up into pairs according to our musical or amusement tastes. The Divisional Intelligence Officer—Eastburn by name, but always addressed as "Brains"—and I favoured the Folies-Bergère!

To all intents and purposes Paris outwardly seemed still the crowded and gay city of pre-war days. It revived memories of my last visit on returning from a Rugger tour with a Gloucestershire XV. We had played at Narbonne—a French Garrison town—where we were hospitably received as temporary members of an Officers' Mess. Here, perhaps for the first time I had realized their strong conviction that war between France and Germany was inevitable, and that Britain would be involved in it. It had a sequel in Paris whereby I had narrowly escaped being hauled before the Gendarmerie, when I tried to dispose of a coffin-like package. It contained a decorative basket-stand trophy presented to me on the field by the President of the Narbonne Club. Unfortunately the driver of our ancient horsed cab got the impression that it contained "un enfant mort"! It is perhaps only fair to record that I had similar memories of almost embarrassing hospitality in Germany on a Rugger Tour with the Harlequins' Club XV under Adrian Stoop's leadership. Thus I had no pre-war prejudice against the German people.

As our train for Italy did not leave till 8.25 p.m., we spent the next day in sight-seeing with tea at Rumpelmayers. We travelled in a reserved coach for Officers, with the luxury of a couchette, the rest of the coaches and corridors being packed with humanity. I was puzzled at the presence in our carriage of a man in British uniform. He proved to be the well-known war correspondent, H. Warner Allen. In his interesting book, *With the British in Italy*, he records: "In our carriage was a British Captain fresh from the horrors of Ypres and happy to be going to Italy. At first he was obviously suspicious of the badgeless uniform then worn by a War Correspondent, but by a commonplace coincidence of travel he proved to be the brother of an old Oxford friend with whom in undergraduate days I gained my first taste of the joys of Italy." My suspicions were perhaps due to the many warnings we received on the need for guarded talk and strict secrecy as to movements of Divisions. This was responsible also for holding back all home letters from the Division for about two weeks.

The senior members of our party had received little information as to the location of the new British Headquarters in Italy, which were to be established under the command of Sir Herbert Plumer. However we travelled hopefully and comfortably via Dijon, changing trains at Modane for Turin. It was good to see again the gorgeous views of the snow-capped Swiss mountains. The streets of Turin in the evening were crowded with the workers from the big engineering works. Good-class restaurants, opera and cinemas gave little impression of a nation facing a war crisis.

The first definite instructions from G.H.Q. in France reached us late in the evening of our arrival at the Palace Hotel, telling us to go to Mantua. Early the next morning a slow, unheated train, stopping at every station and for long periods between stations, took four hours to reach Milan. In all it took nearly twelve hours to reach Mantua. Here with difficulty we found sleeping quarters for our whole party in two big rooms at an hotel, and for two days were left in ignorance of our or the Division's future destination.

General Plumer and his Army Staff had not yet arrived in Italy, but we learned that he was expected the following day, and that British Army H.Q. would be established at Legnano.

In these two days in Mantua some of our Gunner Batteries passed through the City. I recorded: "They received an exuberant welcome from the populace, who crowded the streets, and ran at their side shouting themselves hoarse for the 'Inglesi.' I can't help feeling that many of them ought to be doing something other than mere shouting. The womenfolk threw flowers, and there was the unusual spectacle of a British Gunner sitting on his limber, looking distinctly self-conscious, with a garland of flowers round his neck. There could be no doubt about the effect on the morale of the civil population brought about by the presence of the British Troops, with their march discipline, well-horsed transport and cheerful demeanour. It makes me feel proud to be a British soldier."

We learned also that our Divisional Headquarters were to be located at Cologna Veneta, about 50 kilometres North-East of Mantua. We found comfortable quarters in the Albergo della Rocca at Cologna. Two days were spent in touring parts of the area allotted to the Division to assess and report on the billeting accommodation likely to be available in the villages and farms. Mounted on a bicycle of un-doubted antiquity, and accompanied by an Italian N.C.O. Interpreter, a new vista of life seemed to open up.

I recorded: "The countryside here is flat and presents a marked change from that which we experienced in France. Oxen have taken the place of horses in the fields, with teams of four or more to one plough. Lumbering carts with high wheels and heavy axles crawl slowly along the roads. The narrow country-type roads are built up on a high formation with a pronounced camber, as the land is low-lying with a stream or water-filled ditch on either side." We were to learn later that they quickly became churned up by our 5-ton lorries, owing to inadequate bonding. "In the villages small groups of women are busily washing clothes in one of the mountain-fed streams which abound in the district. Using a trestle-supported plank it is—'scrub, rinse in the stream and beat the clothes violently on the plank.' Wherever we go we are the object of the curiosity and questing gaze of many eyes, but the voices are merry, and the glances friendly and welcoming. We lunch in a village inn, and enjoy an excellent egg omelette produced with remarkable speed. In the quietude of evening we ride slowly back by the light of the moon as our bicycles have no lamps. The war seems blissfully distant."

My role now changed to that of a Station-master and Detraining Officer. On 25th November I rode in a lorry to our new XIVth Corps H.Q., where I received my instructions. I was to take on the following day a convoy of 8 lorries with supplies of rations to the village of Cerea, and establish myself as detraining officer for the Units of our Division scheduled to arrive there. Cerea was one of 3 detraining stations allocated to it.

Thus on the 26th November I billeted myself in the Cerea Station-master's house, adjoining the station, and reviewed on the platform my new command. This consisted of about 20 Italian soldiers under a Senior N.C.O. They were English-speaking interpreters, who were to be allocated to units on arrival. All spoke in a pronounced American accent. Cerea was a village on a single-track railway line with one platform, and no facilities of any kind for detraining vehicles or horses.

The position on the Italian front was still both critical and obscure to us. We knew that the defeated Italian 2nd Army was being withdrawn and replaced by fresh Divisions. The Austrian advance was being held up, at least temporarily, on the line of the Piave River. The crucial question in our minds was whether the Italian Armies could hold out till the British and French Divisions could arrive and move up to support them, before the Austrians could mount a fresh attack in strength.

The Italian railway authority had provided a detailed place and time schedule for the arrival of our Divisional Units. Unfortunately these arrangements broke down completely. Owing to the absence of detraining facilities the off-loading of vehicles and horses proved painfully slow. The line became blocked. Trains were diverted to other stations, or into sidings, or were held up unable to move for hours on end. Part of a Unit's personnel or transport, travelling on a different train from the rest of the unit, might find itself turned out at an unscheduled station 20 or more miles distant from its other part. In some cases units were detrained 40 miles away from their appointed arrival station.

The Cerea Station-master was very friendly, but overwhelmed by the unprecedented flow of traffic. One duty that he never failed to observe was to put on, whenever a fresh train arrived, a most elaborate decorative hat, which signified his high status in the railway organization.

The arrival of units lasted over three days and nights. Without any prior notice of their imminence, train-loads, some intended for us, others not, deposited their human and other freight on our little platform. Each unit was then provided with one of the Italian interpreters, instructions were given them as to the location of their billeting area; emergency rations from our lorry supplies made available, and the unit finally dispatched on its way as quickly as possible. In spite of their long journey the men were in high spirits. They had enjoyed what was to most of them the novel experience of travelling by the coast route along the French Riviera.

I had one unexpected and pleasant surprise at Cerea. On the first day, before the troops arrived, two English ladies appeared on the platform. With two other ladies, one of whom came from my native Bristol, they had been running a mobile canteen for the Italian troops, operating most pluckily close up to the northern battle zone. They had travelled south with the Italian retreat, and planned to open up elsewhere, but were persuaded to bring the canteen to our station. They could not complain of lack of custom. They kept open day and night, and for about eighteen hours out of the twenty-four there was a steady stream of men waiting to get a cup of hot tea and biscuits.

My old unit—475 Field Company—arrived at 3 a.m. on the last day, and were clearly surprised to find their late member waiting to welcome them to Italy.

The same evening I received orders to return to Legnano, and the following day a field ambulance wagon took me to Montagnana, a most picturesque town with mediaeval walls round it. Here we were able to give some expression of our thanks to the four canteen ladies by inviting them to dinner. They had been most helpful and efficient with their canteen. Off duty we found them equally charming and friendly, and the dinner proved a very pleasant change from our normal bachelor existence.

20   Winter in Italy

December 1917–January 1918

On 2nd December 1917 I rejoined Divisional R.E. Headquarters at Cologna Veneta. The billeting area of the Division had been changed, but by the 4th December the Division had been sufficiently concentrated for a move northwards. Adequate co-ordination in regard to troop movements had not yet been achieved by the Staffs of the Italian, British and French Higher Commands. This resulted in units receiving orders to move into new areas, and on arrival finding units of the other nationalities in possession. With the railway system completely overloaded the A.S.C. had an almost superhuman task in transporting, assembling and taking forward supplies of rations, ammunition and other necessary stores. Difficulties were accentuated by congestion on the roads caused by the large numbers of the Italian 2nd Army, who were being withdrawn to the South. Practically all the formations involved in the retreat were taken back to an area a long way behind the Reserve Line, to be re-organized and re-equipped. Many of them in the following year took part in successful battles in defence and attack, with their morale fully recovered.

On the 17th December we experienced our first fall of snow in Italy. This was a signal indicating that offensive operations, except on a very minor scale, were unlikely over the next two months. The Division moved up into a reserve position behind the Italian-held front on the Piave River. We were about 25 miles North-West of Venice, with our Headquarters in the small village of Pozzoleone. In the first stage we moved to Piazzola, close to the Brenta River, where we remained for a week. On one day we walked to a pontoon bridge across the river, built by the Italians as a diversion route for their 2nd Army troops withdrawing from the North-East. Here we watched large straggling parties on their trek southward. It was a sorry sight! I had seen in France many groups of enemy prisoners being marched back with set

142

faces, mud-bespattered and seemingly taking no interest in their surroundings. This was something quite different. With no pretence of marching formation or discipline they slouched along, nonchalant, unkempt, uniforms awry. Few carried any arms. In some cases an officer or uniformed guard shepherded them along, riding in a high-wheeled type of dog-cart. The temperament of the Latin race is far more mercurial than ours. It can sink to the lower depths and rise again to the heights in a remarkably short time.

In the sixteen months which we were destined to spend in Italy we were housed in extremely varied types of billets. Being attached to the Staff, I reaped the benefit of my Colonel's seniority, and as our Mess was a small one we were usually able to find comfortable quarters. Of the Albergo at Cologna Veneta I wrote: "Tonight I am sleeping in a charming old inn, scrupulously clean, with tiled floors, whitewashed walls, old oak doors and rafters almost black. The quaint narrow street has side colonnades with a second storey built out over them, so that from the upper windows you can almost shake hands across the street. An occasional arch spans it, while heavy lumbering carts drawn by oxen creak and groan over the cobbles. We seem to have been transported into a mediaeval era."

We did our best to establish good relations with our hosts. At Piazzola we were billeted in a private house. In a letter I wrote: "Last night we invited our billet host to mess with us. Afterwards he stated that he would like to play bridge with us. Accordingly we all moved into the kitchen, the only warm room in the house, and all our host's family and retainers crowded round to watch the play. We asked him, but apparently misunderstood his answer, what stakes we were to play for. We had to converse in Italian. At the end of two rubbers, my partner and I worked out that we had won threepence. He indignantly insisted that it was over ten lire (then the cost of a good turkey). We were hesitant to accept it, whereupon everyone in the room broke out in an amused babble of advice to us. Altogether the evening ended on a most cheery note, with many good-night salutations."

Our move to Pozzoleone on 14th December, following orders received late in the previous evening, was an example of the lack of organization and co-operation as yet achieved by the Staffs of the respective higher commands. I recorded: "Yesterday proved a hectic day for our Divisional Staff, and the least said to them in the evening was the wiser policy. On the Division arriving in the new area allotted, it was found to be crammed with Italian troops, with no apparent intention or orders to move out." In fact it took a further week before all our units could be accommodated under adequate shelter, and in this mid-December the nights were bitterly cold. "The C.R.E., sensing that the state of affairs was chaotic, promptly intimated that he had an important reconnaissance to carry out in the forward area. We hurriedly departed on a 60-mile tour of the area close to the Piave front between Bassano and Monte Belluna. We had a pleasant day, the Colonel standing me an excellent lunch in a small town quite close to the front. The lunch included fish, guinea-fowl and macaroni. We have not yet mastered the Italian expertise in steering a nearly continuous flow of the latter into our mouths. We were the object of much curiosity on the part of the town inhabitants, no English Officers having been seen there previously. On our return we found that the C.R.E. and I had been allocated sleeping quarters in an old mill with a huge water-wheel at one side. It is run single-handed by the miller, who is nearly eighty years old. We shared a tiny room upstairs, so small that we had to get up at different times. We hope to get a good house billet for our Mess and sleeping tomorrow.''

On our tours by car, obtained from the small Divisional pool, we were able to visit the small towns, and in the early days buy country produce for the Mess very cheaply. I noted down: "Bought thirty eggs in the market from a toothless old lady for 11·25 lire. The old lady, however, expected us to carry the thirty eggs loose in a sheet of newspaper. With some of the rough roads ahead we pictured mangled egg remains decorating the interior of the car, grudgingly allotted by the Staff for our lawful reconnaissance purposes. After experiencing some difficulty in explanations she produced a good basket for the princely sum of threepence." Not unexpectedly prices rose steadily in the face of the heavy requirements of our Forces.

One of our chief deficiencies was the lack of fuel. Coal was almost unobtainable, and priced at about £16 per ton—to us an unheard of price. The Italian Railways had to depend on wood for the fuel for many of their trains. The scanty coal ration reaching units was insufficient for cooking purposes, and supplies of wood equally short. This winter shortage of fuel was, I think, the only factor which affected adversely the goodwill relationship between the country inhabitants and our troops. Scrounging to provide warmth in billets brought some complaints, as farmers and villagers reacted to the disappearance of their timber resources, both growing and otherwise.

For the past month we had suffered an almost complete cessation of letters from home, and those at home had received none from us. Fortunately, about ten days before Christmas, letters and parcels containing Christmas fare began to arrive. With provisions purchased in the neighbouring towns we were able to give all ranks an excellent dinner of the traditional English type. Our two previous Christmas Days had been spent with the possibility of a few enemy shells dropping around us. This year we were in complete peace and well out of range. Also, during the whole of our service in Italy we

144

were very seldom troubled by enemy aeroplane bombing. Believed to be by German squadrons, bombing was carried out with considerable severity almost entirely by night, and directed at the bigger towns. In our small country villages and farm billets we had little to fear.

We remained in Pozzoleone from mid-December until nearly the end of January. Our billet and office was in a farm, sufficiently distant from Divisional H.Q. to prevent members of the Staff dropping in too frequently, and the three Field Companies were in small villages in the area.

Work in my office was relatively light. The first heavy falls of snow had come just before Christmas. The Companies' work on the Corps line was reduced, and in January I spent several days with them in practising rapid light bridging. Our reconnaissances of the forward area continued. On the last-but-one day of the year I recorded: "A good day has nearly come to its close. On a lovely Sabbath morning we set off by car for a recce of our reserve line in the foothills area. With a bright sun shining we had a long tramp, making our notes, amidst the most beautiful and impressive scenery. We were both in excellent spirits, the Colonel whistling and chatting as we walked. At lunch time we sat on the grassy hillside munching sandwiches and an orange. Then, as we were ahead of our time for the rendezvous with the car, we lay on the grass and basked in warm sunshine. It was difficult to believe that the morrow would be the last day of the year. As we looked across at the enemy-held territories the views were glorious. The snow-capped mountains were towering in the background; over the nearer slopes men moved like tiny black specks. Below us lay a small village with its white buildings standing out against the green fields. Over all a blue sky against which the high peaks stood out in massive grandeur, and in the clear atmosphere seemingly close, save in the furthest distance where they merged into a purplish mistiness. There could hardly be a greater change from the desolation of the tree-scarred and mud-based terrain of the Ypres Salient, over which it had been our lot to tramp together a few months earlier."

We had opportunities, also, for lorry-lifts into Verona, Vicenza and Padua, with their historic architectural features. Here shops and restaurants acted as a magnet for the mingling of British, French and Italian officers and other ranks. In one café I copied one of the many greetings to the British troops which abounded in the towns and villages. It was printed in three colours on a large poster on the wall, with the flags of the three nations draped round it. It read:

"Fellow Citizens—As in the countries of Flanders, as in the sacred roads of Jerusalem, English People is carving with glorious, indelible

145

words his unshaken determination to break the block of the foe, his legions full of gallantry, of loyalty and bravery are coming among us, so as to scorn German base falsehoods suggesting cold mercantile egoism.

"Let us welcome them with Italian rejoicing, faithful to the historical tradition according to which the names of Foscilo, Mazzini, Carlyle, Gladstone, Garibaldi, Ruskin mingle together with gratitude and admiration for our immortal art, as well as with affinity for the triumph of oppressed nations.

"The coming of the English Army to our Country be the sacred seal confirming the union which will lead England, France and Italy towards a complete victory. Hurrah for Italy! Hurrah for England!"

In a small village on the same day I noted: "Good health the England."

These expressions of goodwill inevitably brought a smile at the obvious difficulty experienced in translating their sentiments into our language, but we appreciated the underlying motive and spirit, and were grateful for their expression.

In contrast our conduct towards Italian officers must often have seemed cold and even discourteous, although not intentionally. We had to learn to reciprocate. When lunching one day in Vicenza we ordered from the menu 'veal cutlets'. As the waiter disappeared with our order, his young assistant, aged about fourteen, and clad in the usual short white coat, sidled up to us. Probably remembering previous above-average tips from the British, he murmured "No have veal cutlets! Veal cutlets is dead horse." We countermanded our order, but, thanks to the good Italian cooking, I doubt if we should have found it unpalatable, or less tender than young camel, which I have eaten in Tunisia.

"We have been much impressed by the Italian Cavalry horses—a very fine breed, long-limbed, built for speed and always beautifully groomed. In contrast, their draught-horses are not nearly so well kept, and like their donkeys and mules frequently overloaded. The country inhabitants look wonderingly at the few heavy draught-horses which still operate with our transport. Apparently they have not previously seen this type of horse." After the end of the war a number of them were sold to the Italians and fetched very high prices.

At this time I commented in a letter: "Compared with our way of life the Italians appear to me as a curious mixture in their temperament and actions—good in many points, but lacking in others which we regard as important. I think few of us who have taken part in this move into Italy can have done so without a constant feeling of pride in our British origin. There is the realization that the honour of a

Nation's people is not an empty phrase. It is a heritage for which we owe a big debt to those generations who have preceded us.''

I was, perhaps, more fortunate than most officers in being able to explore the mediaeval towns and palaces in this part of Italy, containing so many rich examples of historic interest and beauty. Owing to delays in time and difficulties of transport, we had to purchase quantities of tools and R.E. stores in the towns within reasonable lorry distance. We were also in continual search for timber. Quite unexpectedly near a small country village I discovered a small wood-pulping factory. The power was derived solely from a stream. After much persuasion through an interpreter, we were able to buy considerable quantities of rough timber at a very cheap price. I must admit that, with the full connivance of the Colonel, we took care not to divulge the source of our supplies. We had no qualms as to whether any accounting officer would attempt to establish whether it was used for structural R.E. works or for more quickly perishable purposes!

These visits to the various towns were made most enjoyable by our being accompanied by one of our interpreters, who was a cultured Frenchman fully conversant with the Italian language. He had come with us from France, and had a wide and enthusiastic knowledge of architecture and painting of mediaeval times. Under his guidance we were able to appreciate such works as the frescoes painted by Giotto, representing a milestone, about 500 years ago, in the development of painting, a breaking away from the old formalism, and heralding the spirit of the Renaissance. In a letter describing some of the architectural features which we had seen I concluded with: "There is so much to delight the eye—and yet these are the targets on which the Boche has cheerfully dropped his bombs. The world indeed seems upside down.''

Early in January the Colonel took me on a visit of inspection to the more Westerly part of the front line, where the Italians still held positions among the high mountains fringing the Asiago Plateau. "It was a most interesting experience. My hair must have been trying occasionally to push my cap off my head as we swung round double hairpin bends with a sheer drop of up to a thousand feet below us. There was a bluish haze over the plains from which we had come, but on the mountain peaks ahead bright sunlight on deep snow.''

"After a tour round part of their front, we lunched with a party of very hospitable Italian officers, living in a small mountain-side house to which they had added a wooden extension. From here there was a wide-ranging view to the South covering the whole Plain of Northern Italy, and stretching Eastwards to a distant Venice. The return journey at a faster downhill pace seemed more hair-raising and a tempting of providence. Cheerfulness was not enhanced by occasional glimpses of the mangled remains of a car or Fiat lorry, which had skidded off the road and lay on the rocks below us. The Italian engineers are excellent builders of mountain roads, but seem prone to erect small protecting concrete posts on edges where there is only a small drop, whereas places where a car can slip over the edge and roll down several hundred feet are left unprotected.''

One lesson that we learned was the importance of all R.E. and Pioneers being fully trained in the handling of explosives. Dugouts and trenches were no longer a simple matter of digging. They had to be blasted out of the solid rock of the mountains. Explosives are an invaluable aid to field engineering in the mountain areas. They must, however, be handled with respect for their potentialities. Unfortunately, later on in the campaign, the Pioneers, who had little previous training in their use, paid the penalty of several casualties by not observing the necessary precautions for their use.

Another feature that we noticed was the provision of numerous camouflage-netting screens hung across the roads and tracks leading to the front line. These were essential as the enemy had excellent observation from the higher peaks in their areas.

In the last week of January we moved northwards, with our Headquarters first at Vaccarino, and after a few days at Levada, a village West of Treviso. Here we were in close support of two British Divisions, the 41st and 7th, who were holding part of the Piave front line.

21   On the Piave Front (the Montello)

February–March 1918

At Levada our Mess was reduced to four—G.T.H., the two interpreters who had come with us from France, and myself. The C.R.E. had gone back to England on fourteen days leave; just previously he had not felt well. He obtained permission from the G.O.C. for my deputizing for him, without calling in one of the senior Majors. Unfortunately it did not carry with it any increase in my pay and allowances as Lieutenant, acting Captain. This gave me the opportunity of a minor cleansing of the Augean Stables, as represented by the clerical side of our Headquarters Staff work. It involved a reorganization of our handling documents and messages, a new filing system and allocation of work among the Staff. My one hope was to get it functioning adequately by the time the C.R.E. returned. If it failed to do so I should be well and truly told off by him.

To my regret in other respects, it was never put to this test. The Colonel wrote to me to the effect that he had a fortnight's extension on medical grounds. Shortly afterwards we were advised that the trouble was more serious, and that he would not be coming out again to us, as he was undergoing a serious operation at Guy's Hospital. I was very sorry to hear this, and appreciated and prized a long letter in which he said farewell and referred in the most kind terms to our having worked together. I had learned to appreciate and admire the outstanding nature of his quick-witted brain, coupled with decisive action and thoroughness in all his work. Normally tactful he could lash out vehemently and effectively where incompetence demanded it, but there was always an underlying human kindness. His stout-hearted Scottish batman would, I am sure, have accompanied him cheerfully through hell-fire. In my experience the relationship between a good batman and his officer is often no mean criterion of the latter.

In the second half of February my anxiety as to the successor to Colonel Giles was resolved by the appointment of Major E. Briggs, who originally came out as second-in-command of my old Company. Through the last three years he had proved himself an able and inspiring company commander. Far more outspoken than Colonel Giles, he also did not suffer fools gladly. An individualist with strong convictions on how a job should be done, and prepared to brush aside any opposition, he disliked office paper-work. However, when, as hitherto customary, I put before him draft orders for the Field Companies and Pioneers he remarked rather truculently "Isn't the C.R.E. allowed to make up his own orders and also to sign them?" I meekly submitted that they were drafted and submitted for his approval and amendment as required to spare him from detail work. That was one reason for my attending with him at Divisional and Corps Conferences, and accompanying him on reconnaissances to take appropriate notes. Would he wish to be tied to the office for signing orders of an urgent nature which he had already approved? For a few moments he stared at me, then a broad smile came over his face, followed by "Well! Have it your own way." I mention this little incident as it marks a point where, for the first time, every one of the R.E. officers in the 48th Division had been nurtured in a civilian business or professional occupation, but now translated into the maelstrom of war. Personally it marked also for me as his Adjutant a very happy understanding and association with my new Colonel.

At the beginning of March our Division took over a sector of the Piave front line from the British 7th Division. We held the trenches on the eastern sector of a hog's-back ridge named the Montello. The latter extended for about 8 miles, rising from the plain to a height of 1,000 feet, with the Piave River bed curving round its Northern face. At some points the river bed was over half a mile wide, with the river flowing in channels between numerous small islands, which would be covered later when the mountain snows melted. Hence the front was a quiet one with restricted opportunities for raids from either side. The Austrians on the higher ground, sloping up to the mountain ranges, had excellent observation on all our movements, but indulged only in casual intermittent shell-fire. The three Field Companies and Pioneers were kept hard at work on improving the defences. Strategically the Montello was obviously a key point of attack in any further Austrian advance. Twelve weeks after we were relieved the Austrians in their massed Piave offensive succeeded in capturing the greater part of the Ridge, as one of their principal bridge-heads. It was only after seven days' fighting that the Italians recaptured it. In this they were aided by heavy rain flooding the River, and sweeping away the Austrian bridges.

This area of the North Italian Plain, close to the mountains, provided delightful riding over a wide-spaced open countryside. Thus I wrote: "Not feeling quite so fit as usual, I went for a long ride this afternoon to shake it off. It was again a gloriously clear day with an unsurpassed panorama of the snow-capped mountains. To me they seem always to justify the epithet of 'eternal.' They hold secrets of the world before the history of man was written. They have looked down in bygone centuries on the struggling army of Hannibal, with its new and terrifying form of 'living tanks,' as represented by the elephants. They can bear testimony to the masterly campaigning of Napoleon, and now they look down on our own modern brand of warfare."

Our tenure of the Montello sector did not last long, and on 16th March we handed over to the 58th Italian Division. The difficulties of ensuring a smooth take-over, between two divisions speaking different languages, became apparent. In numerous cases the Italian units' advance parties were inadequately briefed, and reported at the wrong rendezvous, or at times other than those notified previously to us, resulting in much confusion.

On being relieved we moved back to our old billet in Piazzola in two stages. We were still encountering problems in billeting. 18th March 1918: "It is past 3 p.m. and we have just finished our lunch in new surroundings. Yesterday I was told that owing to rearrangement of billets we had to move out this morning, and apparently so far as the Division was concerned we should be homeless. However, I found that the D.A.A.G. was prospecting, and got a lift in his car. We found a village (Carturol) and in conjunction with the village authority fixed up occupation of a partly-furnished house, the owner being absent. Picture to yourself a white-walled villa with green shutters, standing in a fairly large garden. On one side our horses tethered to a short fence. In a corner of the garden three tall cypress trees shadow a small wooden arbour from the rays of the sun. Numerous small lizards crawl along the low wall and up an old vine, or sun themselves complacently on the flagged path.

"I had arranged for an early car lift this morning to take possession of the billet, but my companion was delayed. On arrival on horseback I found part of an Italian Hospital Unit installing themselves in the house. Without the services of an interpreter assertions of our rights of occupation were involved and lengthy. A compromise was reached whereby the Italian unit's party should retain one big room. Our Headquarters party has since arrived and taken possession of the remainder. A little game is still going on anent a bed which was in our part, but was removed by the Italians into their room. It is now back in ours, and probably each side will endeavour to secure possession till the evening."

Later the same day I added: "One other little incident has caused us considerable amusement. Four of us were sitting out in the garden relaxing in the sunshine beside the little arbour. Enter an Italian officer. He was in difficulty with his small-van vehicle. His knowledge of the English language seemed to extend to the one word 'good-bye.' It is not easy to avoid smiling when an officer whom you have never seen previously suddenly appears in front of you, salutes and by way of being friendly opens the conversation with 'good-bye.' He then solemnly bowed and shook hands with each of us in turn, murmuring 'good-bye' on each occasion. This was followed by a protracted torrent of explanation of his difficulty spoken in Italian. However, we were able to provide what he wanted, and he departed with many smiles and handshakes accompanied by a spate of 'good-byes.' Now we have just heard that the owner of the house is expected to arrive here tonight!''

My own turn for the normal ten days leave was coming round, and it was permissible to put in for an extension in special circumstances. The family business with its oil-importing interests was passing through a difficult time, with a very depleted staff. My three years' continuous service overseas stood me in good stead and 19 days leave was granted. There was an additional objective in my mind, following much introspection and correspondence on the subject of marriage when one of the participants was on war service.

I reached my home in slightly under four days, travelling in comparative comfort. A lift in a Staff car with the A.P.M. took me to Padua, whence I arrived in Paris after changing trains only at Milan and Turin. Delays occurred around Paris and Boulogne owing to small air raids. Eight days later I was a married man. I was fortunate in another respect. British officers on leave from France were recalled in the face of the big German offensive in April, but those who were serving in Italy at that time were not recalled.

On my return journey I was detrained at Thiene, a small town a few miles from our Division's rear Headquarters at Fara, which lay at the foot of the mountains of the Asiago Plateau. From a telephone conversation with G.T.H. I learned that the Division, after a quiet period in reserve, had taken over a sector of the front line on the Plateau three days previously; also that it was quite time I took a share in the work on hand in our new sector. We were now facing the actualities of a new experience—a war among the mountains.

22   War in the Mountains (Asiago Plateau)

May 1918

The Asiago Plateau lies about 50 miles North-West of Venice. It was more in the nature of a high-altitude valley or trough 3,000 feet above sea level, ringed round with mountains up to 1,500 feet higher. It extended for about 7 miles in an East–West direction, and up to 2,500 yards in width. Asiago—a peace-time skiing centre, little more than a large village, and by now in ruins—lay nearer to the higher northern fringe of mountains. In front of it on the plateau level were the first-line Austrian trenches, with a second main line behind it—known as the "Winter Line" or "Stellung"—on the lower slopes of the mountains.

Our new 3,000-yard front, held during the winter by the Italians, was on the slopes of the southern fringe of mountains. The position was a somewhat precarious one, in that the area held was only 4,000 to 5,000 yards in depth before the steep descent to the Northern Italy Plain. An enemy advance of this extent would give complete observation over the Plain, and the opportunity of outflanking our Piave front. The mountains forming the range behind our front line rose to peaks varying from 4,000 to 5,000 feet, the greater part being covered by tall pine forests. On the Austrian side the frontier with Italy was only a few miles North of Asiago, the old Italian province of the Trentino having been annexed by Austria in the latter part of the nineteenth century. The mountains on this side were higher and stretched in massive array, with the high peaks of the Venetian Alps backed by the Dolomites and those of the Tyrol.

We learned quickly that a number of new problems were imposed by a war conducted under high-altitude conditions. The Italian Army had specially trained regiments to meet such conditions. In the extreme North-West part of the front their hardy Alpini units held positions in the Ortler Mountains, where the peaks rose to heights between 11,000 and 12,000 feet. Throughout the winter months on

153

our new front persistent snow and ice covered the whole area. We had been mistaken, perhaps, when we smiled on being told by the Italian Engineers that barbed-wire defences should be 12 feet high in places where snow-drifts could form. Even on the 5th June my diary records a heavy fall of snow.

There were few buildings of any description in which to house troops. The solid rock of the mountains for the most part was either bare, or covered with only a small depth of earth. Hence the difficulty of making dugouts and trenches, other than by the slow process of blasting them out with explosives. This also affected the ability to bury cable lines from the front to Brigade and Divisional Head-quarters. Accommodation for the various headquarters and all Divisional units behind the front line area was in wooden huts, relying on concealment for the most part among the pine forests and defiles.

Water supply for men and such horses as were working in the mountains depended on a single pipe-line, through which it was pumped up the mountain-side from the Astico River in the Plain into small reservoirs. Its final delivery stage often entailed being carried considerable distances in petrol cans. There was always the risk of the pipe being broken by shell-fire. Fortunately during our stay in the area we were never without supplies, but were supposed to be rationed to a gallon per man per day. Fortunately, also, there was an unlimited supply of forest timber for fuel in the huts.

The major administrative problem was the maintenance of sup-plies to the units on the Plateau. In France we had been accustomed to an almost clock-like regularity in the arrival of our daily food rations. The vast quantities of ammunition, ordnance and R.E. materials, held in the back areas, had been distributed to the forward areas by a widespread rail and road network. Here, apart from the inherent difficulties arising from the heavy overloading on the North Italian railways, our own supply transport was unsuitable for climb-ing the steep mountain ascent. Neither our heavy lorries nor the heavy draught-horses of our supply wagons could be utilized. The Italians had relied on the use of 15-hundredweight Fiat lorries, which were both fast and easily manoeuvrable round the hairpin bends. That there had been numerous casualties due to skidding off the road was evident from the many battered remnants lying on the mountain-side. It was not an uncommon sight to see anti-skid barbed wire wound round their solid rubber tyres. Light lorries of this or similar type could not be made available for our use. Further, the condition of our draught-horses deteriorated rapidly if they were kept in the atmosphere and cold conditions of the Plateau, combined with the shortage of grazing and water. As a result we had to rely on the more hardy big mules. They were utilized mainly as four-horse teams drawing light G.S. wagons, but numerous stores, including barbed wire, were taken on Italian pack-mules. The latter made the ascent on the steep and rough mule-tracks up the mountain-side, in charge of Italian drivers.

A very large number of these mules and light G.S. wagons to carry about 15 hundredweight were allocated to the Division. Colonel Barnett has recorded[1] the method adopted whereby our first-line transport was divided into two echelons. It was found that to make the journey to the Plateau and back to the Base on the Plain entailed at least ten hours on the road. Also that the mules required a day's rest every third day. He quotes as an example that a single Infantry Battalion required an allocation of 46 mules and 10 light G.S. wagons to maintain its daily supplies. Half of the latter were based on the Plateau, the other half on the Plain. Every day the empty wagons of each unit, working to a close timetable, travelled down from the Plateau to a mid-way rendezvous with the loaded wagons. Here teams were exchanged, and the loaded wagons brought to the top.

When relieving units on the Plateau, the Infantry were not allowed to use the road. Carrying only light packs they scrambled up the mule-tracks, which reduced very considerably the distance traversed. Even so, the ascent from the foot of the mountains to the Plateau entailed a steady climb of about five hours' duration. Gunner transport using the road took about an hour longer. The actual distance of road traversed was reckoned to be about 15 miles, and the height attained was considerably higher than that of the top of Snowdon.

Apart from this one road as a connecting link with our rear Headquarters, there was a limited use of a teleferica, or aerial ropeway. The Italians had constructed a large number of these telefericas in the high-altitude regions. They comprised an endless steel cable, supported on pylons erected on the mountain side. Small "cars" (so-called) were hung from the cable by a davit-like attachment at intervals. The cars were shallow trays about 6 feet long by 2 feet wide, and travelled upwards as the cable was revolved round large drums electrically driven at the top and bottom of the system. The cars were far from being safe conveyances, especially in a high wind. They depended on their own weight for remaining on the supporting cable, and there was only a small space between the ascending and descending cars as they passed one another. If a load of one shifted and projected over the side it might well knock the other car off the cable. We were told that in crossing some of the deep gorges in the mountains there was a sheer drop of over 2,000 feet. In parts of the front they were used for transporting the wounded or sick.

On my return from leave I had obtained a lift to the Plateau on a

[1] *With the 48th Division in Italy.*

155

light lorry carrying R.E. Stores. A thick mist hung over the mountain area and the Divisional relief and several days following were under the continued impact of snow, sleet, rain or fog.

My first indication of the recent take-over by the British Divisions was a large signpost "Tattenham Corner" at the top of the ascent. Beyond this point the road passed between the mountains through the Granezza Valley, leading towards Asiago. Our Divisional Headquarters and various units in reserve were located in this valley, which was well screened and partly protected from the enemy's fire by the mountains Kaberlaba and Torle. Our front line lay along the forward edge of the former, which was largely covered by pine forests. The road to Asiago, after leaving the Granezza Valley was fully exposed to enemy view, and had to be heavily screened overhead up to the point where it passed through our front line. On the left sector of our front, which was bare of trees, the final stage of delivering rations and water could only be carried out after nightfall by pack-mule transport.

The broken nature of the mountain hill-sides, and the dense pine forests, made it very difficult, from the defence point of view, to ensure an adequate field of fire. Perhaps the most unusual feature for us was the wide distance between the Austrian and our front lines. No-man's-land varied between 750 and over 1,500 yards. There was no need for care in exposing heads above the parapet, and we chuckled with satisfaction while reminding ourselves of Plugstreet days, with enemy snipers a bare 100 yards away, lying in wait for an unwary exposed head. We were equally free from any possibility of an enemy-tunnelled mine exploding under us at any moment. It was obvious, also, that the war on this front had been conducted by the Italians and Austrians on the "live and let live" principle. There was a relative absence of shell-holes, although Asiago and the small hamlets behind the Austrian front had been severely damaged. Our Staff were especially worried at the lack of protective dugouts in our area. The danger under shell-fire was to some extent minimized by the narrowness of the trenches, and to their being cut in rock. To guard against surprise raids under cover of fog or mist, small outposts were usually maintained in front of the trench line.

A more aggressive and harassing attitude was quickly adopted by our Gunners, and by the Infantry in patrolling no-man's-land, as well as raiding by night. Included in our defence system were a support-line and a reserve-line. They were sited at considerably higher altitudes on the sides of a mountain range rising to 4,500 feet.

It was apparent at once that our Staffs were far from satisfied with the general state of the defences as taken over from the Italian Army. Inspired unremittingly by "Fanny," the Division were set to work on new strong-points, dugouts, strengthening the barbed-wire entanglements sited to force attackers over broken ground into pockets covered by fire, and in improving communications.

My letters home during the first half of May strike a somewhat plaintive note. "I have been working late hours to well past midnight on making out reports and office work. Unfortunately the open-air tramps and perhaps the high altitude induce more than normal sleepiness. We are, however, very comfortably housed in an Italian-made hut, and the scenery round us is everywhere a joy to behold." Parcels from home began to arrive, having taken over five weeks to reach us during the fierce fighting period in France. My favourite baccy was restored to my pipe, but cakes and fruit which my family had persisted in sending us were either dry or a squashy mess.

Ten days later I noted: "Still very busy and burning the midnight lamp in my office room. The rain clouds seem to have been sitting firmly on top of us. We are told that the average snow/rainfall is on 140 days out of the 365. To us it seems to be working out at 30 out of 31 per month. The snow on our area has gone but we can always look out on the higher peaks which remain covered with snow."

Some of the Italian heavy-artillery units had remained in our area. No little skill and patience must have been required in hauling their guns up the mountains, and making emplacements among the outcrop of rocks close to the road. The effect of heavy-gun firing among the mountains was remarkable for its reverberations. The sound seemed to be echoed and re-echoed, rising and falling in a well-regulated succession of waves. This also applied to the numerous thunderstorms accompanied by lightning. The lightning, striking out of dark clouds over the massed snow-capped peaks, gave an added and awesome grandeur to the scene. It brought a reminder of the immeasurable forces of Nature, compared with which man's heaviest artillery seemed puny. One less pleasant feature was its effect on our field-telephone system. Attempts to carry on a conversation during a thunderstorm were apt to be accompanied by sharp shocks running up the arm from the receiver.

During the month in which the Division held this mountain sector much hard slogging work on improving the defence system had been carried out by all units. They had adapted themselves to the entirely novel conditions. This had not altogether escaped recognition from the Higher Command. I recorded: "Some balm!! The G.O.C. has advised the C.R.E. that he has received a very complimentary message on the work of the Divisional R.E. and Pioneer units, which has given him great pleasure to pass on . . ., etc., etc."

Two days later the C.R.E. and I accompanied Major-General C. S. Wilson from Earl Cavan's Headquarters Staff on a long and instructive tramp over our area. Afterwards we entertained him in our Mess. We gained a hint that the Division might be taking part in an offensive in June against the Austrian positions on the Plateau. The feasibility of attacking, and securing sufficient depth in the higher mountains beyond the Plateau, seemed to us a particularly unrealistic and grim prospect.

The tides of fortune in a long war inevitably ebb and flow. Following the big offensive by the German Armies in France in the spring, General Plumer with the British XIth Corps Headquarters, and the 5th and 41st Divisions had been taken back to France. The British forces remaining in Italy were thus reduced to the three Divisions, 7th, 23rd and 48th, with Corps and ancillary units. Earl Cavan had taken over from Sir Herbert Plumer as Commander-in-Chief British Forces in Italy.

Rumours as to our Division's future movements, and constantly revised confidential Staff orders, followed in a bewildering pattern. In the recorded events that follow it will be seen that we were destined to remain in Italy, and to spend the next and last six months of the active war among these mountains, or in relief reserve in their foot-hills. In that period we were to take part in two large-scale battles— the first defensive, the second an offensive with a success beyond our wildest expectations.

23   The Carriola Front

May–June 1918

"It is Whit Monday, 20th May. Last night I slept between clean sheets on a real bed! We have exchanged our mountain-side hut for a share of a modern villa, pleasantly located close to a large river. [The village was Tezze near the Brenta River.] Our billet family are very friendly and helpful. But the heat!! It is like emerging from the Arctic regions straight into the tropics. Two days ago, and only a few miles away as the crow flies, we were cussing at the poor heat produced by the stove in our hut. It is now 9.45 p.m. and I am sitting, minus tunic and close to a wide-open window, almost overcome by the heat."

For ten days we relaxed, out of range from enemy gun-fire. "I had a joy-ride today by car to the nearest town (Vicenza), and acquired my pith helmet. They are being issued to all ranks, much to their amusement. Also we now appear in khaki shorts as our normal dress. All activities carried out by units take place in the early morning or in the latter hours of the day." I could get in the saddle for an evening ride, or clamber up one of the rocky foothills in peaceful enjoyment of the Italian scenery. From here we could look down on a big river (the Brenta) winding through the pasture-lands, and then across to other small hills, with an occasional tall campanile lit up by the setting sun, or an old ruined castle or large villa nestling among yew trees."

We also had acquired a badminton set, and found it an excellent game, which we could fix up on any level patch of ground. We were feeding well with supplies from Vicenza, and needed exercise.

On the last day of May, after a regretful farewell to my horses, I travelled up to the Plateau by lorry to take over from my opposite number in the 7th Division. We were relieving them in the Carriola Sector, on the left of the Granezza Sector, which we had held previously and was now held by the 23rd Division. An Italian Division were on our left.

The general characteristics of our new sector, with a front of about

159

4,000 yards, were roughly similar, except that the whole area was more broken up by defiles and rocky mountain-side ground. Observation, mutual support and field of fire were poor and further restricted by several small hills in no-man's-land. On the extreme Western part and on the Italian-held front, the two opposing lines faced one another across a steep-sided watercourse ravine, known as the Ghelpac. On the centre and Eastern parts the distance widened out to as much as 1,700 yards. As with the Granezza Sector, outposts were maintained in no-man's-land. The lack of adequate dugout protection was even more marked. The available road from the Plains via Caltrano seemed steeper and more tortuous than the Granezza road. Divisional H.Q. were in well-made huts near Carriola, with the heights of Cima di Fonti and Magnaboschi on the East and North side rising to nearly 5,000 feet.

I recorded: "Our R.E. Headquarter Mess has taken on an international character. It consists of three English officers, a French and an Italian officer, and an American doctor. The three non-British are men well endowed, who have travelled widely, and their respective outlook on world affairs and the war makes an interesting study. The American does not hide his light under a bushel, but is new to warfare. At meal times he expatiates on what he has encountered on his walks round the area, in excited and glowing terms, whereas to us they represent no more than a part of our normal life. It makes us feel that we are really hardened soldiers." On one occasion he insisted on offering five pounds to two that one of us could not find his way walking to a certain Headquarters under thirty minutes, taking a route through the forests and never having gone that way previously. The bet was accepted and won with ten minutes to spare. On the proceeds the Mess had a gala night, and no-one seemed more pleased than our American doctor.

On the higher mountain sides behind the British front a number of O.P.s had been constructed. They gave a comprehensive, if distant, view over the Plateau and the Austrian positions on the northern side. In the early morning, when one of the Field Company officers and I were walking along a rough trench leading to the O.P.s, we met two officers. One, wearing Staff insignia, was the then Prince of Wales, afterwards King Edward VIII, who was attached to British H.Q. Staff in Italy. He stopped and chatted brightly, giving us the latest news from the Front in France, and asking questions about our front.

With "Fanny," as always, full of zeal for strengthening the defensive elements of the sector, the Division worked hard on additional wiring and provision of strong-points behind the front line, and also in battalion tactical practices for bringing forward supports, in the event of an enemy attack

A personal note in my diary records a call on the telephone from him, giving me the first news of the appearance again of my family's names in a C.-in-C.'s dispatch, this time in General Plumer's honours list, including the award of the D.S.O. to my brother. They have been among our most prized possessions.

We were at this period under orders to prepare for an offensive across the Plateau. The days passed quickly. The scattered nature of the works on which the three Field Companies and Pioneers were employed meant long hours in the open air. Notes in my diary record long tramps on five out of the first six days in the new area.

Although it was June, the reverse operation of moving from the Plain to the Plateau was even more striking in its climatic effects. At first cold and wet, the weather on 5th June produced a heavy fall of snow. I wrote: "Last week we could not sit out of doors without the risk of sunstroke. Today we can only look out on a white-covered landscape, with snow 5 inches deep all around us. As we sat and shivered in front of our stove, someone brightly remarked—'Oh for the shade of our sun-hats now!'"

During our period of relief in the Plains there was a very bad outbreak of a form of feverish influenza among all units and ranks in the Division. It persisted after our move to Carriola. Most of the Divisional H.Q. Staff and half the members of our Mess, and in some Units twenty-five per cent of their strength, were on the sick list.

Fortunately—or so it seemed to us at the time—there was very little shell-fire activity from the Austrians. Our own artillery fire brought a very limited response during the first fourteen days of June. We were to learn later the reason.

24   The Austrians Attack (Asiago Plateau)

15th June 1918

On the afternoon of the 14th June the O.C. of our 477 Field Company and I had gone out into no-man's-land to select, as far forward as possible, protected sites for forming dumps of R.E. materials and stores. This was part of our preparations for the proposed attack by our Division across the Plateau.

This part of the Plateau was very broken ground, rough stone outcrop and several hillocks rising from 50 to 100 feet in height. There were no British patrols operating on our front. We were making our way over no-man's-land, with our minds more intent on finding a suitable site, when we spotted an Austrian officer with a companion moving round from behind a hillock about 400 yards away on our right front. The officer raised his arm in salute to us, then they turned back and were lost to view behind the hillock. I did not attach the least importance to it. Obviously both of us were out for reconnaissance purposes, and neither was armed in the role of a fighting patrol, so we merely continued on our respective tasks. We had been rather prone to look upon no-man's-land as our preserve, thanks to the more active patrols from our front-line companies. Writing to my brother a few days' later I said: "It was rather a curious feeling to look back at our own front line nearly 1,000 yards behind us." Perhaps it would have been more accurate to describe it as a momentary spasm of that sinking feeling which I had experienced in comparative loneliness in daylight with nothing between me and our enemy. This might have been more pronounced had I foreseen that within the next fifteen hours many Austrian battalions—probably that officer with them—would be sweeping over where we were standing, with an impetus that carried them two-thirds of a mile within our defensive system.

When, however, we returned to our hut the C.R.E. informed us that the plans for an early attack by us were unlikely to materialize. At a Conference held that afternoon the G.O.C. had said that definite and reliable information had been received by the Italian High Command that a major offensive would be launched on the following morning by the Austrian Armies. It would extend over a front of about 50 miles, from North of Venice along the Piave River front, and the mountainous Mt Grappa area of the Brenta Valley, as far West as the front of the French Corps on the right of our two British Divisions on the Plateau. The Asiago front held by the latter would not be attacked in force.

In the event this offensive comprised a series of strong attacks at a number of selected points along the whole of the above front, in the expectation that some of them would achieve a break-through, and enable the gaps to be widened on either flank, thereby forcing a general retirement. The information received was accurate with one important-to-us exception. At its Western extremity the Plateau was selected as one of the principal points of attack, and, unknown to us the heavy artillery opposite us had been greatly reinforced. These guns had been allowed only a minimum of registration, and up to the morning of the 15th June the enemy's shelling had been subnormal. On our side some of the heavy Italian guns had been withdrawn from the Plateau to reinforce the Piave Front. An important factor in the fighting that ensued was the reduced strength of our Infantry Battalions owing to the still-prevailing influenza epidemic. The total fighting strength of the twelve Divisional Infantry Battalions on this day was under 6,000. Two of the 143rd Brigade were less than 400 in numbers.

Unlike the night preceding the opening of the Somme and Passchendaele offensives, there was no feeling of tension among us. The C.R.E. was recovering from an attack of the prevailing fever, two other members of the Mess were still under its effects. We played bridge till late in the evening, but slept in our uniform. A few days after the battle I recorded an account of it. "At 3 a.m. I was awakened by the sudden roar of a very heavy bombardment. Although nothing heavy was dropping in the immediate vicinity of our hut, it was evident that the Austrians were sending over a steady stream of 8-inch and 5·9-type shells all round our area. A little later we realized that some gas-shells were dropping close to us, and we put on our gas-masks. Luckily a few days previously I had arranged for all our H.Q. Staff gas-masks to be tested. Not without some disparaging remarks, the C.R.E. had been persuaded to try out his own mask in front of the gas N.C.O. It happened to be defective.

"For a time the bombardment seemed as intensive as any we had experienced in France. This first phase of the enemy shelling was obviously directed at our battery positions, and nearly all of them received hits. Later it was concentrated more on our front line, causing heavy casualties in the forward companies, owing to the lack of adequate dugouts."

The day had dawned with a thick mist hanging over much of our area. We had not the least idea of what was happening. It transpired subsequently that the cable lines from the forward area to Divisional H.Q. had been cut by the heavy shelling at an early hour in the morning; wireless failed and visual signals were not received owing to the mist. Orders, however, had been sent for the support battalions of the two forward brigades to take up their battle positions. The first definite news of an infantry attack was said to have been brought to 143rd Brigade H.Q. by a wounded signaller. It was to the effect that the front left Battalion and H.Q. and Signal Station were surrounded, and the enemy were pressing forward towards Cesuna. Definite information of an infantry attack in strength did not reach Divisional H.Q. till about 8 a.m. All units in the Division were then alerted and ordered to move into support or reserve positions.

"Shortly after 8.30 a.m. my telephone rang. It was my brother speaking from the Pioneers' Camp on the mountain-side behind us. 'Can my fellows go out on their job now? The shelling seems to have died down a lot.' I replied that I would ask Division and let him know. I walked across to the Divisional 'G' Staff Office hut, which was only a short distance away. When I gave them the message the answer was 'Good God! Are they still there! Orders were sent them and they should by now be in position manning a gap by the Cesuna Switch, opposite where they have broken through our front.' A D.R. message containing the order, for some reason, had not reached them. This was the first intimation I had that the enemy had actually attacked.

"From various sources we learned gradually that the Austrians were fighting their way forward in great strength directly in the area in front of our Headquarters.

"Briefly told—the first waves of the Austrian infantry attack reached our front line about 7 a.m. In this they were aided by the thick mist, and the cover given by defiles and broken nature of the ground. They quickly penetrated at two points, one on our extreme right in the 145 Brigade sector, the other more seriously on our left, 143 Brigade, in front of our Headquarters. On our right sector at least seven Austrian Battalions attacked the front held by the Oxford and Bucks Battalion, the two forward companies of which had suffered very heavy casualties from the enemy bombardment. Passing fresh troops through the gap the enemy fanned out and established a number of machine-guns under cover of the woods. The remainder of the Oxfords formed a semicircular defence in front of their battalion headquarters, with their flanks bent right back. There they held on grimly till supports and counter-attacks halted the enemy's advance.

"On the left 143 Brigade Sector, part of which fronted the deep Ghelpac ravine, the infantry holding our front line posts were practically wiped out by the initial shell-fire, and the same tactics were adopted by the Austrians. Here again the Battalion Headquarters near Perghele House put up a most gallant defence under the R.S.M., after all the senior officers were put out of action. The right company of the 5th Warwicks had suffered a similar fate, and the enemy advance on that side continued till they were a full half mile to the rear of Battalion Headquarters. Ironically phrased perhaps, the valley of which they took advantage was marked on our trench maps as 'Happy Valley.' This valley was protected by two well-wired trenches running in a wide V shape from the southern end towards the North-West and North-East. Known as the Cesuna Switch and Lemerle Switch, they were designed to force an attacking enemy into a kind of pocket towards the Southern end of the valley. Two of the battery positions of our 240 Brigade, which were in advanced positions, with a view to our prospective attack, and heavy trench-mortar battery positions were overrun. Taking with them breech-blocks and dial-sights the Gunners fought back with rifles alongside the infantry. Other guns were manhandled into the open. A 4·5 howitzer battery was firing shrapnel over open sights at a bare 700-yards range against advancing Austrian infantry.

"Immediately to the North of our Headquarters the village of Cesuna was very heavily shelled, and must have been one of the main objectives with its road connections. At this point the penetration had reached about 1,000 yards, with the Austrians reported as advancing in large numbers. They did not succeed in reaching the village. Laterally they were occupying our front-line trenches over a length of 3,000 yards.

"As the situation became clearer, our supporting units moved up and reinforced the forward Battalions in the positions where they were holding off repeated enemy attacks. Gaps in the line were covered, and by midday the enemy advance was halted.

"The infantry fighting was practically continuous during the afternoon, with strong artillery support on both sides. The 7th Battalion Warwicks under Colonel Knox regained a key position threatening further advance on Cesuna. In this they were aided by one of our guns manhandled into position and firing over open sights. Other local attacks enabled a gap between the two forward Brigades to be filled and our line made continuous and straightened out. A Brigade of the 7th Division, then in reserve in the foot-hills, was brought up to the Plateau, and concentrated centrally behind the two Divisions, but took no part in the battle.

"At 6 p.m. two Battalions of the 144 Reserve Brigade made a

determined attempt to regain ground to the North-East of Cesuna, and made some progress, but were met by heavy machine-gun-fire.

"The G.O.C. then issued orders for a concerted attack by our three Brigades at 4.30 a.m. the following morning. During the night there was almost continuous machine-gun and rifle-fire along the whole front. There were few on either side on the Plateau who had more than brief snatches of sleep, as they waited in trenches or improvised positions. My brother, after returning from a day and a night in the trenches, was found to have a temperature of over 104. In spite of the heavy small-arms fire, parties were searching for wounded and strengthening defences; others were bringing forward rations and replacing ammunition supplies. In our minds was the question—who will strike first when dawn comes? Will our own attack be met by a similarly determined advance by Austrian reinforcements brought forward during the night?

"Our counter-attack was completely successful, and by 7.30 a.m. the whole of our original front was cleared of enemy troops, other than the dead and wounded. The retreating Austrians were followed up into no-man's-land, and driven off the outcrop hillocks. Orders had been received from G.H.Q. that attacks on the enemy's front line were not to be pressed forward if strong opposition was encountered. Moving forward in Company, or half-Company, strengths Units of the 143 and 144 Brigades gave the enemy no opportunity to make a concerted resistance. Crossing the Ghelpac Ravine, the enemy front-line trenches near Canove were entered at two points. From there a further 200 prisoners were captured and brought back, and a number of our own men who had been taken prisoners were rescued. Many machine-guns, flammenwerfer and other Austrian equipment passed into our hands.

"About midnight of the 15/16th June I had fallen asleep for a couple of hours. In the early hours of the following morning I went forward over the area where the fighting had taken place, to estimate the effects of the bombardment, and ascertain what essential work was required from the R.E. point of view. In the wake of our counter-attack parties were everywhere searching the woods and open ground for the wounded, and collecting the dead.

"In the area in front of the pocket formed by the Cesuna and Lemerle Switch trenches, particularly, the Austrian dead lay in large numbers. As a memento I added an officer's fine Steyer pistol and holster to my personal armament. In their retreat the Austrians had left behind large quantities of arms and equipment. Although most of their wounded must have been evacuated during the night, many were still lying in the woods."

It had been a fight in which all Units of our Division, other than the transport and details stationed in the foothills area, were called on to take up their positions in the defence. The Divisional Artillery were in action almost continuously for over thirty hours, in spite of unexpectedly heavy counter-battery fire from the Austrians. In the light of previous experience, the little incident recorded earlier, in which two of us had chosen to stroll peaceably and unescorted across a large part of no-man's-land, less than twelve hours before a battle opened, seems unrealistic. There must be few old campaigners who could not moralize at length on the unexpected twists and turns of events which so vitally affected their lives. One lesson again brought home to us was that the personnel of all armed units, such as Gunners and Sappers, must be trained and ready to fight with their rifles alongside the Infantryman. In this instance our Field Companies were not brought into the actual fighting, except for a small party under the R.S.M. working at the R.E. Dump near Pelly Cross, in the right sector. They successfully held off enemy attacks on their position in what had become the front line.

It should be borne in mind that the battle events which I have described were confined to a single Divisional front of approximately 4,000 yards. We learned subsequently from prisoners that, apart from the normal troops holding their front, a crack Austrian Division had been brought up from the rear in lorries to make the initial breakthrough. A second fresh Division followed behind them to carry forward the impetus of an attack, which was confidently expected to sweep their enemy off the Plateau, and open the way to overrun the North Italian Plain.

The cost in casualties sustained by our Division, within the period of approximately thirty-six hours, were—killed, wounded and missing —70 Officers and 850 Other Ranks—a total of 920. The known casualties of the Austrians were 576 killed and buried by our troops, 34 Officers and 694 Other Ranks taken prisoners, of whom 188 were wounded. During the night of the 15/16th June the Austrians had ample opportunity to evacuate their wounded, and undoubtedly did so. On the basis of a comparative ratio of 5 wounded casualties to 2 killed (ours were higher than this), their evacuated wounded would have numbered not less than 1,250, making a total, on a conservative basis, of around 2,550, compared with the British 920.

In estimating the ebb and flow of this battle, four factors may be taken into account. (1) The natural difficulties of front-line defence due to the broken nature of the field of fire. (2) The inadequacy (judged by British/German standards) of the work done during the earlier Italian occupation in providing dugouts and protective wire. (3) The 48th Division units had a bare fourteen days, prior to being attacked, in which to effect improvements, and become fully conversant with

167

the forest-covered area in which they had to operate. (4) The reduction in the heavy Italian Artillery units, who had normally been supporting this front, but had been withdrawn to strengthen the Piave Front.

In face of the difficulties of appraisement of the situation as the enemy attack developed, due to early breakdown of communication, "Fanny's" tactical handling of the Division in timing and disposition was, in our opinion, all that could have been wished for. The courage shown by the Battalions holding the front line, who bore the brunt of the bombardment and initial weight of the enemy's attack, and that of the Gunners was magnificent. I recorded at the time: "Our G.O.C. made the remark in my hearing that it was probably the best fight the Division has ever made."

To complete the outcome of this, the last large-scale offensive by the Austrians, the following may be briefly recorded. The 23rd British Division, on our right on the Plateau in the Granezza Sector, were also strongly attacked on the morning of the 15th June. Their front was similarly penetrated at two points, but to a lesser depth than that in our sector. Determined counter-attacks were successful in restoring their front. As the Italian Division on our left was not attacked, their front being protected by the greater depth of the Ghelpac Ravine, the Allies' hold on the Plateau remained firmly in their possession.

On the front of the River Piave the fighting continued for a week before the Austrians were finally driven back across the River. They had succeeded in establishing three bridge-heads on the South bank, the most important being the capture of the greater part of the Montello. The Italians holding this sector carried out a number of counter-attacks extending over seven days, finally regaining the whole of their previously held positions on the South bank. The difficulties of the Austrians in reinforcing and bringing up supplies were accentuated by a rise and swifter current in the flood-water of the Piave. Their casualties in crossing the River were accordingly high. The total Italian casualties in the battle have been quoted as about 90,000, an indication of the weight of the Austrian attack.

Lord Cavan's Despatch records that "The result was a complete and disastrous defeat for Austria." Historians accept the view that it had a great effect in lowering the morale of the Austrian troops, and in the capability of Germany to win the war.

25 Interludes from the Front (Granezza, Venice)

July–October 1918

In the week following the Austrian attack on our front we learned with the greatest regret that "Fanny" was leaving the Division, and taking over an appointment in England. For over three years he had inspired all ranks with a fighting spirit, and had won their confidence as a leader.

On 26th June we were relieved by the 7th Division and returned to our old billet in Tezze on the Plain. For the next three weeks the depleted Infantry Battalions were allowed to rest and reorganize. Similarly the work of the R.E. Field Companies and Pioneers was light, consisting mainly of training in the cooler hours of the day, owing to the extreme heat. Flies became our chief enemies, and a continuous source of annoyance, particularly in farm billets. A slab of butter left on the table would become practically black in five minutes

left uncovered. At night time we lay on our beds, in the costume which Adam wore before becoming tailor, and perspired. The C.R.E. was sent on a month's sick leave to England, as he seemed unable to shake off the effects of the recent epidemic, and Major Crawford joined our Mess as Acting C.R.E. For the three weeks we were free from being under daily shell-fire, and from operational tasks. Our badminton set in the early evenings gave us pleasant exercise.

On several occasions kindly-disposed Staff Officers on their lawful (!) occasions provided lifts into the bigger towns. G.T.H. and I had been given special passes for towns outside the permitted area. This had arisen from our being authorized to purchase tools and R.E. requirements from the big city stores on a far more extensive scale compared with our experience in France. On one such occasion I was severely hauled over the coals by the Military Police for not carrying the pass with me.

There is a happy recording of the A/C.R.E. and myself being taken to Verona, one of the most interesting old towns in Italy. From there we went on to Sermione on a small peninsula on the Southern end of Lake Garda. Here a short-leave rest camp had been set up for British Officers. A curious feature was that the extreme Northern end of the Lake, backed by high-altitude mountains, was Austrian territory, and held by them. Thus small naval units patrolled on each side of the boom stretching across the lake and forming part of the front line. We returned to Verona for the luxury of a splendid dinner at the Europa, followed by a visit to a large cinema and a return in the early hours of a Sunday morning.

Most memorable and enjoyable was a visit to Venice. A limited number of special passes were issued for a twenty-four hour period. I managed to secure passes for Lieutenants Bessant and Barrat from 475 Field Company and for myself, to start on Friday 12th July. Venice in the last year of the 1914–1918 war was a city entirely devoid of visitors from the outside world, other than a few Officers from the British and French Forces. The following account is extracted from a long description written after our visit.

"Late in the evening prior to our projected afternoon departure nemesis loomed up in the shape of two messages. One demanded the presence of the A/C.R.E. with the Divisional G.O.C. for the whole day. The other indicated that the British E.-in-C. was coming to our Headquarters, and required to be escorted on visits to our three Field Companies. The latter had to be my job. Luckily he arrived early, and I managed to hustle him round the Companies before lunch-time. He came back to lunch, at which we brought out all our choicest delicacies and drinks, such that he went away in a very gracious and complimentary spirit. That is what we call 'tact' on both sides. Having previously packed my toothbrush in a haversack, I quickly rode away to the station (Tavernelle), where—wonder of wonders—the train started punctually.

"On arrival our passes were scrutinized by several officials, who scrawled their names on them with huge pen flourishes, and filled up any blank spaces with official stamps. We hired a gondola to take us straight down the Grand Canal to our hotel near the Piazza of St Mark. It was then about 6.30 p.m., and the evening sun immediately behind us gave a warm softening tone to the buildings along the Canal, now mostly with shuttered fronts.

"Following a quick dinner, while it was still light we dawdled along the Piazza and Riva fronting the Canal. Only a relatively few British officers had been to Venice up till this time, and it was a renewal of our early experiences in Italy, when everyone turned round to stare at us as if we were a new type of fashion-plate. On this occasion we frequently overheard the remark 'Americani!' This may have been due to the effect of our sun-helmets, of the African explorer's type, and drill tunics. It was certainly not a Bond-street pattern. We sat in the Piazza at an outdoor café, and watched the stream of the city's war-time residents strolling past. They included men in the blue-grey uniform of the 'Soldati,' the grey costumes of the Marines, and the clean white rig of the Sailors, in contrast with the trim Venetian girls with black shawls over their shoulders. There was not a single tourist to be seen. It was a Venice populated only by the humbler dwellers belonging to the city. As darkness fell we hired a two-oarsmen gondola, in which we were steered for an hour through devious and narrow canals, linked with the Grand Canal. Normally the cafés and waterside must be lit up with numerous lights reflecting on the waters. Now the only lights visible are an occasional blue coloured lamp at corners or under archways, or a red lamp to mark a 'Rifugio' in case of an air attack. It was a bright starlight night, with no visible moon. The city that we saw was a mystical outline of domes and towers, or, in the narrower and darker waterways, shadowy outlines of arched bridges, and masses of tall buildings, between which only a patch of starlight was visible.

"In the morning I was up at 7 a.m. for a pre-breakfast stroll. In our tour of the city during the day we were much helped by Bessant, by profession a devoted architect, who had known Venice in pre-war days. The strong sunlight, with its effect of light and shade on the Piazzas, buildings and lagoon made a very different but wonderful impression on me, compared with that of the previous evening. The lower part of the façade of St Mark's was boarded up and sandbagged, but its mosque-like domes and marble facings and the reconstructed Campanile cannot be hidden or lose their beauty. Inside, the mosaics that have covered the walls and roof for perhaps hundreds of years remain untouched, but the High Altar and the Screen are carefully protected. We were able to see all the rooms in the Doge's Palace, but the pictures and monuments had been taken away. We were temporarily incarcerated in the torture chamber, and crossed the Bridge of Sighs.

"Almost all of the expensive type of shops were closed, but around midday the narrow shopping streets were thronged with the native population. A few of the pre-war 'touts' remained, and eagerly advanced to the attack when they saw us. Appeals to show us over silk or Venetian glass factories were, however, unavailing. One in hurt tones claimed to be the proprietor of a famous and most interesting glass-works. We hard-heartedly came to the decision that despite the war effects, the proprietor of so famous a factory should not have permitted himself to parade the streets in grimy linen and frayed garments. Our twenty-four hours in Venice passed all too quickly. As we recrossed the Lagoon on our return journey the sun was shining on the white envelope of an Austrian observation balloon. It reminded us of the narrow margin by which the city had so far remained in Italian possession."

On the 22nd July a lorry took me and my kit to the Granezza Camp on the Plateau to arrange taking over. With the C.R.E., and G.T.H. who normally acted as Stores Officer, both away on leave I found myself heavily tied to office work. I noted that the entries in our in-coming documents register more than 200 in three days. For the first ten days or more, after taking over, the R.E. are usually inundated with inquiries and with allocating priorities for works required. Shortly after the C.R.E.'s return I received a dressing-down from him for tackling a job when I had more than enough to do. He also asserted that he proposed to bring in one of the Company subalterns to help and understudy headquarters work.

We had already been instructed to plan and erect extensive hut accommodation for winter conditions. We were also told again to accumulate on the Plateau a full supply of R.E. materials likely to be required for an attack by us on our front. We were not very happy over the prospect of the latter, after studying the strength of the enemy defences from aerial photos.

In the first week of our taking over the front there was very little shelling by the enemy. Our own Gunners quickly became more active, and raiding by the Infantry was intensified. Some of these raids were on a considerable scale, with similar action by the Divisions on our left and right. In a subsequent dispatch Lord Cavan wrote: "When the British Divisions took over the Asiago Front orders were issued for the complete command of the broad no-man's-land to be obtained and retained. Between 29th March and 14th September 41 successful raids had been carried out. In addition to inflicting heavy casualties, 871 prisoners and 24 machine guns had been brought back to our lines."

Increased artillery activity by either opponent almost inevitably resulted in retaliation. Otherwise the morale of the troops at the receiving end of the shelling deteriorated. Thus life on the Plateau was always subject to the whims of the Austrian Gunnery Depart-ment. Unexpectedly, instead of the anticipated three or four weeks, the Division's period of front-line contact with the enemy was destined to continue for an unbroken fifteen weeks.

In this period the Austrian shell retaliation increased in intensity spread over a wide-ranging area. It may be wondered why our troops behind the front-line area had to depend on huts, albeit sheltered as far as possible by natural landscape features. The answer lies in the sheer impossibility of blasting out sufficient dugouts in the solid mountain rock. Thus throughout the 24-hour day we were exposed to the chance shell "having our number on it." In a letter written shortly after the Armistice I admitted: "The leaks in the roof of my bedroom in the hut, of which I complained in earlier letters were due to various punctures from enemy shells. On one occasion a shell decapitated, at a height of about 20 feet, a pine tree growing just outside my bedroom window, and deposited the top of the tree on the roof. The shell then travelled another 30 yards before entering a cook-house (not by the usual door) and exploding." These we had learned to regard as normal minor hazards, and they did not worry us unduly.

In mid-August the C.R.E. brought in J. A. Henderson, one of the 475 Field Company Subalterns, to help in the work of our Headquarters staff. Older than most of the junior officers, he was capable, a great lover of horses, and a most likeable addition to our Mess.

In this period, also, we were to a greater extent dependent on Italian transport from the Plains for our R.E. requirements. I was not altogether happy about the heavy loads allowed by their officers on their pack-mules and light wagons. The pack-mules scrambled up the rough mountain tracks with almost incredible loads—e.g. of barbed wire. A note records: "I have been poring over an arithmetical sum. 3,982 foot run of $9 \times \frac{3}{4}$ inch timber—what is the approximate weight? A pair of Italian Army mules, starting in the morning from the Plains, hauled it in a light wagon up the 4,000 feet to the Plateau, covering 20 miles, and reached our stores dump by 2 p.m."

August passed into September with only normal front-line activities. On 8th September we learned that the plans for a large-scale attack on the mountain positions opposite to us had been cancelled. There were no regrets at this decision on our part.

With preparations for our own prospective attack cancelled we entered on a relatively quiet period apart from raids. We learned that Lord Cavan, British C.-in-C. Italy, was going on leave for a fortnight. From this we deduced that no major events on our front were anticipated in the immediate future.

Three Infantry Battalions from each of the three remaining British Divisions in Italy were withdrawn and sent to France in mid-September. From our Division they were the 8th Warwicks, 8th Worcesters and 5th Gloucesters.

So far I had been fortunate in surviving over four years of army life without any absence due to sickness. I had, however, been advised to have a small surgical operation which would entail about ten days in hospital. Our Divisional A.D.M.S. suggested my taking this opportunity of a likely quiet period on our front. The following day, in mid-September, an ambulance deposited me at No. 24 C.C.S. at Montecchio, about five miles from Thiene. The C.C.S. proved to be a big modern country-house, with a fine terrace and large gardens, situated on a hill overlooking the Plain. Owing to some casualties being brought in, the operation was put off for a couple of days, and to my annoyance I suffered the normal pre-operation semi-starvation.

It was my first experience of being in a hospital ward, and after a few days I thoroughly enjoyed the restful period. Our surgical ward contained about eighteen beds in a lofty and well-lit room, but most of the occupants, if badly wounded, were sent on to a base hospital as quickly as possible.

"Opposite to my bed is a lively young Austrian Officer with a cherub-like face. He has been shot through the thigh, and was captured in one of our infantry raids. The Sister in charge of the ward caught him out of bed last evening. Jerry—as we call him—cannot speak or understand the English language, and a most amusing pantomime ensued. She tried to explain to him that he was a very wicked Austrian, and if he got out of bed again he would be badly straffed. He, meanwhile, thought it all a tremendous joke when Sister seized a large poker and playfully pretended to brain him. There are now no serious cases in the ward, and in my corner we get rather obstreperous, with consequent strafing by Sister. Next to me is a most humorous Irishman with an ankle damaged while playing soccer. His other neighbour is an Airman, whose head was cut open by anti-aircraft fire. When he laughs he has to hold his shaven head to prevent it opening at the crack—as he expresses it. As the Irishman continually makes him laugh, we are hoping that the stitches hold fast. As a dire threat we have been told by Sister that the Padre will be sent in to keep us in order."

With nothing to do, and the Padre distributing copious supplies of Y.M.C.A. Red Triangle notepaper, I wrote home describing various little incidents of life in a C.C.S. close to the front. "Although it is still very hot, we get warm soup twice every day with our meals. Unfortunately it is always the same brown and rather indistinguishable variety, the only difference being when it is burnt. An appeal to Sister as to whether the variety was changed monthly or quarterly elicited the reply that it had never changed since she had been there! *Ergo*—it is probably triennial, or for the duration of the war!" Another incident noted: "To-day the contents of the ether bottle apparently got into the teapot—we hope by mistake!"

In a later letter, when other casualties had come in, and I had reached the walking-about stage, I wrote: "The week here has opened my eyes to the scope of hospital work close to the front; and what a grand work it is. With modern surgery even men badly hit seem to be relieved quickly of pain, and all the wounded in the wards are as cheerful as can be. I have noticed a carved motto on one wing of this house, the front of which is in typical painted and decorative Italian style. The motto is 'Post Fata Resurgo'—remarkably apt for a C.C.S., where the wounded are patched up, and rise again to carry on their lives!"

Also few of us during the war or afterwards fully recognized the extent of the work and sacrifice of life made by the Army Chaplains. Although High Authority restrained them from what may be termed the close conflict area—an inhibition which was often disregarded— they shared many of our dangers and shell-fire. Official records show that 97 were killed, and 69 died as the result of the war. Of these 98 were members of the Church of England.

I did not lack visitors. Major-General Sir H. B. Walker, our new Divisional Commander, came in as the result of a mild form of sickness, and I had several interesting talks with him. He impressed me as a first-rate successor to our "Fanny." Colonel Howard, our G.S.O.1., and Colonel Barnett, A.A. and Q.M.G., whom I had got to know well as fellow members of our small advance party in the move to Italy, came down to see the G.O.C. The C.R.E. also came to have an eye-test. I gathered from them that the war was progressing very well without my services, and that there was no need to hasten my return. One sad piece of news was that Colonel J. M. Knox, the O.C. of the 7th War- wicks had been killed by a direct hit on his Battalion Headquarters dugout. An outstanding and successful Battalion Commander, he and his Battalion had worked from the earliest days in the fullest co-operation with 475 Field Company, and he had become a firm friend of all our senior R.E. Officers.

I was rather surprised to find that the C.C.S. seemed generous in keeping the patients in hospital—other than serious cases which were sent down to the base—rather than returning them quickly to duty. The R.A.M.C. Colonel in charge of the C.C.S. even suggested that I might like to go down to a convalescent home for a few days before returning. However, I felt perfectly fit, and by 28th September my last stitches had been taken out and my diary of the following day records: "Am discharged to duty. Return to G. (Granezza) by ambulance, and am quite cheerful and pleased to be back." I arrived in time to bid farewell to our departing American M.O. A special dinner in his honour had been arranged in the Mess, with good-bye and good-luck toastings all round. Including our interpreters, we represented four nationalities, each of which had to be duly toasted in turn. The C.R.E.'s subsequent comment, "Quite a bright evening," may be taken as a mild understatement.

During the latter part of September our Divisional Staff had been advised that the Division would probably return to France in October, following in turn the 7th and 23rd Divisions. Also, as the result of cancellation of the planned attack across the Plateau all surplus am- munition and stores, brought up for the attack, were to be evacuated to the Plain. Work to effect this had gone steadily forward. By early October they were advised that the return to France was definitely postponed. Instead a large-scale allied offensive on the Piave Front was planned. British G.H.Q., who had been located at Lugo in the foothills, and the 7th and 23rd Divisions would move some 60 miles away eastwards of the Plateau to take part in this offensive. Great secrecy was enjoined regarding these moves.

From the 11th October we found that our Division had been transferred from the British Corps to the XIIth Corps of the Sixth Italian Army for tactical purposes. Our 477 Field Company was also detached and sent to the Piave Front for bridging operations, and we were told that the whole Division would follow in a week or two. Meanwhile we were dependent for administration, special transport, ammunition and stores on the now distant British G.H.Q. One result of our being under Italian orders was a succession of visits from Italian Generals and Staff Officers. They were largely foisted on us by Divisional H.Q. to be escorted round our defence system. Assisted by interpreters they asked innumerable questions on our organization and dispositions, and of our experience in France. I noted: "It is all rather fun, as we are slack in the office and field work, and no-one seems to know what is supposed to be happening to us."

Our complacency received a shock when, after a week under Italian tactical command, we were ordered to take part in a general attack in the next few days, to obtain a footing in the mountains across the Plateau. At the same time we received completely contradictory advice that we were to rejoin the British Corps on the Piave, and would not be attacking on the Plateau. Incidentally a note of mine records the first fall of winter snow on 9th October, and, a week earlier, night frost at 22° F. with thick ice on ponds.

Soon after my return to duty I had been presented with a personal problem. Major G. E. A. Richards, who had commanded 474 Field Company since Major H. C. Clissold had been killed in the battle for Passchendaele, became seriously ill, and was evacuated to England. The C.R.E. offered to recommend that I should take over the command, with the temporary rank of Major, if I so wished, as my name had been on a recommended list for the past year. On the other hand he was content if I preferred to retain my post as Adjutant. I liked the work I had been doing, and from the point of view of my wife and parents I ran less war risks, compared with those of the Field Company officers. On the other hand, with three years' experience of Field Company work, in all junior stages of rank, would I not be pulling my weight more fully in a company command? I accepted and my name went forward for confirmation.

At this period heartening news of the Allies' successes in France had been reaching us. My diary of 12th October records: "Strong rumours that Germany has put out 'feelers' intimating that they were prepared to evacuate Allied Territories. In the evening some beano in Signals' Mess!" The latter may be interpreted as a high-spirited rough-and-tumble with no holds barred, and our hopes that it represented Germany's realization that they could not win the war. It would, however, be a mistake to think that the great majority of those serving overseas would have been content with an inconclusive ending to the war. In spite of war weariness and a longing to get home, there remained a determination that the sacrifices of those who had given their lives in it could only be honoured by final victory. Also that there must be recompense for the stupendous loss of the Nation's manpower and resources.

On the 21st October we were notified by the XIIth Italian Corps Command that the projected attack across the Plateau was cancelled. It was far from being an easy period for any of the principal Staff Officers of our Division. Although the Iatlian XII Corps Staff were most friendly, and ready to do all they could to integrate our British Division with their own units, there were numerous inherent differences in procedure, apart from language difficulties. These were intensified by the dual control under which our Staff were operating. As an example we were at this date under orders from British G.H.Q. to continue evacuation of ammunition and stores not immediately required, with the understanding that we would be moved to the Piave at an early date. The Italian XIIth Corps, on the other hand, clearly expected us to remain attached to them on the Plateau.

Isolated from the other British Units in Italy, and with delayed letters and newspapers from England, we seemed out of touch with the war and with impending events. Thus, up to the 24th October, so far as we were concerned, we were merely holding a small sector of the Allied Western Front in a war which might well continue for many months or even years. We had not the slightest premonition that within the next eleven days the 48th Division would have become "the first British Division to enter enemy territory on the Western Front" (Lord Cavan's dispatch), and an armistice would be signed under which Austria admitted defeat.

Before recording our totally unexpected experience in that period, it may be helpful to summarize briefly the changing fortunes which had characterized the war in France during 1918. Between February and June the German armies, greatly reinforced by divisions no longer needed on their Eastern Front, following the collapse of Russia, launched three main offensives. With about a hundred divisions available they had attacked on 21st March on a broad front from near Arras to south of the Somme. They regained the ground which they

177

had lost on the 1917 Somme battlefields. They overran Bapaume, Péronne and Ham, and forced the Allied line back to Albert.

From 9th April, in a month's fighting they swept forward further North in the area between Messines and La Bassee. Two days later Haig had written his famous order of the day, "With our backs to the wall, and believing in the justice of our cause, each one of us must fight to the end."[1] General Foch had been appointed Allied Generalissimo. At the end of May had come a further German offensive south of the Somme. Soissons was lost, and again the enemy reached the Marne River. Amiens and Paris were severely threatened, but by the middle of June the impetus of the attacks had been halted. Throughout those three months the Allied Armies in France had been very near to disaster, in face of the supreme effort of the German High Command to strike a final successful blow.

In mid-July they made one more attempt at a break-through in the area of the River Marne. In the intervening month reinforcements from England, and the sailing from America of large contingents of new troops, had given Foch the necessary strength to strike back. After three days of initial success, the Germans were driven back by the Allied counter-attack. It proved the vital turning-point of the tide in France. This time it was a tide of successful advances in France and Belgium, the flow of which not even the stubborn courage of the German soldier could stem in the fourteen weeks that followed.

[1] A facsimile copy of Haig's order as originally drafted in his own handwriting hangs in Clifton College library.

26   Our Last Battle (Asiago)

27th October–2nd November 1918

"A fight on and me not in it!" This perhaps libellous complaint imputed to an Irishman no longer applied to most of us. It had been swept away by experience of the realities of war. The instinct of self-preservation is in constant conflict with the action that war demands. In this personal conflict anticipation may well be the most disturbing emotion. On the Asiago Plateau in the fourth week of October 1918 the events erupted so suddenly and unexpectedly that anticipation had scant time to materialize.

We knew that an offensive on the Piave Front was planned. Of its date and scope we knew nothing. We appeared unlikely to be involved in any large-scale attack, at least in the initial stages. In this we were proved to be very wrong.

A considerable quantity of the British ammunition and stores on the Plateau had been taken away into the Plains. The provision of forward R.E. dumps in no-man's-land, which I had considered futile, had been cancelled, and were never needed. There was little shelling, and apart from raiding we were left to routine tasks. Thus my diary records (21st October): "C.R.E. and G.T.H. return from leave to Venice." On the following two days: "Tramp with C.R.E. over front and reserve lines recording unfinished works." On one of these we came across an old bronze cannon embossed "Ex Napoli. 1886." I was now also acting O.C. 474 Field Company, and spent the 24th and 25th October in the Company wagon lines at Fara in the Plain, getting better acquainted with the personnel and horses. On the 26th and 28th I watched the R.E. and Pioneers playing inter-Unit soccer matches. The only offensive action on a considerable scale had been on the night of 23rd–24th October. Under orders from the Italian Sixth Army Command each of the three Divisions on the Plateau Area had raided the trenches opposite to them. The 4th Glosters raiding Ave and S.M. Maddalena brought back 6 officers and 223

O.R.s at the cost of very few casualties. The French Division on our right captured over 700, and the Italians on our left 14 in a smaller raid.

It was not until the afternoon of Sunday, the 27th October, when the C.R.E. held a Company Commanders' Conference that we learned that a major offensive by the Allied Armies had been opened on the Piave Front. At 23.30 the previous night a bombardment of the enemy positions had opened, and early in the morning the British 7th and 23rd Divisions had crossed the Piave and gained a bridge-head across the river, east of the Montello. In his subsequent dispatch of 15th November, as C.-in-C. British Forces in Italy, Lord Cavan recorded that orders had been issued that no British gun should fire a single shot previous to the general bombardment. Also that all British troops visible to the enemy should wear Italian uniform in order to conceal their presence. The two British Divisions formed part of a British-Italian Army of two Corps, which was placed under the command of Lord Cavan by General Diaz—the Italian Supreme Commander. The latter, in stressing the vital importance of secrecy, had suggested that the 48th Division should remain on the Plateau to make as little apparent change as possible. Lord Cavan had agreed to this, with the stipulation that the Division should rejoin his command at the earliest opportunity. This somewhat indeterminate arrangement was clearly the cause of the conflicting instructions under which our Divisional Staff had been suffering.

Turning now to events on the Plateau, raiding parties from all three Divisions on the night of the 29th/30th October found that Austrian troops had withdrawn from their positions in the trenches in front of Asiago earlier that evening. Only a few men had been left in the trenches to fire Vérey lights. Patrols were sent forward into Asiago, and during the day it was established that the enemy were holding in strength their main Winterstellung defence system. On this and the following day probing patrols were met by rifle and M.G. fire along the entire front. The whole of our area received unusually heavy shelling, including gas-shells. There was no indication of any general retirement, the indications being only that the Austrian Command had preferred to hold the immensely strong positions they had prepared on the forward slopes of the mountains behind Asiago.

Thus the general position, as known to us on our front on the 31st October was as follows. We had meagre information of the Allied Forces on the Piave Front having successfully penetrated into enemy-held territory, and captured a very large number of prisoners. All Units in our Division were warned to be prepared to move forward, and to bring up from the Plain their "B" echelon transport vehicles essential for any advance. 474 and 475 Field Companies and the

Pioneer Battalion were employed in making passable for transport the road leading forward through Asiago.

At 02.50 hours, 1st November, Divisional Orders were issued for the 144 and 145 Brigades, each on a two-battalion front, to attack the Winterstellung in conjunction with the French Division on our right. The attack was timed for the Infantry to make the assault three hours only after the issue time of the detailed order.

This was to be fighting of a totally different character from that previously experienced by the Division. Nature's obstacles of rivers, heavy rain and clinging mud were replaced by mountains to be scaled, and narrow roads to be traversed through the mountain passes. From my experience the average officer indulged in surprisingly little contemplation or assessment of the underlying higher strategy which directed his movements. We were still parochial in our outlook. To plunge into a barren land of mountains gradually increasing in altitude, and stretching seemingly into infinity, appeared to us to be without reason. Or were we merely attacking in order to pin down troops which might otherwise be sent to the Piave Front? In this again we were proved to be totally wrong. There was a strategic objective, however unlikely of attainment it seemed then. A rapid advance could cut off from its basic supplies an entire Austrian Army in the Altipiano area.

The Austrian front which the 48th Division now faced extended some 4,000 yards. On the Division's right immediately North of Asiago, the defensive system included Mt Catz (4,000 feet) with a strong redoubt on the summit. Behind it a succession of peaks rose to over 6,750 feet. On lower ground immediately to the West of Mt Catz, the small village of Bosco was guarded by all-round defences. From this point the main trench line, named in our maps Purge, Nette and Goodwood trenches, ran in a south-westerly direction to the deep Val d'Assa Ravine. In front of Goodwood trench, and behind it, were defences in depth including the larger village of Camporovere as a forward bastion. These guarded the entry to the all-important road leading to Caldonazzo and Levico, which for many miles ran alongside the northern edge of the Val d'Assa Ravine. Behind Goodwood trench this road was also dominated in turn by Mt Rasta (4,250 feet) with a fort, and Mt Interrotto (4,600 feet).

In a Divisional order issued early on the morning of 2nd November, the objective of our advance was that of "reaching Caldonazzo and cutting off the whole of the Altipiano." Through this small town in the old Italian Trentino Province ran the vital life-line rail and road supply route serving the Austrian Army Eastwards in the Val Sugana and Brenta River area. But Caldonazzo was 22 miles distant from our camp at Granezza, as the crow flies. It was probably nearer double the distance by the steep and twisting transport roads in the passes between the mountains.

The joint bombardment by the French Division on our right and our own Division opened at 05.00 hours (1st November). At 05.45 the barrage was laid on the Winterstellung and the Infantry attacked. On our right the 145 Brigade broke through the defences on the lower slopes and scaled the heights of Mt Catz, against stiff resistance. The garrison holding the summit were all killed or captured. Several hundred prisoners were captured, and a number of field-guns, howitzers and machine-guns. The guns had been well served by the Austrian gunners before they were forced to retire, taking the breech-blocks with them. The French Division on our right had also advanced and kept in touch with our flanking battalion.

The attack of the 144 Brigade against Goodwood trench on the eastern lower slopes of Mt Rasta and Mt Interrotto was met with strong resistance. After penetrating the main line the attacking battalions were driven back by counter-attacks, but held on to the forward bastion area round Camporovere, 1½ miles North-West of Asiago. They were unable to retain the village of Bosco, and their losses on this front were heavy. One Section of my Company were attached to the forward Brigade during the battle, and were employed in consolidating the Camporovere trenches against further counter attack, and operated with the Brigade to the forward limit of the advance. All other available R.E. and the Pioneer Battalion were continually employed in clearing the road across no-man's-land and through the chaos of Asiago. By the evening of 1st November it was sufficiently cleared as far as Camporovere, and the reserve 143 Brigade, with their light transport, were brought forward and concentrated in the Asiago area.

General Walker had decided to exploit the success of the 145 Brigade on the right by a turning movement. Reinforced by the reserve Battalion of the 144 Brigade they attacked again at dawn of the following morning (2nd November). Swinging left-handed in a Westerly direction they broke through the more lightly defended line North of Bosco, and gained possession of the twin mountains Mt Dorbellele and Mt Mosciagh, with peaks rising over 5,000 feet (Snowdon 3,568). They were then in a position of outflanking all the enemy positions in Goodwood trench and on Mt Rasta and Mt Interrotto. To avoid being cut off, the Austrian troops, who had hitherto put up a stout resistance, evacuated their positions and retired up the Val d'Assa road. The 144 Brigade moved forward again, and by about 08.00 hours were in possession of Mt Interrotto. All barriers to entry on the Caldonazzo road had been swept away.

In any story of the 48th Division's operations in the war the two operational orders Nos. 55 and 56, issued at 09.45 and 18.00 hours on this day, must rank as presaging its most exciting episode, and the one with the most far-reaching effects. The morning order, after giving the objective of Caldonazzo, ordered the 143 Brigade, with three Artillery Sections and a half Company R.E. (475 Field Company) under Brigadier-General Sladen, to move forward as the Advance Guard. The other two Infantry Brigades, R.E. and Pioneers were to follow them up the Val d'Assa Pass, and would concentrate for the night in the forward area beyond Asiago. The later order indicated that the Advance Guard had reached a point nearly six miles beyond Camporovere. Enemy resistance had been weak, with every sign of a rapid retreat. The 48th were in front of, and out of touch with the Italian Divisions on both flanks. Prisoners had reported that the Austrians intended to retire to and stand on a line a short distance inside the border, or one guarding the upper area of the Val Sugana. The Division was ordered to continue its advance in the morning, and gain the high ground overlooking the Val Sugana. If this was successful, Caldonazzo and Levico would be captured, and the Val Sugana blocked. No times for moving in the morning were indicated.

The only order I had received was one from our R.E. Headquarters to the effect that the Sappers were not to return to their Granezza camp after finishing work on the roads, and that our light transport vehicles were to be brought up to Asiago. Soon after it had become dark I left the three Sections of Sappers ensconced for the night in a trench near Goodwood, vacated by the Austrians early that morning, and brought forward our transport vehicles and Officers' horses from Granezza to Asiago. The latter, as seen by day, was reminiscent of the worst-hit areas of Ypres, with the gaunt walls of roofless houses standing in a sea of rubble. I found a big yard adjoining some ruined buildings where we could bivouac for the night. It was just half an hour short of midnight, after a strenuous and tiring day, when I crawled into my valise. My batman had laid it out on the concrete floor under an archway. On looking round under the light of my torch I saw that it was in the middle of scattered heaps of Austrian bombs, machine-gun cartridge-belts and rubble. It did not affect my immediate relapse into sleep.

27   The White Flag (Val d'Assa)

3rd November 1918

This description of my personal experiences in the 48th Division's advance into Austrian territory on the 3rd and 4th November follows closely a detailed record written shortly after the events.

Sunday, 3rd November 1918.   At 03.30, after four hours untroubled sleep I was awakened to receive a D.R. message with orders for moving forward. The Company, less one Section in advance, were to reach the Val Portule road junction on the Val d'Assa Road about 5 miles from Asiago by 06.15 hours, and follow in the wake of the main body, consisting of the 144 and 145 Infantry Brigades.

By the light of two blazing fires, made with timber from the rafters of Asiago houses, we packed up and booked in shortly after 04.00 hours. It was a ghostly march through the ruins of Asiago and Camporovere, in the darkness of a November night. After the heavy firing of the day there was an uncanny stillness. The guns were silent; there were no sounds from machine-guns or rifle-fire. The rapidly changing movements of the past sixteen hours, and the fall of darkness had made the precise positions of friend and foe a matter of guesswork. There remained only the crunching rumble of wagon wheels and the rattle of horses' hooves on the rough road. The Sapper sections were waiting for us after their night in Austrian trenches. After absence from Field Company comradeship it felt good to be barking out the familiar walk-march order to a hardened Company, with nearly four years' war experience. A short distance further on, the road ran along the edge of the Val d'Assa Ravine, with a cliff-like wall of mountain on its right-hand side. The great depth of the Ravine in some parts, and its narrowness, make it one of the gloomiest gorges in Europe. For only the briefest periods can the sun penetrate to the swift-flowing waters of its river. It is said to have inspired the famous Italian poet and patriot, Dante, in his conception of the *Inferno*.

It was a steady climb up the pass between Mt Meatta (6,050 feet) and Mt Montule (6,400 feet) in succession on the right, and Mt Verena (6,600 feet) on the other side of the Ravine. Possession of the summit of Mt Meatta had been gained the previous day after a sharp fight with the Austrian garrison. As dawn grew into daylight, the Ravine, with its rugged or steep pine-clad slopes, gradually opened its depths to view, and the early morning mist floating over them dispersed. We marvelled at the fact that the roadway had not been previously mined. There were numerous places suitable for it. We encountered only one half-hearted attempt to block the road by blasting out the rock face of the side of the mountain, where the road was very narrow. This had already been cleared by the R.E. party with the Advance Guard. The further we progressed the more the signs of a hurried Austrian retreat became evident. Rifles and equipment had been thrown away on the roadside. At various points, where side-valleys joined the road, there were open spaces. We passed occasional buildings, huts and dumps of stores. Some of these were still burning, others had been left untouched. At intervals there were large boards on posts at the side of the road, with traffic instructions painted on them. The complex composition of the Austrian Army was brought home to us by the lettering being set out in five different dialects. For several miles the road had been a steady uphill climb, and throughout skirting the edge of the Ravine.

By about 10.30 hours we found a place where we could pull well off the road on gently rising grass-land, at the entrance to a small side-valley. I halted here for fifty minutes to give a needed water and feed to the horses, who had by now been trekking for six hours, and a rest for the marching Sappers. On the slopes above us were a number of big log huts. From one of these a dog was howling piteously. Thinking that he had been left behind without food, or that there might be a wounded man there, two of us climbed up to the huts, but the dog would not let me get near him. Inside the huts there was every sign of a hurried evacuation—food left in mess tins, clothing and equipment scattered around in confusion. One hut had been used as a photographic studio, and was littered with plates and prints. Behind was a well equipped hut obviously used as quarters for Officers. From another a man ran out, calling us in English. He was not an Austrian, as I at first supposed, but an Italian who had been a prisoner for four months. He looked very thin and weak, but his eyes shone and he insisted on wringing our hands. I asked him whether he had been getting sufficient food. "Never enough," was his reply, "but we used to cut grass every day and add it to the food they gave us." This was said in a perfectly matter-of-fact way, and I do not doubt he was speaking the truth. He told us that the Austrians in the camp here had put up a resistance with four machine-guns, but their shooting had been wild, and held up the advance for only a short time. He had run away and hidden on the hillside. Before moving off again we annexed a light spring cart to which we harnessed (!) a pack-pony and mule, and transferred to it some of our additional load of road tools. Over the latter part of our march we had met batches of prisoners coming down the road, some of them under guards, but many of them trudging slowly down unescorted and at their own will and pace. Several of our Divisional Staff cars and D.R.s had also passed up and down the road.

Later on I was marching alongside the officer of the leading Section when I saw a big grey open car travelling slowly down the Pass towards us. A white flag was flying from a pole fastened at the side of the windscreen. In it were an Austrian General and two other officers and a British officer! Surrender? Is this the end? It was one of the most thrilling moments of my life! Instant thoughts raced through my mind of what it might portend. And then my thoughts were of my two predecessors in command, and all those others of the Company who had similarly given their lives to achieve it. If only they could have seen this day!

From a passing D.R. I learned that some of the Divisional Staff were at an Osteria a short distance ahead. I rode forward to get details of the situation, and if possible orders as to our movements. The Osteria was the "Osteria del Termine"—in British parlance "the last Pub in Italy," before crossing the frontier. Outside on the road were the A.P.M. and several officers attached to the Divisional Staff. "What's the news and doings?" "The Old Man [General Walker] is in there"—pointing with his thumb—"with an Austrian General. They're begging for an Armistice."

I learned that the 143 Brigade Advance Guard in the early hours of the morning had continued their advance. At Vezzena, about 2½ miles from the Osteria the Austrians had attempted to make a stand. Their resistance had been overcome and large numbers were surrendering. The Brigade were now moving on towards Caldonazzo, and possibly Levico beyond it.

It was only subsequently that we were able to piece together the full story of the drama that was being enacted round us. Following the collapse of the Austrian resistance a few hours earlier, General Von Ritter Romer had been sent in under the white flag. He had been wounded in the leg. He is said to have claimed that a general armistice over the whole front was under negotiation. General Walker, who had come forward to the Osteria, thereupon sent Colonel Howard, G.S.O.1., and an Intelligence Officer to the Third Austro-Hungarian Army Headquarters with a written reply.

In this document he stated that no order to suspend hostilities had been received by the British Forces. Acting under orders received by him, he had issued orders to his troops to occupy Levico, Pergine and Trento. He demanded unconditional surrender of all hostile troops in that area. General Romer would be held as a hostage against any hostile action during the operations necessary for the occupation.

The timing of this document—09.35 hours—is important in relation to General Walker's responsibility for action at this time. Owing to the rapidity of the advance of the 48th Division, he was completely out of touch by signal communication with the Italian Corps and Army H.Q., under whose higher command we were operating. The Division was also out of touch and well ahead of the Italian Divisions on our right and left flanks. In the face of far superior enemy forces, the sole responsibility for the decision to order the Division to press forward with the advance, and not give them time to reform, must have been a heavy one. Realizing that the stake at issue was a high one he took the initiative.

It was not till later in the afternoon that communication with the Italian Sixth Army Headquarters was re-established. The orders then received stated that no general armistice had been signed, and confirmed that the advance as ordered by General Walker was to be pressed forward with the utmost vigour. I was told at the Osteria that it was unlikely that our rations for the next day could catch up with us. We must manage as best we could. A quarter of a mile beyond the Osteria I was able to tell the Company that, for the first time since the war started, we had arrived on enemy territory—in fact we were the first British Division to do so on any part of the West European Front. The Sappers livened up, but were obviously tiring. I had anticipated that we should find clear space off the road at Vezzena, where I proposed to halt for at least a couple of hours. I did not know that the area round it was an Austrian Corps Headquarters, serving three Divisions, with a large camp and hutments. It was about 12.30 hours when we reached the village and found flat open ground, where we pulled in and outspanned. Nearby was a big army field bakery and storehouses. In these we found a quantity of flour, potatoes and forage, and also some rabbits, which met a speedy death and were handed over to the cooks. The latter succeeded in cooking a good hot meal for the Company, although the R.E. Field Companies were still at a disadvantage, compared with the Infantry, in not being issued with travelling cookers.

After a short "look round" the Sapper Sections and transport animals and vehicles, I had a good wash. Then we lay on the grassy bank overlooking the road. Tired as we were, the constant passing of batches of prisoners was too interesting to permit our sleeping. Parties numbering between 200 and 500 were being escorted by about a dozen

British soldiers. The contrast between the demeanour and movement of the latter and that of the men they were shepherding was very marked. We were told that over 5,000 had already surrendered. The Austrian officers, some of whom were being driven down in horsed vehicles, were well turned out. They looked at us with a perhaps assumed supercilious or disdainful glance, understandable in their ordeal. It was impossible not to feel some sympathy for them, and we never had the same sense of personal enmity for them that we had for the Germans. Most of their rank and file looked unkempt, with no signs of pride, or of a desire for further resistance. They carried with them into captivity non-military packages of varying type. One man had a violin case under his arm, but the most unexpected was a man who marched in the middle of a large batch leading by a cord a full-grown unshorn sheep! Whether it was a mascot, or an insurance for rations must remain anybody's guess. A striking contrast in demeanour was provided by a number of released Italian prisoners laughing and cheering us as they passed.

When we set off again on our trek at about 15.00 hours, we had added a good consignment of flour, potatoes and forage, loaded on our "borrowed" transport. We were surprised at the extent of the Vezzena Corps H.Q. Camp, which we were now passing. Here earlier in the morning our Brigade Advance Guard had met a short but lively resistance. Evidence of a defensive line included on the right of the road a formidable-looking stone-built fort, perched on a small hillock. The mountain slopes here had receded from the road, leaving a big flat area of grassland. We were told that some 3,000 Austrians, outnumbering the whole of the Brigade, had come out and surrendered. A great mass of Austrians had been roughly herded together, and were being guarded by our old friends the 7th Warwicks Battalion. Two field-guns were trained on them while their arms were taken from them. The Pioneer Battalion arrived later at Vezzena under the command of my brother, and arrangements were made for them to take over control of all prisoners still in the area—fresh numbers were continually coming in—and to guard the Corps H.Q., where the Commander of the IIIrd Austrian Corps and three Divisional Generals were confined temporarily.

A party of the Warwick Battalion, who had been fighting in the morning, and had now been relieved, had captured a set of band instruments. As we drew near, they lined the roadside and played us through, to the accompaniment of a discordant bleating of their instruments from unskilled musicians, each attempting a tune of his own.

From now onwards the road presented an extraordinary scene of confusion. The sides were strewn with abandoned rifles, steel helmets, respirators and larger equipment of all kinds. Field-guns, wagons and carts, an occasional lorry, presumably without petrol, and dead horses were scattered along the grass verges. Many of the horses lay on the roadside in pools of blood, with large chunks hacked out of their rumps for food.

We were now over the highest part of the pass. After about one and a half hours' march a car from the rear drew up alongside me, with General Walker inside. He asked what were our instructions. I told him that our last were to make for Levico. "No," he said. "That can't be done. You had better push on towards Caldonazzo for a bit, and then move to Levico in the morning." He told me that he had ordered 144 and 145 Brigades to concentrate for the night at Caldonazzo, and that 143 Brigade were going on towards Levico. He was on his way to the former town to ascertain the general position, before returning to Divisional H.Q. He left us with the warning that our advance had far outstripped the Italians on our left and right (an Italian Division had relieved the French Division). We must be responsible for our own protection as there might be Austrian forces operating on either of our exposed flanks.

We had travelled beyond the limits of our large-scale maps, and I had to rely on one with a 1/100,000 scale. It showed a reasonably direct route to Caldonazzo, but with many twists indicating a steep descent. But when we reached a road-fork we were met by a Staff Officer who told us that the more direct road was only a rough mountain track, and very steep and precipitous. The Infantry had gone that way, but it was quite unsuitable for transport vehicles. The weight behind the four mules drawing our double tool carts was over two tons, and darkness was close upon us. Realizing that we could make sure of reaching Levico the following morning I decided to take the alleged better road, although this appeared to entail a detour of about 5 miles, round the southern base of Mt Cimone (4,350 feet) which blocked our way.

Our 475 Field Company Sections with the Advance Guard had gone with the Infantry down the track road in full daylight. We heard later that in doing so one of their double tool-carts, with its four-mule team, had skidded over the edge with a drop of some 400 feet into the Ravine below. The two postillion drivers and the brake-man had a miraculous escape—one of the former managed to jump off and save himself, the other two went over the edge with the wagon, but were both caught on a bushy ledge 50 feet below, and lived to tell the tale. The party who were sent the next day to search for the cart could see only splintered pieces of wood. One mule, however, was seen to be alive, and had to be shot from above.

The "better" road proved far from being an easy route, and

comprised, over several miles, a series of ascents and descents, with many hairpin bends. The Austrians used it as a one-way road only. One long up-hill stretch, with a very steep slope, was more than the tired toolcart mules could tackle. It meant "out with the drag-ropes," and hooking in extra leaders from the other wagons in turn for each of the tool-carts. A light Fiat lorry that had passed us came back with the information that the road ahead was completely blocked for transport by fallen teleferica cables and two cradles. On riding forward I found that the cradles were of a much heavier type than those used by the Italians and were fixed firmly to the 3-inch cables, which stretched across the road at a height of about 3 feet. A strongly built wooden tower, over 40 feet high, erected in a clearing about 100 yards away, had supported the cables. This structure had been set on fire, and had partly collapsed, bringing down the cables with it. It was still burning, and had obviously been set on fire recently, so that I wondered if an enemy party might have prepared an ambush. I sent a screen of Sappers up the pine-covered slope on one side of the road—on the other side there was a steep fall in the ground-level—but there was no sign of an enemy. In the darkness the job of clearing the road took a full half hour. It was lucky that we were available with the necessary equipment, as it was then the only road available to the Division for bringing forward supplies, including ammunition and our rations.

With the darkness a fairly thick mist had set in. The time was now around 19.00 hours, and we had been on the road for nearly fifteen hours. I had been getting anxious as to finding some building in which the Sappers and Drivers would obtain shelter for the night. It was obvious that some of the men and horses had nearly reached the breaking-point. The transport vehicles at the rear of the Company column had spread out. While the Company halted to close up, I rode forward with Lieutenant Ivey, two Corporals and an Orderly to reconnoitre a village (Lancin) which I guessed from my map to be about half a mile ahead of us. An Italian ex-prisoner on the road had informed me that he had seen British troops there.

After a few hundred yards we came to a big farm house, with yard and outbuildings. There were no lights visible and the house door opening on to the yard was not locked. We went into two furnished rooms, without a sign or sound of any inhabitants. It seemed a heaven-sent haven for the night. I sent the Orderly to bring up the Company, and told Ivey to search the house, while I looked round the barns and other outbuildings. A minute or two later Ivey ran across the yard exclaiming "I opened the door of a room leading from one we were in, and there are half a dozen Austrian soldiers there, lying on the floor." We went back to the house, loosened our revolvers and gently opened the door. When I flashed my torch round the room we saw that there were 8 of them, all peaceably sleeping, with their rifles by their side. We took these away, and when the Company arrived a few minutes later made the outer room our "guard-room" for the night, with the prisoners locked in their room.

Thinking I might get into touch with some other British Unit in the village of Lancin, I rode on with my batman to find it consisted of a very few cottages, and no signs of troops. Just beyond it our road met in a T-junction a North-bound road in the area of the Italian Division on our left. In the darkness and stillness of the mountains I heard the distant confused sound of a large body of marching troops. It was difficult at first to decide from which direction they were coming. Were they the Italians coming up from behind on our left? Or could they be Austrian reinforcements? We were still at war and I was not without a few tremors as I waited. I drew back from the road junction till they came closer. The relatively brisk but nondescript marching step and cheerful chattering sounds soon indicated that they were coming up from the South, and allayed any doubts. In answer to my query, one of the Italian officers told me that the British troops were "avanti."

My field-message book contains the copy of the report timed 19.45 hours sent back to the C.R.E., indicating our location at Lancin, $\frac{1}{2}$ kilometre N.E. of Lavarone, and of my intention to move at 07.30 hours in the morning to Levico. We interviewed a man and three women who had been found upstairs. They were Austrians, but one of the women spoke Italian, and we made them understand that they were confined to the house during the night, and that no harm would come to them. We also found a number of rifles, swords and other equipment in one of the barns.

Captain A. G. Maclellan, 2nd in command of the Company, had found good shelter in barns and outbuildings. Foot inspection disclosed only two or three cases needing treatment. Horses were well rugged-up; each man had two blankets carried in the Sections' forage-carts. Company orders were issued. They concluded with a brief reminder for maintaining the reputation of the British soldier in dealing with the enemy civilian population—a new factor in our experience. A large room on the ground-floor had been appropriated for the officers' quarters. It was comfortably provided with a couch, table and chairs. We were in relative luxury. Hot tea and a good supply from our mess food and drink stocks were produced. It was over eighteen hours since we had started our day at now far distant Asiago. The events which we had witnessed had been so surprisingly unexpected, so far-reaching in their results and in the hopes they had aroused in us. I was proud of the stamina and response of the Company to the arduous conditions of the march—not a man had fallen out, neither horse, mule nor vehicle was left behind. With a thankful heart I slid into my sleeping-bag, my British warm over it.

The tricks of memory are many and curious. With all the changing panorama of our march, and its involvements, there stands out vividly a simple picture. It is that of an old grey-haired peasant, in the fading light of the day, lying on the sloping grassy bank on a lonely stretch of the mountain road. He lay on his back, groaning deeply, his eyes staring but unseeing, as the marching troops toiled up the hill past him. How had he been caught up in the maelstrom of fighting men? Why does this remain fixed in memory, when over nearly four years we had known the impact on our senses of shell-torn human bodies, of mutilated horses, of the destruction of men's own erections by shell-fire? Did pity still survive in our hearts? The answer perhaps lies in our belief in those days that the major hazards of life and death and destruction belonged to the fighting forces, without the indiscriminate involvement of civilian lives. Did we not look upon man's callous inhumanity to his fellow-men as a relic of the 'dark ages,' unthinkable in a twentieth century? Is it due to a world-wide weakening in moral fibre that succeeding generations have seen that conception even more widely shattered?

28　Austrian Surrender (the Trentino)

4th November 1918

　　All astir at 06.00 hours on this the 4th of November 1918, the Company took the road for Caldonazzo at 07.30 hours. To my surprise and relief our G.S. ration-wagon drove into the yard shortly before we left. The driver and his mate's feat in travelling from the ration-dump at Asiago through the night and finding the Company was in itself a remarkable achievement.

　　We gave some food to our eight prisoners, and indicated that the Asiago road was the only way to their next meal. They went off in a bunch, seemingly happy.

　　Turning northwards again at the T-road-junction, we were now skirting the Western side of Mt Cimone. My map indicated a drop of over 2,500 foot in about four miles from this point to Caldonazzo. A Staff description of the road was that of "a one-way mountain road, with about twenty-five hairpin corners, no guard-rails, a precipice on one side most of the way, and decidedly dangerous for lorries or 1st-line transport." After two days its use was banned, and a longer route through the Italian area substituted. My own description included that of a narrow shelf-like road, only 12 feet wide in some parts, cut out of the side of the mountain, and a sheer drop of up to a thousand feet on the other side. At times the road was tunnelled through the solid rock. Passing places were some distance apart. I was thankful that we had not attempted it the previous night in the darkness and mist.

　　On our march down the steep descent, the Divisional Intelligence Officer—"Brains," my stable-companion in the Divisional advance-party from France to Italy—riding a motorcycle stopped beside us. He carried a copy of an order to all Units. "An armistice has been signed to come into effect at 15.00 hours this afternoon." A message to this effect had reached Divisional H.Q. at Vezzena at 03.00 hours this morning. "All units will carry out their forward movement orders, but will not move beyond the line gained by the Advance Brigade at 15.00 hours. All Austrians within this line are to be considered as prisoners of war. The Infantry have advanced well beyond Levico, completely cutting off large numbers of Austrians, and there are several thousand prisoners already at Caldonazzo." Such was the substance of the great news he brought us.

A few minutes later I was able to halt the Company and tell them that an armistice would come into effect in a few hours' time. A big cheer went up. As it finished an echo, clear and distinct, came floating back from the mountain sides, raising a general laugh. The further whimsical thought came in my mind, that the ancient Italian guardian gods of the mountains were joining in acclaim at their release from foreign domination.

We managed to get past an Italian Battalion resting by the roadside and reached Caldonazzo soon after 09.00 hours. It had become a brilliant sunny morning with the mist swept away, yielding mountain scenery as impressive as any we had seen previously. We learned later that we had been lucky in our timing also. A Staff car, which left Vezzena at the same hour as we had left Lancin, did not reach Caldonazzo till two hours after our arrival. Two tractor-drawn 6-inch howitzers attempting the descent, contrary to orders, had blocked the road, taking half an hour to negotiate a single hairpin bend. For the time being this road represented our life-line for rations and ammunition!

At Caldonazzo we found that we had caught up with the 144 and 145 Brigades, still providing the Main Body. They were under orders to move forward at 10.00 hours, so we were well up to time.

While waiting for them to move off we watered and fed. I walked round some of the vast Army store-sheds adjacent to the railway. We learned later that this was the railhead supply-base for the Third Austrian Army. There were over two hundred heavy and field-guns, which had been prepared for blowing up with guncotton slabs and fuse fixed in position, several thousand machine-guns, rifles and army equipment of all kinds. In an open yard were several hundred wagons. There were sheds packed with saddlery and harness. I noted one shed about 120 feet long by 30 feet was stocked nearly up to the roof, solely with horse-shoes. One of the 145 Brigade Battalions had discovered two trucks filled with cases of Zeiss binoculars. As a result many passed into temporary possession of British hands, but I believe orders were issued for their being given up; whether successfully or not I do not know. There were several trains and lines of unloaded wagons in the sidings, which had failed to get away before the rapid advance of our troops, and the breakdown of Austrian morale. It transpired, subsequently, that an Austrian Red Cross train had got away at the last minute and had met disaster. It was not till two days later that the wrecked train was found by one of our mopping-up parties in a deep cutting about 6 miles from Caldonazzo. The three front coaches which had telescoped were filled with dead bodies. In the rear part of the train about a hundred wounded with doctors and nurses were found practically without food of any kind. A very large proportion of the wounded were stretcher-cases, and had to be carried over three-quarters of a mile to the nearest accessible road.

The most remarkable sight in Caldonazzo was that of a wide open space packed with a great mass of prisoners squatting or walking aimlessly around. About 10,000 were corralled inside roughly erected wire fencing rectangular in shape. At the corners machine-guns were posted to sweep the lines of the fences, with the Oxford Battalion providing guards facing them at intervals. Big bonfires which had been made outside the enclosure were still burning. During the long nightfall, in the light only of the blazing fires it must have been the most bizarre and unique spectacle of the 1914–1918 war, with the prisoners hungry and restless. Later in the day, with the arrival of battalions from two Italian Divisions—a number of whom had been brought up by lorries using more Westerly routes—the charge and feeding of the prisoners was taken over by them. Other Italian Units went on westward to make a formal entry into Trent, the capital of the Province.

The 144 and 145 Brigades moved off at 10.00 hours. We followed in their wake. While waiting at Caldonazzo we had looked round with a view to augmenting our transport and spreading our loads. We commandeered four extra Austrian horses—they were little more than sturdy ponies—and three light carts. We found all the harness we wanted in the stores. In addition we swapped a pony which we had impressed the previous day for a better-looking one. We might have a circus-like appearance, but it worked excellently and lightened the loads of men and horses.

Levico proved to be a far more attractive place than Caldonazzo. It was one of the Sports Centres in the Trentino. We were told that two days previously the life of the little town had been normal. When, in the evening, news had come of our rapid advance, the Austrian troops were apparently told to take what they could from the shops. As far as foodstuffs were available the shops appeared to have been sacked thoroughly.

After leaving Levico for Pergine I was watching the Company go past, following a ten minute halt. To my surprise I saw, coming along the road behind us, the Brigadier leading the Brigade, which had set out in front of us two hours previously, and whom we were supposed to be following. They had taken a wrong road. We continued ahead till we were checked by a Gunner Unit in front of us, who were disregarding the canons of march discipline. The Brigadier came along and "choked them off" in no uncertain terms. They were halted and the Brigade went through and we followed behind them.

For some 3 miles our route lay along the side of the Lake of Caldonazzo. In its mountain setting, with the westering sunlight on it, the scenery represented the unspoiled beauty of nature at its best. In striking contrast, the scene of confusion on the roads must remain one of the most unforgettable memories of those who were witnesses of the débâcle of an Army. The previous day had involved the retreat of two or possibly three Austrian Divisions. On this 4th November's fateful day in the history of the Austrian Peoples, with the collapse of its Empire, we were witnessing the attempts of three Austrian Corps to escape before the 15.00 hours expired.

Our 143 Brigade early in the morning had moved forward from Levico. They occupied Pergine, and rapidly covered a further 5 miles to Baselga di Pine, a village on the escape road leading North from Trent, which lay about 6 miles West of Pergine. This effectively cut off the supply and escape routes for the transport vehicles of the three Corps. In endeavouring to pass through the bottle-neck of the defiles in the Pergine/Trent area their transport had become completely jammed. On our route and its connecting roads guns and hundreds of vehicles had been abandoned. In many cases parts of their loads had been scattered on the roadside, with discarded rifles and equipment. There was the same sad spectacle of dead and mutilated horses. Others had been freed from their harness, and stood pathetically by their vehicles.

The small town of Pergine seemed considerably more pro-Italian in its sympathies. Italian flags were flying outside the windows in many of the houses. In the central square the Chief Official of the town, wearing his chain of office round his neck, stood with a large assembly of cheering and waving inhabitants. A couple of Fiat lorries containing Italian soldiers had come up by another route, and were in front of us, cheering and shouting in reply. "Italy had regained its lost Province of the Trentino after many years under Austrian rule." The British troops marched stolidly through the village without stopping.

About 3 miles North of Pergine the Company side-tracked to Vigalzano, a small and poor type of village, in which we had been told to billet ourselves. There were no other British units in it. Here again the inhabitants seemed strongly pro-Italian. The Head-man welcomed us, and all the villagers crowded round us when we halted. They tried to shake hands with everyone, talking excitedly and so fast that we could hardly understand a word. We supposed that they were saying nice things, but they were quite lost on us. The usual acknowledgement from the troops was in the strain of "Cheer-i-oh, old bird—it's all right now," "Don't get excited," and "Give our love to the family."

It must have been about an hour before the armistice deadline of 15.00 hours, that I heard the last brief outburst of firing that marked the end of the 48th Division's fighting service overseas. It had covered three years and seven months in Belgium, France and Italy. For the 474th Field Company it had entailed an additional three months, and a further four months were to elapse before we returned as a cadre, 50 strong.

The sobering thought was how few members of the Company that went out in December 1914 were left to take part in this final victory, and that now I was the only Company officer, out of the original complement of 12, still serving in the two Companies.

In this days advance about 2,000 Austrians were made prisoners in the Pergine area. Throughout our march we passed small parties of stragglers, with and without their weapons. They were being rounded up and directed to the collecting-point at Caldonazzo.

It is difficult to estimate the actual road distance covered by the Company on such twisting roads from Asiago. It lies probably between 40 and 45 miles in the space of thirty-six hours. After the initial attacks in which the 144 and 145 Brigades, supported by the Gunners, had played a full part, the final phase had been the achievement of the Infantry Battalions of the 143 Warwick Brigade under Brigadier-General Sladen's forceful leadership. They had responded magnificently to "Fanny's" training and inculcation of the spirit of the offensive.

For the Company, our billet in Vigalzano was to be the end of our road. We established our Officers' Mess in a comfortable little room with a big logwood fire. Our stock of Mess provisions and drinks was sufficient for our needs. We were tired. We were happy with a deep unspoken thankfulness. There was little merriment. In the evening we sat round the fire and talked of the events of the two days' advance. We were still bewildered at what seemed to us almost a miracle. Did it mean that Germany was also on the point of collapse? (The German surrender came exactly a week later.)

Whatever basis the Higher Commands might have had for the assurance of final victory in the war, the humbler ranks, who had been engaged in it, had learned to their cost the constantly changing uncertainties of war. It was not many weeks since the Austrian Army on the Plateau had carried out a determined offensive against us, with the conviction that they would overrun the principal northern cities of Italy. For the past four days we had been cut off from all outside news. This applied to the Allied offensive on the Piave Front. In fact they had forced what became a general deep retirement of the

Austrian forces north of the river, and captured many thousand prisoners. The achievement of our advance into the Trentino—so unexpected by us, and seemingly by the Allied Higher Command in Italy—must be considered in conjunction with the all-important success on the Piave Front. But this was some 60 miles distant. How had the breakdown of the Austrian morale spread so rapidly among their troops? I do not know the full answer.

On this same night General Walker issued this "Order of the Day":

"Officers, N.C.O.'s and men of the 48th Division. Your achievements during the last few days of the most profound military events deserve unstinted praise. After fourteen weeks of trench warfare and arduous work, chiefly at night, combined with frequent raids of the most difficult though successful nature, you have undertaken an attack on a front originally allotted to two Divisions against what ought to have been impregnable mountain positions; you have swept away the enemy rearguards, and acting as the vanguard of the Sixth Italian Army, you have advanced so rapidly and with such resolution that the retiring enemy have had no time to reform, and have left over 20,000 prisoners, hundreds of guns, and immeasurable booty in the hands of the Division.

"The mere performance of the march in the time and under the conditions you endured would have been, even without opposition, considered a creditable feat. You can justly claim that the favourable situation of the Italian Armies on this front at 15.00 hours to-day, when one of the most memorable armistices in history was signed, is largely due to your exertions and resolution.

"As your Divisional Commander I cordially thank you.
"4th Nov. 1918.   H. B. Walker.

Major-General Commanding 48th Division."

A few days later a message to General Walker from Earl Cavan was published in Orders. In it he sent to all ranks his intense appreciation of their great services and victory. Also to General Walker personally his thanks for the drive and determination with which he conducted the arduous operations. He added that the Chief of the Imperial General Staff had that day sent his special congratulations to the 48th Division by King's Messenger.

The responsibility carried by General Walker had been a heavy one. On the news that the Austrians had withdrawn from their advanced positions in front of Asiago to their Winterstellung line, he had mounted the initial attack, at very short notice, in conjunction with the French Division. When his outflanking attack had proved successful, he had committed the Division to an objective in which the high stake represented the cutting of the enemy supply route for three Corps.

He had pressed the attack forward, although at a vital period out of touch with his Higher Command, and when his troops had outstripped by several miles the Allied Divisions on both flanks. It was November, with the heavy winter snowfalls much overdue. At the furthest point reached on 4th November his Advance Brigade were (as officially quoted) 76 miles distant by road from the Divisional rail-head. From the latter all supplies had to be transported forward over a single treacherous mountain road with gradients varying from a starting-point in the Plain at a 350-feet level, rising to 4,600 feet. The achievements of the Divisional R.A.S.C. Units in organization and efficiency of men and vehicles had been outstanding.

On the following two days the Company were left to their own devices, cleaning up equipment and resting, followed by inspections and a little drilling. On the morning of the 5th November I rode over to Divisional H.Q., which had moved forward to Civezzano, in order that I might glean the latest news. Everyone was in the cheeriest of moods. The tension of the past few days was over. I was invited into their Mess, where I was surprised to find an elderly Austrian General. He was the Duke of Braganza, Commander of the Sixth Austrian Cavalry Division. Orders had been received that he was to be escorted that afternoon over the armistice line as a free man. He had the appearance of a fine old English country gentleman, and talked freely and with the utmost courtesy in excellent English. Colonel Barnett has related that he had surrendered to General Walker on the evening of 3rd November, saying as he handed over his sword "I am indeed proud, General, to be able to surrender to such a distinguished British Officer as yourself, and permit me to congratulate you on the wonderful marching powers of your magnificent Division. The advance of the 48th British Division will go down to history as one of the most splendid feats of the British Army."

As Colonel Barnett aptly commented: "For an example of a really tactful speech under awkward circumstances this can hardly be equalled!"

29   Finale (Northern Italy)

November 1918–March 1919

On the 7th November the Company started on its march back to the Plains, destination Thiene, a distance by road of about 65 miles. It was taken in stages, stopping for the night at Caldonazzo, Vezzena, Val d'Assa Camp, and the Company's old camp at Granezza. The roads were still littered with abandoned Austrian equipment. At Vezzena we were able to quarter ourselves in the Austrian Corps H.Q. huts. The Mess hut was most comfortably furnished, including a large piano. I was somewhat mystified at finding in it a recent copy of the *Bristol Times and Mirror* newspaper. The subsequent explanation was that my brother, with his officers, had occupied the suite prior to our arrival. We also had the luxury of a full-size porcelain bath cum hot water. I spent some time walking round the huge reserve stores of weapons and equipment. In one section there were now over 14,000 unused or surrendered rifles and several hundred machine-guns.

Shortly after our evening meal, Maclellan's bedroom, adjoining mine, was found to be on fire. It took about fifteen minutes to extinguish it with the aid of buckets of water, and an axe, which I wielded with such vigour that it brought down nearly half one side of the room. However, I did not anticipate a bill for damages from the Austrian Army, nor making a counter-claim for cleansing my tunic and trousers.

Late in the evening we heard that the Italian papers were reporting that Kaiser William was abdicating.

From Granezza Maclennan took the transport by road, while the Sappers and I went down the mountain side via the mule tracks. Our hopes that Thiene was the end of our journey were quickly nullified. Next morning we were on the road again at 08.00 hours bound for Tezze, about 14 miles distant. On the march I was on foot in front of the Company when I saw a red-tabbed officer step out into the road from a side turning. It was the British Corps Commander. It seemed an occasion to which the "no compliments" on the march did not apply. We eyes-righted and he came over and marched with us for about a quarter of a mile, asking numerous questions about our experience in the advance into the Trentino. He told me details of the German surrender, which we had not previously heard.

Four days later the Company made what was to prove the last trek with a full personnel, before gradual dispersion for demobilization. Our two pontoon wagons had rejoined us with two pontoons on them, but we gathered that the Company's original ones were lying somewhere on the bottom of the Piave River. This final move brought us near Vicenza, to the little village of Il Palazzeto.

The thoughts and hopes of all ranks now were centred on an early return to England for demobilization. A scheme giving priorities for individual early release had been worked out, but in general Unit Commanders were expected to remain until their unit was reduced to cadre strength. The original plan appeared to be that the cadre would take back their unit equipment. This was subsequently changed, and all our horses, vehicles and stores were left behind in Italy. The equivalent of two Infantry Battalions, made up of volunteers and low-category men, also remained to form part of the Army of Occupation, and were later transferred to Egypt.

With the large numbers of overseas troops involved, the dispersal for demobilization was inevitably slow. In our case it represented a period of nearly four months before the cadre reached England. As a Territorial Unit we were not professional soldiers, and only a few were anxious to continue in the Army as their career. Hence, with the task completed for which they originally volunteered, the incentive for training no longer existed. The problem before us was to keep the dwindling number in all ranks as contented as possible pending their release.

The necessity was strongly impressed upon us for maintaining a high standard of discipline, drill and general appearance. I found in 474 Field Company a similar devotion to that in 475 given by the mounted section drivers to the horses and mules under their charge. The condition of our vehicles and harness had suffered in the almost continuous movements of the Trentino advance and return. General Walker rightly insisted on all personal equipment, horses and vehicles being speedily brought up to a standard of which we could all be proud. On 20th November our turn came for a searching inspection by him. Those Units which failed to come up to the standard required were made fully aware of it, and given a short period before a further inspection. I recorded: "The G.O.C. was very affable and paid the

Company one or two compliments. The draught-horses have recovered remarkably well, considering that they have emerged from three months' hard work while we were in the line on the Plateau, ending up with as severe a test as they are every likely to meet."

Five days later, at very short notice, we had a further full inspection of the Company by General Wilson, Engineer-in-Chief, I.E.F., on the Castelgomberto aerodrome. The following extract from a letter perhaps exemplifies the less formal nature of our Army life. "We were due to arrive on the aerodrome at 09.40 hours for inspection at 10.00. We were forming up the Company transport in the approved pattern when a red-tabbed Staff Officer strolled up to me. I happen to know him well. [He subsequently became a close friend and business associate]. His official announcement of the nearby presence of the Engineer-in-Chief, British Forces in Italy, with a long string of letters after his name, and of the Corps Chief Engineer, was as follows. 'Morning, Eberle! I've got two tame Generals running about in the background. We're beastly early, so just tip me the wink when you're ready for me to trot them forward! Right-ho?"

The E.-in-C. seemed quite pleased, and instructed me to inform the Company that it was a very creditable turn-out. For this the credit lay with the Second in Command, Captain A. G. Maclennan, who had kept the Company in excellent form after Major G. E. A. Richards had been evacuated. Later we received a very complimentary "Special Order."

27th November 1918. "Today I was a spectator at a big review of Allied Troops on the aerodrome by H.M. The King of Italy. The troops represented the equivalent of about a Division, the 48th providing a composite Infantry Brigade and other Units including 475 Field Company, Major J. R. M. Crawford, O.C., being the senior Major. I had a very good view from close to the King's standpoint. After a short inspection in line by the King, the Troops marched past, returned to their line and finally advanced in review order, halted and gave the General Salute. It was a most impressive sight on a bright day, the British contingents being exceptionally good, both in respect of smartness in their turnout and in marching.

"Our Officers have also each received a commemorative medal given by General Mantuori to the British and French Officers who took part in the battle of 15th June. The inscription engraved on it in Italian is translated for me as being "To Brotherly Trust and to Victory—Army of the Altipiani."

Spurred on by Divisional H.Q. orders we had set about the organizing of time-filling tasks. We formed three committees with representatives of all ranks on them—Sport, Entertainment and Education.

Outdoor activities were restricted by weather conditions, but competitive football, basketball (to our own revised rules), treasure hunts and compass and map-reading exercises were organized. With great zeal we arranged numerous classes in engineering, craftsmanship and general education. I found myself adopting the role of a Professor of Mathematics. In this I was able to obtain advice from my wife on the syllabus, ranging from fractions and decimals to logarithm tables. It had been her principal subject at Cambridge, and she had accepted an offer from Dr King, Headmaster of Clifton College, to take a wartime post teaching mathematics in the Upper School. Until our numbers dwindled too low in February, these classes were successful in providing an alternative interest.

On Sunday, 17th November, a Divisional Thanksgiving Parade had to be cancelled owing to snow falling heavily all day. Instead two services were held in an old disused church in Brogliano for limited numbers. The following Sunday our Company attended a service there, with the Senior Chaplain—a brother-in-law of Lord Cavan—giving us an excellent and heartening sermon.

My next Sunday morning was spent in riding up a valley amidst magnificent mountain scenery. "I have spent two days with one of the Company's Sections detached for work at St Querico on the Agno River. From here we rode up the valley past Recoaro, about 3 miles only from the Austrian boundary near the top of Lake Garda. It is a curious mixture of an old mountain village and part mountain holiday resort. Ahead of us rose Mt Pasubio (7,300 feet), a great rugged and scarred mountain with the sun shining on its covering of snow. The road wound up the valley with the deep ravine on one side, in which the Agno rushed fiercely down over its stony course. With every bend of the road fresh views unfolded of the mountains stretching ahead to the Dolomites. In the quaint cobbled street of Recoaro we passed the village menfolk in their long, black, fur collared ulsters, folded across the body on to the shoulder. The smiling womenfolk were neatly dressed in black, with black shawls over their hair, and prayer-books in their hands. There had been no English troops up here, so that we attracted considerable attention. Everywhere the men's black broad-brimmed hats were raised to us, and a soft-spoken greeting offered. It seemed that Peace at last had linked with nature in bringing back the joy of life into their hearts and ours."

Fourteen days leave to England was still being granted, and I was fortunate in that my turn came so that I could spend Christmas at home. It was the first time in five years. On the return journey, after being held up at Cherbourg for three days, we froze for four days in a troop train which had at least one broken window in every compartment, and no heating.

11th February 1919. "The Company strength has dwindled from 215 to 3 Officers and 110 O.R.'s, of whom 23 are transferring to the Army of Occupation. I have refused to keep back a single man on the score of being indispensable to us, if he is entitled and wants to go. We still have 47 horses. We are told that 23 trains are earmarked for February for evacuating the British forces in Italy."

22nd February. "We are down to our Cadre strength. One other officer, Lieutenant D. M. Wilson and myself, with 50 O.R.s. It seems likely now that the Cadre will not bring back to England any of the horses, wagons or technical equipment. All except 9 of the horses will be taken away in a few days, and we should leave by 9th March at latest. The three Field Company Cadres have linked up and we have a combined Officers' Mess."

The chief task remaining was to hand over and obtain clearance from D.A.D.O.S. (Ordnance) for all our equipment and stores. The Ordnance check was a long and full one, but this hurdle was satisfactorily overcome on the 3rd and 4th March.

"An Augean sorting and clearance of Orderly-Room papers has been carried out. I have paid a sad farewell to my two horses; one is going to the Army of Occupation, the other is being sold in Italy. Less regretfully I watched the departure of a 3-ton lorry, packed full with our explosives, nowadays including a quantity of unscheduled and more vulnerable types. I would not like to have been in the vicinity if the lorry suffered a big crash. We have nothing to do, and nothing to do it with! Surely it can only be a few days now before we leave!"

In this we were disappointed. The unfortunate Italian railways could not stand the prolonged strain on their resources. Previously scheduled dates became nebulous. They could not produce sufficient trains. Thus our departure was delayed till the 24th March. For the last ten days we were left without a horse or vehicle of any description. Major Crawford, who was acting for the C.R.E. suggested my going to Florence, which I had not previously visited. Travelling through the night I had two splendid days in Florence. Incidentally the railway fare cost the equivalent of twelve shillings, and the all-in "en pension" terms at the Helvetia thirteen and fourpence per day. The British and American community had an organized committee for showing Officers round the treasures of Florence, and acting as hostesses for teas and dancing. Avoiding the latter, I was privileged to enjoy the expert guidance of Professor Powell. On the return journey I had a few hours in which to explore both Bologna and Padua.

We duly set out for England on the 24th March, two days before the 48th Divisional H.Q. Overseas ceased to operate. At Southampton we received orders to return to Bristol, and billet at the "White City."

This was a large building erected originally as an exhibition centre, near Ashton Gate, and taken over by the War Office. I had sent a telegram to our R.E. Headquarters asking for transport for the Sappers' packs, and our other small impedimenta; apart from this our arrival was apparently unexpected. Thus we were unrecognized as we marched through the busy Bedminster streets. It was hard to realize that four years and seven months had elapsed since the Company had left Bristol on the first stage of its war service. The Cadre, consisting of lower demobilization category men, did not include a single member of its original complement.

At the White City we were given a warm welcome from Colonel Seymour Williams, a pre-war C.O. of the Company. The following morning I had a stormy interview with a demobilizing officer in Bristol, to whom I applied for warrants for all the Cadre to travel forthwith to the Dispersal Centre at Chiseldon. He claimed that his allotment was for a few men only each day, whereas my instructions were for immediate release for all. Fortunately the issue was finally decided in my favour; the warrants at once made available, and a generous apology from the officer.

Farewells were exchanged with all the members of the Cadre, and they departed to resume the garb and employment of "Civvie Street." Formalities with our R.E. Headquarters in Bristol were concluded. As O.C. of 474 Field Company, the only person left to whom I could issue orders was myself. Under these instructions I travelled on the 4th April to the Dispersal Centre. I exchanged my Territorial Army commitments for those of the Territorial Army Reserve of Officers. This service lasted for a further eighteen years until terminated under the age limit. In 1940 I was translated into raising and commanding a Company of the Home Guard—initially L.D.V.—which very quickly became an over-size Battalion of my native County Gloucestershire Regiment.

Thus that 4th April 1919 marked the end of my wartime Sapper Venture. I do not regret its impact on my life. During four and two-thirds years I learned much of man's humanity and of his inhumanity, of the potentiality of his underlying courage, of the strength in the bond of comradeship, and its reactions to good leadership. As a perpetual reminder among my most treasured possessions are a silver cross and two sheets of inscribed paper, with the facsimile signature of Winston Churchill, Secretary of State for War.

30   Post-War Retrospection

My story is not complete if I fail to express my debts of memory and gratitude to those, named and unnamed, who were my closer comrades in the 48th Division. There can be few stronger bonds of friendship and dependence than those forged on active service. Nor can I forget the loyalty of those who acted as my batmen; one of whom in these days unblushingly addresses me by an apparent wartime nickname.

There is another acknowledgment due. It is to my old School at Clifton, where I spent six years. This was the true starting-point of my Sapper Venture as a Cadet Royal Engineer Volunteer. (At the annual Public Schools' Camps we were nicknamed "The Parsons," due to our shoulder-strap titles bearing the initials R.E.V.) Arising from this a possibly unique record may be cited. When the South Midland Division went overseas the C.R.E., the Commanding Officers of the Signal Company (at that time in the R.E. Corps), and of the two original Field Companies were Cliftonians. As casualties occurred in the Field Companies—two C.O.s were killed—the successive appointments to the Commands were ex-members of the School, six in all, covering the whole period of the Division's service overseas.

The original H.Q. and two Field Companies of the South Midland R.E. had a total establishment strength on mobilization of 447 all ranks. These were expanded during the War to serve the needs of the 48th and 61st (2nd Line) Divisions. The combined total of those who were killed was 233.

Present-day generations may not realize the extent to which the British Nation, in the early days of the 1914/18 War, depended on the ex-members of the public schools and grammar schools for filling the junior commissioned ranks in the New Army Units, and the casualty gaps in the Regular and Territorial Forces. Relative to the Continental Armies, Britain was unprepared and untrained for a war on a major scale. It was not merely that these schools had provided the basis of early training in their Cadet Corps. In the closely-knit

206

community of School and House organization, and in the playing-fields, the seeds of service, discipline and leadership were sown. Perhaps only those who saw them in action at the Front can appreciate fully the measure of their successful leadership in the vital roles of junior officers. The price paid for it in the number of their casualties was a high one. The Clifton War Memorial Gateway is inscribed "To the memory of 3,063 Cliftonians who served, and of 578 who fell in the War 1914–1919." The names of 275 who fell in the 1939/45 War were added subsequently. Similar figures were to be found in the Schools throughout the country.

Among post-war memories, inevitably perhaps, those of Clifton's first two Field-Marshals—Haig and Birdwood—stand foremost. I first heard these two names under circumstances which indicate a remarkable sense of foresight on the part of the speaker. The date was the 25th June 1904. As members of the Cadet Corps we were drawn up facing the wide steps above which stood the newly erected statue of St George commemorating the Cliftonians who had fallen in the South-African War of 1899. General Lord Methuen, who had held a high command in the war, had been invited to unveil the memorial. At the start of his address he said that there were Cliftonians who might have claimed it as their birthright to stand in his place that day. He had in mind particularly Colonel Haig and Colonel Birdwood, who had been with him in South Africa. Eighteen years later, the then Field-Marshal Earl Haig stood on the identical step for his speech— now, also as President of the College—after unveiling the names on the 1914–18 War Memorial.

One valued recollection is that of a small private dinner party at Clifton, at which Haig was present. The outward impression which I received was that of a broad-shouldered, powerfully built man, deliberate in every movement or action, as if a heavy burden of responsibility still rested on him. Inwardly a man richly endowed with the moral fibre and resolution of his Scottish ancestry. He was not a talented or ready conversationalist, but what was said carried conviction and confidence. The underlying sympathy and simple kindness of his nature had been amply shown in his untiring activities for the reinstatement of ex-Servicemen in civilian employment, and in establishing the British Legion on a strong national basis.

There was a strong contrast in the outward personality of Field-Marshal Lord Birdwood of Anzac, who had commanded the Anzac Corps in Gallipoli, and the Fifth Army in France. After his return from India in 1931, where he had been Commander-in-Chief, he became a Member of the School Council, and later its President. He was four years younger than Haig, and survived him by twenty-three years. When visiting Bristol he stayed usually with an old friend living not far from my own house, and frequently I acted as his chauffeur after meetings at the school.

He did not possess the physique of Haig. His strong personality arose more from an exceptional liveliness of spirit and alertness of action. Always ready of speech, his approach to his fellow men in all walks of life was of the friendliest nature. This was exemplified by a preference, to an unusual degree, for addressing those he met by their Christian name rather than by their surname. He possessed a happy gift of making them feel that what they said was of real interest and importance to him.

In Haig's speech to us of June 1922, to which I have referred above, he used these words: "War may let loose the worst passions of human nature, but a war that is just, that is imposed upon a peace-loving nation by the desire to protect and further the safety of the homeland, and justice and liberty among the peoples of the earth must always call forth the highest qualities of men. . . . Tanks, guns and aeroplanes would not have sufficed to bring us victory in the Great War if the *character of our people had been other than it was.*"

In the above words there lies, perhaps, the justification for my attempting *My Sapper Venture.* I am certain that they represent the message and challenge which he wished most ardently to pass on to succeeding generations of the British People.